Transformations in Ancient Judaism

Transformations in Ancient Judaism

Textual Evidence for Creative Responses to Crisis

JACOB NEUSNER

HENDRICKSON PUBLISHERS

© 2004 by Jacob Neusner

Hendrickson Publishers, LLC
P. O. Box 3473
Peabody, Massachusetts 01961-3473

ISBN 1-56563-705-4

Printed in the United States of America

First Printing — October 2004

Cover Art: The image used on the cover is of a menorah engraved into the lime floor of a house built around 40 B.C.E. not far from the Temple of Jerusalem. The house was burned down during the destruction of the Second Temple in 70 C.E. and its ruins excavated in 1969. Israel Museum (IDAM), Jerusalem, Israel. Photo Credit: Erich Lessing / Art Resource, NY. Used with permission.

Library of Congress Cataloging-in-Publication Data

Neusner, Jacob, 1932–
    Transformations in ancient Judaism : textual evidence for creative responses to crisis / Jacob Neusner.
        p. cm.
    Includes index.
    ISBN 1-56563-705-4 (alk. paper)
    1. Judaism—History—Post-exilic period, 586 B.C.–210 A.D.
2. Judaism—History—Talmudic period, 10-425. 3. Judaism—
Sacred books. 4. Judaism—Relations—Christianity. 5. Christianity and other religions—Judaism. I. Title.
    BM176.N4866 2004
    296′.09′01—dc22
                                                2004017184

Table of Contents

Preface   vii

Abbreviations   xi

Introduction   1
The Public Side of Faith   1
What Is at Stake in this Book?   4
Why Judaism in Particular?   5
The Program of Exposition   6
What Exactly Do We Mean by "Judaism"?   8

1. Exile and Return and the Response of the Torah   13
Reorganizing the Past to Face the Crisis of an
     Uncertain Future   13
The Turning Point of 538–450 B.C.E.   19
The Torah in Context: Exile and Return   25
First Comes the System with its Inner Logic   26
How the Pentateuch Met the Challenge of 538–450 B.C.E.:
     Why Did Pentateuchal Judaism Endure?   28
Sacred Persistence   32
A Successful System for this Israel's Social Order   34

**2. The Loss of the Jerusalem Temple and the
    Response of the Mishnah**   37
From Disaster to Despair   37
The Mishnah's Response to Despair   38
The Mishnah's Modes of Thought: Hierarchical Classification   40
The Mishnah's Six Components   42

The Mishnah's System Seen Whole   52
Drawing Nourishment from the Past, Thinking about the
    Future—Always in the Here and Now: The Mishnah's
    Eternal Present-tense Paradigm   55
How the Mishnah Resolved the Crisis of 135 and Defined
    Normative Judaism: Israel and Adam Once More   57
Judaism without Christianity   60

3. Asymmetries: Gaps in the Pentateuchal-Mishnaic System   62
Systemic Silences: Gaps between the Systems   62
The Contrast between the Pentateuch's and the Mishnah's
    Media of Expression   66
The Mishnah's Systemization of Singular Historical Events
    into Components of a Paradigm   70
The Mishnah's Teleology without Eschatology   81
Asymmetries: A Different Kind of History   88

4. Rabbinic Judaism and the Emergence of the Christian Empire 91
From 70–135 to 312–363: The Crisis of the
    Fourth Century C.E.   91
The Basis for this Inquiry   94
The Age of Constantine and Its Meaning for Judaism   99
From Enemy to (Illegitimate) Brother: The Transformation
    of Rome   103
Writing History: The Temple and the Failure of Julian's
    Project in Jerusalem—A Null-Hypothesis   116
Rabbinic Judaism and the Meaning of History   135

5. Symmetries: History and Messiah in the
    Talmudic-Midrashic System   137
History Returns and Rabbinic Judaism Takes Shape   137
The Conception of History in the Talmud of the Land of Israel   139
Genesis Rabbah and Israel's History   142
From Scripture's Historical Thinking to Rabbinic Judaism's
    Paradigmatic Structure   148
The Messiah Comes to Rabbinic Judaism   155
Judaism despite Christianity   165

6. Stability and the Next Turning Point   168
The Beginning of Western Civilization and the Birth of
    Christianity and Judaism   168
The Christian *Défi* and the Success of Judaism   170
Christianity and the Indicative Traits of Normative Judaism   173
The Stability of Rabbinic Judaism and the Next Turning Point   176

Index of Ancient Sources   179

Preface

The Judaism that is defined by its canonical writings—the Pentateuch and Prophets, Mishnah, Talmuds and Midrash—tells the story of how hope overcomes despair. That message coming to us from the formative age of normative Judaism proves remarkably relevant to the Judaic situation beyond the sorrowful twentieth century. When defeat turns to despair, Judaism comes to a turning point. And with the response to despair resulting in an act of stubborn affirmation, Judaism is transformed.

Here, to tell that story, I contemplate the three generative transformations in the formation of rabbinic Judaism—three transformations that responded to and shaped definitive changes in Israelite politics, society, and culture—all three precipitated by enormous public events of a catastrophic order. At the three principal turning points in its unfolding, normative Judaism—the Judaic religious system embodied in the Pentateuch (ca. 450 B.C.E.), the Mishnah (ca. 200 C.E.), and the first of the Talmuds and its companion Midrash-compilations (ca. 400–450 C.E.)—shows how, in the case of one particular religion, people respond to critical moments in the social order by rethinking received paradigms of piety and practice. This they have done, and now continue to do, through recasting the received tradition by means of the resources of its own interior logic. When chronic issues turn acute and come to crisis by catastrophic events, the rabbinic sages explore anew the potentialities of the received system and discover truth both continuous with the past and responsive to the unanticipated crisis.

Each of these three principal turning points in the formation of Judaism signals fundamental changes that were recorded in writings of enduring impact and were reflected in public policy as new theological forms of lasting importance. All represent responses to critical issues confronting the faith, and the people who embodied the faith, and these responses were written down in canonical books of an innovative character appropriate to the crisis at hand.

What is at stake in the story that I tell? This book represents religion as an act of shared culture, the critical component of the social order. Religion is understood in this book as comprised of public things thought, said, and done. These are matters that can reasonably and critically be studied, not merely reported on as a subjective fact of one's personal condition. Here I lay emphasis on the public structure and the corporate, social system contemplated by religious ideas. I interpret transforming events in Judaic religious or political thought as the response to a common problem, whether chronic or critical.

I view religion as acting upon society, defining culture, and shaping the public interest. Religion is not merely acted upon and configured by other forces in the shaping of that interest. In my judgment, one of the most engaging traits of religion is the match between systems of religious ideas and the social world of the group that frames and responds to those ideas. It is here, in its applied reason and practical logic, that religion transforms itself from a corpus of abstractions into a body of social doctrine capable of securing the common good. So at stake at these three turning points—these moments of transformation—is the public expression of the inner life of the community, the expression of life that claims to embody the religious ideas of the community and explain itself through them.

What is the significance of recognizing religion as an expression and act of public policy? I present religion here as an independent variable in the formation of the social order. That is to say, religion in its inner logic explains—it is not explained away by—other social forces, whether economics, psychology, or politics. When we recognize how people formed into a community by common faith and custom work together to solve critical problems, we see one of the principal reasons for the enduring role of religion in shaping civilization, today as well as throughout history. It lies in the power of religion to form community and bring about common action in the public interest.

This essay in interpretation draws upon many of my previously published books and brings together some of their principal ideas in a manner that none by itself yields.

Chapter one recapitulates some of the theses found in *Self-fulfilling Prophecy*.[1]

Chapter two restates ideas found in *Judaism: The Evidence of the Mishnah*.[2]

---

[1] Jacob Neusner, *Self-fulfilling Prophecy: Exile and Return in the History of Judaism* (Boston: Beacon Press, 1987; repr., Atlanta: Scholars Press, 1990).
[2] Jacob Neusner, *Judaism: The Evidence of the Mishnah* (Chicago: University of Chicago Press, 1981; 2d ed., Atlanta: Scholars Press, 1988).

Chapter three builds on *Judaism: The Evidence of the Mishnah,* on *The Mishnah: An Introduction,* and on *Judaisms and their Messiahs at the Turn of the Christian Era.*[3]

Chapter four reworks central points of *Judaism and Christianity in the Age of Constantine.*[4]

Chapter five continues the exposition initially undertaken in *Judaisms and their Messiahs* and in *Judaism and Christianity in the Age of Constantine,* as well as drawing heavily on the ideas found in *The Presence of the Past, the Pastness of the Present.*[5]

Chapters four and five also both rest on the results of *The Foundations of Judaism.*[6]

Chapter six readdresses findings in *Self-fulfilling Prophecy,* in *Judaism and Christianity in the Age of Constantine,* and in *Death and Birth of Judaism,* my field-theory of the history of Judaism.[7]

The work as a whole restates in clear terms what I hold to be the interior design of the movement of the Judaic religious system from a philosophical to a religious character as laid out in *The Transformation of Judaism.*[8]

Echoes of other works of mine resonate throughout. The items specified here are the principal monographs that contribute to this interpretative account of how normative Judaism has come to formation in the context of public events. What of the interior context of theology: the

---

[3] Jacob Neusner, *Judaism: The Evidence of the Mishnah* (Chicago: University of Chicago Press, 1981; 2d ed. Atlanta: Scholars Press, 1988). Jacob Neusner, *The Mishnah: An Introduction* (Northvale, N.J.: Jason Aronson, 1989). Jacob Neusner, William Scott Green, and Ernest S. Frerichs, eds., *Judaisms and their Messiahs at the Turn of the Christian Era* (New York: Cambridge University Press, 1987).

[4] Jacob Neusner, *Judaism and Christianity in the Age of Constantine: History, Messiah, Israel, and the Initial Confrontation* (Chicago: Chicago University Press, 1987).

[5] Jacob Neusner, William Scott Green, and Ernest S. Frerichs, eds., *Judaisms and their Messiahs at the Turn of the Christian Era* (New York: Cambridge University Press, 1987). Jacob Neusner, *Judaism and Christianity in the Age of Constantine: History, Messiah, Israel, and the Initial Confrontation* (Chicago: Chicago University Press, 1987). Jacob Neusner, *The Presence of the Past, the Pastness of the Present: History, Time, and Paradigm in Rabbinic Judaism* (Bethesda: CDL, 1996).

[6] Jacob Neusner, *The Foundations of Judaism: Method, Teleology, Doctrine* (3 vols.; Philadelphia: Fortress Press, 1983–1985; repr., Lanham, Md.: University Press of America, 1988).

[7] Jacob Neusner, *Self-fulfilling Prophecy: Exile and Return in the History of Judaism* (Atlanta: Scholars Press, 1990). Jacob Neusner, *Judaism and Christianity in the Age of Constantine: History, Messiah, Israel, and the Initial Confrontation* (Chicago: Chicago University Press, 1987). Jacob Neusner, *Death and Birth of Judaism: The Impact of Christianity, Secularism, and the Holocaust on Jewish Faith* (New York: Basic Books, 1987; repr., Atlanta: Scholars Press, 1993).

[8] Jacob Neusner, *The Transformation of Judaism: From Philosophy to Religion* (Champaign-Urbana: University of Illinois Press, 1992).

construction of religious ideas in a systematic framework? My under-standing of the counterpart construction—the theology that animates the inner precincts of Israel's social order—is set forth in *The Theology of the Oral Torah,* in *The Theology of the Halakhah,* and discussed in detail in *The Halakhah: Encyclopaedia of the Law of Judaism.*[9]

Both the title of this book and its program I owe to Professor William Scott Green of the University of Rochester. From the cases I had selected, he showed me how to frame the field-theory of the formative history of Judaism that is adumbrated in these pages. The relevance of this book to contemporary Judaism hardly requires articulation beyond what is broadly implied in the opening paragraph of this preface.

Jacob Neusner

---

[9]Jacob Neusner, *The Theology of the Oral Torah: Revealing the Justice of God* (Montreal: McGill-Queens University Press, 1999). Jacob Neusner, *The Theology of the Halakhah* (Leiden: E. J. Brill, 2001). Jacob Neusner, *The Halakhah: An Encyclopaedia of the Law of Judaism* (5 vols.: The Brill Reference Library of Ancient Judaism; Leiden: E. J. Brill, 1999).

Abbreviations

ᶜAbod. Zar.	*ᶜAbodah Zarah*
b.	Babylonian Talmud
Ber.	*Berakot*
m.	Mishnah
Ketub.	*Ketubbot*
Miqw.	*Miqwaʾot*
Neg.	*Negaᶜim*
Nid.	*Niddah*
Qidd.	*Qiddušin*
Roš Haš.	*Roš Haššanah*
t.	Tosefta
Taᶜan.	*Taᶜanit*
y.	Jerusalem Talmud
Yebam.	*Yebamot*
Zebaḥ.	*Zebaḥim*

Introduction

Religion responds to historical crisis because it forms a critical component in the shaping of the public order of society and culture. Forming and re-forming, a religious community embodies what people do together to solve problems, and thus the political decisions of the group flow from their religion.

This book illustrates that fact by examining three case studies provided by Judaism in its formative history. These case studies are turning points—occasions of transformation—in the historical unfolding of what became normative Judaism. Each turning point signals a defining moment in that history, starting in the fifth century B.C.E. and continuing to the definitive statement of that Judaism with the formation of the Talmud about 600 C.E. In each case a wholly new corpus of coherent ideas took shape and provoked an unprecedented kind of canonical writing—Judaic writing—to embody the fresh statement. In this fashion Judaism addressed a chronic problem when it become acute and responded through its own transformation. That is, Judaism revised the received system and structure of its religion. Its new canonical writings were intellectual initiatives taking entirely unprecedented forms. These writings, then, signal the transformation of Judaism at each of its turning points.

The Public Side of Faith

Why highlight the public aspect of religion—exemplified by Judaism—as a medium of problem-solving in the Israelite social order? The recognition of the public character of religion competes with another view, which sees religion as a private practice or philosophy to the exclusion of its application to issues of social order. In this latter context people speak of "my God," not "our God," of personal conversion to the exclusion of the social mores demanded of the community and for its nurture, and, in the case of Judaism, one hears the oxymoron, "my Judaism," as though public "Judaism" could sustain quite private versions. Whatever for? Now the religion of this other view takes shape in the encounter between God and the individual in quest of God. Religion consequently is deemed not public nor accessible to universal reason and criticism. So at most it can be reported upon, but not studied as a set of facts about what people say and do together.

In principle none who holds the view advocated here denies that religion takes place in the arena of private life. But once people one-by-one find God, they ordinarily seek out others who affirm the same encounter. They forthwith form a community of like-minded persons to explore the consequences of the encounter with God. The result of the personal encounter therefore persists in public activity and gives shape to enduring institutions. Thus religion is not only private, representing individuals' response to the inner searching of the heart, but soon changes public behavior and in time informs public policy.

Once we recognize that religion does not fulfill itself wholly through the personal quest for direct encounter with God, the public side of faith emerges. When this occurs we can address religion as a social, shared enterprise in social or political setting: religion does become a formative component of culture. In this book I wish to show how at three critical junctures in its history, successive systems of Judaism addressed and resolved critical issues that Jews faced as a community. From the resources provided by the history and texts of normative, that is rabbinic, Judaism I mean in this book to right the balance of our appreciation of the contribution of religion to both private and public life. And in so doing, I highlight the power of religion to confront crises in society and culture and particularly in the case of Israel to allow its people to transcend despair.

Three qualifications require attention. They are framed in answer to questions or objections that often arise. I do not offer here on behalf of religion arguments usually characterized as apologetics, utilitarianism, or reductionism.

First, this book is not an exercise of apologetics for Judaism, rabbinic Judaism, religion, religions, or religiosity. I do not claim that because religion shapes society, religion is more than merely relevant, that it is true, or that it accomplishes worthy goals, e.g., in the case of Judaism, the perpetuation of the Jewish people. In affirming the public side of faith, we need not engage with the truth-claims of any one of the religions, let alone of religion viewed whole. We only recognize why it is that religion—religions—endures as the definitive factor in humanity's social order. Religion endures through the entire history of humanity. It is not going to go away, and it demands close study by anyone who wants to understand the human condition and its future. Whether we place a positive or negative evaluation upon religion in no way pertains.

Second, I do not mean to suggest that religion serves only because it is useful. My goal is to understand what religion is and how it works. It is not my purpose to advocate for religion over irreligion, let alone one religion over others. Religion is a principal formative force in society and culture for much, though not all, of humanity. If we cannot conduct public affairs without studying politics, economics, organizations and institutions, and other secular activities, we cannot understand the human condition without some theory in mind of what religion is and how it makes its impact on the human community. Religion is treated here as an independent variable and its ideas as unmediated responses to public issues.

Third, I do not propose to reduce religious faith only to an exercise in communal problem-solving through manipulation of religious attitudes and convictions. I do not represent religion as the upshot of a collective fantasy indifferent to actuality. I do not suggest that, in the service of this-worldly tasks, people willfully manipulate eternal, revealed truth that they believe God has vouchsafed to them. I am not claiming that they change their faith to accommodate reality. Such a collective resort to cynicism treating religion as instrumental would mock the convictions with regard to revealed truth that animate the faithful. It also contradicts human nature, which does not take kindly to deliberate misrepresentation. Religious people are not to be denied the fundamental integrity of their conviction nor the sincerity of their piety—certainly not in these pages nor by me, a practicing Jew.

That is why the processes of accommodation, adaptation, and redefinition traced in the three case-studies set forth here are easier to describe and analyze than to explain and interpret. Three times over we shall see how Judaic religious systems responded through reform and renewal of the received Judaic construction ("Judaism") to manage critical turnings in the Israelite social order. What I argue for here is the power of self-evidence to camouflage reform as renewal. In reflecting on what in their original context are perceived as obvious meanings and inescapable doctrines, people take for granted that earlier expressed religious truth addresses their very immediate dilemmas and pertains to what engages them. Religious responses to crisis represent a massive exercise in "self-evidence."

Let me explain what I mean through a simple case of broadly conceded self-evidence: the Holocaust and the state of Israel are the givens of contemporary Judaic consciousness. It is impossible to imagine a contemporary community within Judaism that was studying the book of Job or Isaiah's suffering servant (Isa 53–54) that would not once refer to the problem of evil represented by the people of Israel who were confined in Auschwitz. This is because the Holocaust defines one of the givens of contemporary Judaic consciousness. Nor can one imagine a group considering Ezekiel's prophecy of Tel Aviv (the hill of Spring) and his vision of the dry bones that would not invoke the miracle represented by the creation of the State of Israel. These people understand that Isaiah and Ezekiel prophesied to another age long ago. But they also take for granted that the prophets speak today. That is why they study the record of their prophecy and what has been imputed to that prophecy. With religion we deal not with what people argue as a plausible proposition, but with what they know as absolute, categorical fact.

To generalize, Jewish people (though not they alone) take for granted that Scripture speaks to them: that is why they turn to it to begin with. Their contemporary condition then instructs them on what they should seek. The given condition shapes their reading and response to what they find in Scripture. It is not what they profess, but what they take for granted, that defines matters. The contemporary facts of life impose form and meaning on the self-evidence that shapes religious faith. Holocaust-theologians do not manipulate Job to their task, nor do Zionists force Ezekiel to serve theirs. To them, the relevance of Job or Ezekiel is inescapable. The faithful do not manipulate truth; they build on the foundations of fact as the survey of their understanding of reality defines those facts.

What Is at Stake in this Book?

Why should we think at just this time about religion, here exemplified by Judaism, as a tool for problem-solving? And why should we study the transformations in the history of Judaism in the context of the challenge of crisis and the response by the religious community of its reconstruction and renewal of the received faith? It is because, these days, throughout the English-speaking world, people are placing too much stress on the personal side of religion, its benefits to the individual and its impact upon him or her. What makes the matter timely is the contemporary stress within religious life upon the individual and the personal and private experience reported by the faithful.

I therefore deem it worthwhile to take Judaism as an example of the traits common among religions, specifically its impact upon the public, social, and communal life; how religious ideas formed by those that hold them relate to the social world, and how the faithful confront the political world. Since I wish to show how through religious doctrine and activity people solve problems, I take up the case of Judaism, among many possible candidates, to make the point. Here I mean to set forth the perspective in detail, if not to prove the principle through a variety of probative cases. I trust that in the future others will contribute examples from other world religions.

Why Judaism in Particular?

Judaism in its formative period serves our purpose because the three turning points in this period of its history are well-documented and are signaled by the writing of new kinds of books. Transformations in the Judaic system and structure correspond to, are recorded in, and ratified by, additions to the canon. Each principal moment in its formative history, embodied in its canonical writings, moreover, are defined by what in retrospect we can see as a time of crisis. Such critical changes—turnings—have threatened the integrity of the faith, its plausibility, relevance, and self-evidence, and have therefore called into question the future of the community of Israel sustained by that faith. But at each of these turnings, the inner logic of the faith yielded ideas that systematically responded to the challenge of the hour. That logic came to solid expression in books of lasting influence. In the present work the books we examine are the Pentateuch, the Mishnah, the Talmud, and the rabbinic Midrash. This unfolding canon of Judaism embodies a sequence of responses to challenges of an intellectual and existential character.

At the three critical turnings we will examine here, we will discover that Judaism solved problems by reshaping itself, its way of life, its worldview, and even its theory of who and what the "Israel" of which the faith speaks is and to which (in its view) its Scripture refers. Through the Judaic religious system, its people responded to, and solved, fundamental problems. This they did by rethinking the received tradition. They reshaped it in accord with a logic they deemed to be found therein, and found a new way of writing it all down. At each turning point a new kind of writing, first the Pentateuch, then the Mishnah, and finally the Talmuds and Midrash, recorded the result of that rethinking and reconstruction. When we consider the cases treated here, we find instructive examples of the thesis announced at the outset: through religion humanity solves problems.

What responses qualify as exemplary, and how are they documented? I focus on three interrelated systems of ideas and the writing that realized them in permanent form, a form that has had ongoing influence for almost two millennia: the Pentateuch (ca. 450 B.C.E.), the Mishnah (ca. 200 C.E.), and the Talmuds and Midrash (ca 400–450 C.E.). These systems of ideas and their canonical writings I set forth as intellectual records of the religious responses to social and political problems, as well as the cultural dilemmas that transcend abstract theology. At issue, however, are not books alone. I do not portray merely how a crisis prompted someone to write a book. The thesis that animates this account concerns a religion viewed whole, the entirety of Judaism, its rites and rituals, ideas and issues. This religion is most readily studied in the books it values as authoritative. That is why I address the governing constructions of ideas as embodied in official writings. I describe the way in which the thoughtful Israelites at several points of crises set forth in documents, in time accepted as canonical, the coherent conceptions needed to guide people in shaping religious expression.

I need not apologize for my stress on books in the study of a religion that has sustained itself through books, beginning, after all, with Scripture. The intellectual expression of religion demands attention whether for its systematic theology or for its unsystematic, episodic religious teachings. What matters is that the intellectual expression of a community is accessible to us in the very language of those that valued these particular ideas. We are able by direct encounter with their own writing to introduce our own questions and perspectives—our interest in the political and social foundations of the community's religious teaching. If we want to know how the ideas that people formed solved the problems that they experience, we are wise to take up the books they wrote in the aftermath of crisis and turning.

The Program of Exposition

I propose no continuous history of ideas, a narrative of the history of the formation of Judaism through its principal writings seen in context. I regard such a project as well worth the effort, but I have a different one in mind. Rather, I wish to make the simple point just now set forth, exploring some principal turnings in the history of Judaism as a public exercise in problem-solving. To that end I select for description, analysis, and interpretation three moments of transformation. Each represents an occasion for Judaism to serve the Jewish people as the means for solving its problems and each comes to realization in writing. There are, of course, other candidates for analysis as transformations in response to turning points in politics and culture besides those treated here. I in no way claim that these exhaust the possibilities. I only maintain that from the contemporary perspective these texts represent the three most significant moments of transformation for the formative age of Judaism. The brief account that follows shows the principle of selection that governed my choices as to canonical writings and intellectual initiatives.

The Torah of Moses

We begin with the formation of the Torah, often called the Pentateuch or the Five Books of Moses, and its statement to a world in flux in the fifth century B.C.E. It was at this time during the exile and return that a system took shape that would define the inner structure of nearly all Judaic religious systems from antiquity to the present day. During this period the first turning point yielded the Torah, attributed to Moses at Sinai and proclaimed by Ezra in Jerusalem about 450 B.C.E.. This initial Judaism turned the inchoate and diverse traditions of pre-exilic Israel, that is, Israel before 586 B.C.E., into the Torah of Moses. This transformation marked the origin of the Judaism embodied by the Torah. By transforming received traditions into a coherent and authoritative story, the first system took shape at the turning point marked by the return of the Israelite exiles to Jerusalem—often called Zion—following the destruction of the temple in 586 B.C.E. by the Babylonians—the temple built by Solomon almost four centuries earlier—and the restoration of Israel to its land in 538 B.C.E. by the Persians.

The Mishnah

The Mishnah was the first document of normative Judaism beyond Scripture itself and contains the initial writing down of the Oral Torah. The Mishnah took over the Pentateuchal system recapitulating its main points in a fresh way and in a new medium of expression. This new systematic statement emerged as a response to the despair precipitated by the failed wars against Rome in 66–73 C.E. and in 132–135 C.E. and their aftermath. The Pentateuchal paradigm had failed, signaled by the loss of the reconstructed temple in Jerusalem and by the resulting permanent cessation of the blood atonement rites of animal sacrifice that the Torah had prescribed in 450 B.C.E. following their restoration by the returning exiles in 538 B.C.E.

The Talmuds and Midrash

These texts reflect the work of what is now called rabbinic Judaism. There are two Talmuds, one composed in the land of Israel (ca. 400 C.E.) and the other in Babylonia (ca. 600). Through the Talmud the earlier Mishnah would find its way into the social world of the Jewish people. The system of rabbinic Judaism with its distinctive traits—sanctification in the here and now as the condition of salvation at the end of time, the whole embodied in a system of action-symbols and rules of conduct—emerged not in the Mishnah but in the first of the two Talmuds, the Jerusalem Talmud, usually referred to as "Yerushalmi." That same system also imposed itself on the Judaic reading of Scripture in such compilations of midrash—texts of scriptural interpretation such as *Genesis Rabbah* and *Leviticus Rabbah*. The Talmud and the Midrash emerged as responses to two challenges, first, as a response to the rise of Christianity to political hegemony in the Roman Empire, and second, as a response to a systemic anomaly and asymmetry in the Pentateuchal-Mishnaic system. The shift in the external political situation of Judaism marked by the recognition of Christianity as the state religion of Rome (discussed in chapter four) and the internal logic of the then-existing Judaic system (discussed in chapter five) combined to produce these texts of normative rabbinic Judaism.

The completed rabbinic system established a theology of history congruent with that of Scripture and an eschatology realized in a doctrine of a Messiah. In this final synchronization of the Pentateuchal and the Mishnaic systems with its inclusion of history and Messianic eschatology, however, the historical narrative was understood in terms of the Mishnah, not those of the earlier Pentateuch. The Halakhic category-formations governed, their theology endured. When, moreover, the Pentateuchal history was "Mishna-ized," and the doctrine of the Messiah adopted and the sage understood to be the model of the Messiah, rabbinic Judaism was complete. That is the story documented in the fifth chapter. Chapter six asks why the Pentateuchal-Mishnaic system, as reconfigured by the Talmudic-Midrashic system, persisted as it has for a millennium and a half as the single paramount Judaism, and why it continues today to define Judaism for the majority of practicing Jews.

These three turning points do not exhaust the transformations in the history of Judaism that warrant attention. Certainly others present claims as compelling as those chosen. Qabbalah is one example of a reform of Judaism that yielded Reform, Orthodox, and Conservative Judaism. But the three cases in this book mark the most important moments of change in the formation of rabbinic Judaism. They form a continuous story of successive systems. They serve their purpose, which is to underscore the character of religion, exemplified by Judaism, as a shared and public enterprise of believing communities, a way in which people work together to solve problems.

What Exactly Do We Mean by "Judaism"?

Having used such language as "Judaism" and "religious system" and "Judaic religious system" (hereafter "Judaic systems of the social order"), let me now define those operative terms and categories for this book.

Judaism

When people use the word "Judaism" they use it only in the singular, and they assume they refer to a single religion, or religious tradition, extending (if not from creation) from Sinai to the present. By "Judaism" many assume they speak of a single, unitary, harmonious, continuous religious tradition beginning at Sinai and continuing to the present day essentially unchanged. That represents not only a theological construct, which is appropriate, but a historical, descriptive one, which is challenged by facts of history and culture. When they use the word "Judaism" in that way, as people often do, they find the confrontation with change and diversity difficult. Things changed over time and not always in a way consistent with the received tradition. Moreover, different conceptions of what "Judaism" has been, is now, and should be, have competed for the loyalties of the same folk. "Judaism" with its native category "Torah" as counterpart, represents a theological, not a descriptive historical category. This theological category imposes itself on the selection, and then the description, analysis, and interpretation of the data that forms an understanding of Judaism that is single, normative, unitary, harmonious, continuous—all the way back to God's revelation at Sinai. In such a categorization judgments as to what is normative or representative, and as to who decides such matters, abound. Judaism outside such a theological framework then precipitates confusion. Moreover arguments ultimately beyond resolution on what is authentic or true Judaism, and what is false or not normative, take over. Those arguments, which may be critical to theological discourse, impede the understanding through description, analysis, and interpretation of social and cultural facts.

Not only so, but in contemporary discourse (and for some time now) not a few people understand "Judaism" to refer to a secular ethnic culture and not a religious tradition at all. The result is that by "Judaism" people frequently mean "everything and its opposite." Such lack of definition paralyzes secular analytical discourse concerning the religion, or to the religious tradition, to which people make reference when they use the word "Judaism." A different category-formation is required for the social and historical study of religions, for a religions-historical study of any complex religion such as is represented by "Judaism," "Christianity," "Islam," "Buddhism," "Hinduism," and others. These "-isms" and "-ities" make concrete abstract theological judgments and are frequently imposed, to begin with, by outsiders seeking simple constructions for complex data. This tendency to reify is generally understood in the academic study of religions.

Judaic Systems of the Social Order

Instead of using the indeterminate "-ism," "Judaism," I refer to the several "Judaic systems of the social order," meaning by this term, various Judaic systems, commonly but not always of a religious character, when I am defining a determinate group of Jews' social and cultural construction. That is to say, I define the genus of which I speak, a religion, as well as the species of that genus, in the present context, not Judaism pure and simple, but only "a Judaism."

Specifically I understand by a religious system three constituent components, which fuse into one: (a) a worldview which, by reference to the intersection of the supernatural and the natural worlds, accounts for how things are and puts them together into a cogent and harmonious picture; (b) a way of life which expresses in concrete actions the world-view and which is explained by that worldview; and (c) for the purposes of this book a social group calling itself "Israel" for which the worldview accounts, which is defined in concrete terms by the way of life, and which, therefore, gives expression in the everyday world to the world-view and is defined as an entity by that way of life.

A Judaic system then comprises not merely a theory found in texts and distinct from social reality, but an explanation for the group "Israel" that gives social form to the system and an account of the distinctive way of life of that group. "A Judaism" is not a book, and no social group took shape because people read a book and agreed that God had revealed what the book said they should do. Let me state with emphasis: *A Judaic system derives from and focuses upon a social entity, a group of Jews who (in their minds at least) constitute not "an Israel" but "Israel," and hold to their religious system not as "a Judaism" but as "Judaism," pure and simple.*

Why invoke the social entity first, and then the ethics or way of life and the ethos or worldview in succession? It is because a systemic so-cial entity is essential to the construction. For it is conceivable that a Judaic system could treat as not essential a variety of rules for everyday life. In modern times that indifference to rule-making for this morning's break-fast proves characteristic of a number of "Judaisms." Or such a Judaic sys-tem may fail to articulate elements of a worldview to answer a range of questions other "Judaisms" deem fundamental. Contemporary "Ju-daisms" do not treat as urgent many of the philosophical and theological questions found absorbing by earlier system-builders. But no Judaic sys-tem can omit a clear picture of the meaning and sense of the category "Israel" (as a people group, not a national entity). Without an "Israel" (in contemporary terms, an answer to the question, "who is a Jew?"), a social entity in fact and not only in doctrine, we have not a system but a book. And, as I have already emphasized, a book is not "a Judaism," for it is only a book. In this book we will follow a sequence of Judaic religious systems, each set forth in its distinct canon, each addressing a critical issue with a self-evidently valid response. Each of my three "turning points" mark new beginnings: evidence of systemic origins.

How then do we differentiate one "Judaism" from some other? When we identify "Judaisms" in one period after another, we begin by trying to locate, within the larger group of Jews, those social entities that see themselves, and are seen by others, as distinct and bounded. Such dis-tinct groups ("Israels") present to themselves a clear account of who they are, what they do, and why they do what they do: the rules and explana-tions of their shared, collective, corporate "Judaism." "A Judaism" ad-dresses a social group, an "Israel," with the claim that their group is not merely "an Israel" but "Israel" itself, "Israel" in a nutshell, "Israel" in its ideal form, Israel's saving remnant, the *state* of being "Israel," the natural next step in the linear, continuous history ("progress") of "Israel," everything, anything, but always "Israel."

From Judaisms to Judaism

So "a Judaism," a Judaic system, constitutes a clear and precise account of a social group, the way of life and worldview of a group of Jews, however defined. Speaking descriptively, therefore, we can identify no single "Judaism," no linear and incremental history of one continuous "Judaism," for there has never been "a Judaism," only "Judaisms." But as I argue in chapter one on the Pentateuchal transformation, there is a single paradigmatic and definitive human experience that each "Judaism" reworks in its own circumstance and context.

"Judaism" then serves to refer to a particular religious tradition that comprises a variety of expressions. I maintain two complementary propositions: (a) no religious system (within a given set of related religions) recapitulates any other; (b) nevertheless all religious systems (within a given set) recapitulate resentment. A single persistent experience for generation after generation captures what, for a particular group, stands for the whole of the human condition: everything all at once, all together, the misery and the magnificence of life.

What I have said requires the immediate specification of that single paradigmatic experience to which all "Judaisms" everywhere and under all conditions refer. That experience is set forth in chapter one, but it pertains to all three components of this account of how "Judaism" solves a social and intellectual problem—how it resolves a crisis. Thus I maintain we may speak of "Judaism" in a secular framework of cultural analysis despite the diversity of Judaic systems that history has produced, illustrated in this book by the Pentateuch (and Prophets), the Mishnah, and the Talmud and Midrash.

As a matter of fact, we may identify that generative and definitive moment, precisely as all "Judaisms" have, by looking into that same Scripture. All "Judaisms" before modern times have identified the Torah as the written statement of God's will for the Jewish people. I suppose that to start we should specify that formative and definitive moment, recapitulated by all "Judaisms," from the story of Creation to Abraham his offspring, Isaac and Jacob. Or perhaps we are advised to make our way to Sinai and hold that the origin of "Israel" occurs at God's descent from heaven.

Allowing ourselves merely the retelling of the story of the religion deprives us of required insight. Recapitulating the story does not help us understand the religion. Identifying the point of origin of the story as text, by contrast, does. For the text tells not just what happened on the occasion to which the story refers, e.g., the creation of the world, but how (long afterward and for their own reasons) people wanted to portray themselves. The tale in text, therefore, recapitulates the resentment that springs from that point of crisis which the group wishes to explain, transcend, and transform. It is what permits us to speak not only of "Judaisms" but also of "Judaism."

However subcategorized, all "Judaisms" in this sense form a single species of the larger genus, religion. For all religions used some materials in common and exhibit some traits that distinguish each of them from every other species of the genus religion. That is what makes of them a single species. Each Judaism retells in its own way and with its distinctive emphases the tale of the Five Books of Moses, the story of a not-a-people that becomes a people. This people has what it has only on condition, and it can lose it all by virtue of its own sin. That is a terrifying, unsettling story for a social group to recount of itself because it imposes an acute self-consciousness and a chronic insecurity upon what should be the firm foundation of society. The collection of diverse materials joined into a single tale on the occasion of the original exile and restoration from that exile, because of its repetition in age succeeding age, precipitates the recapitulation of the interior religious experience of exile and restoration—always because of sin and atonement. But I have gotten ahead of my story, which unfolds in the initial Judaic system, as I explain in chapter one.

Exile and Return and the Response of the Torah

Reorganizing the Past to Face the Crisis of an Uncertain Future

The decades from 538 to 450 B.C.E. marked the period of the generative crisis that produced the initial systemic statement of Judaism, the Torah, also known as the Pentateuch or as the Five Books of Moses. The Hebrew word *torah* is translated "Instruction." The concept of "Torah" or "instruction" would replicate itself in nearly all subsequent Judaic religious systems of the social order, whether continuous with the Pentateuch, as in the case of the Mishnah, Talmud, and Midrash of rabbinic Judaism, or later. The Torah drew upon older traditions of pre-exilic Israel but came to formation and closure in response to the destruction of the first temple and the exile of the political classes of Jerusalem by the Babylonians in 586 B.C.E. and the subsequent initial return from exile around 538 B.C.E. The Torah reached its final form starting with those who returned to Zion beginning in 538 B.C.E., and came to define what we now call Judaism by around 450 B.C.E., when Ezra proclaimed it the foundation-document of what would be the restored temple of Jerusalem (completed ca. 415 B.C.E.).

The process that yielded the Torah was precipitated not by the destruction of 586 B.C.E., but by the restoration from exile beginning about 538 B.C.E. The period of the formation and closure is in two parts: the first, between the destruction of the temple in 586 B.C.E. and the return to Zion in 538 B.C.E., a time of despair; and second, from 538 B.C.E. to the closure of the Pentateuch by Ezra in about 450 B.C.E., a time of renewal. In the former period, the temple lay in ruins, and the Israelites in Babylonian exile settled down for a wait of indeterminate length. Whether or not they could conceive of returning to Zion is difficult to say; they had no reason, while Babylonia ran the world, to think that they might soon go back to the lost land. But when the Persian world-ruler, Cyrus, conquered Babylonia and restored exiled peoples to their lands, including Israel to the land of Israel, the idea of a return to Zion, lost a half-century earlier, seemed a practical possibility.

Now it was in that latter period in particular, beginning with the return in 538 B.C.E. and ending when Ezra proclaimed the Torah in 450, that Israel found itself facing a profound question, one that could have yielded despair. It was this: if Israel had once lost the land and returned, could the people lose the land again? Then, what defines the condition of its enduring tenure, explaining how to prevent another exile and assuring that the present return would endure? What are the rules, and what is the significance of this sequence of events? For the situation of the people Israel in the land of Israel had been transformed from a given to a gift, an immutable fact of nature into a transient condition, a variable of politics.

What is meant by "from a given to a gift?" The nation restored to its land may be compared to a condemned man reprieved from the scaffold. To such as he, nothing loses its astonishing quality. Nothing ever can look the same as it did before. Life cannot be taken for granted, as a given. It becomes a gift, each day an unanticipated surprise. Everything then demands explanation, but uncertainty reigns.

Returning to Zion beginning in 538 B.C.E. Israel thus found itself in the position of the condemned man accorded a wordless reprieve and removed from the scaffold. For how long? The Torah answered that question and did so explicitly through the story that it narrated and the laws and prophecies that it vouchsafed. Responding to that uncertain moment, the Pentateuch of Ezra, attributed to Moses, resolved the crisis of an uncertain future. The unsettling events experienced by Israel in the aftermath of 586 B.C.E. and then 538 B.C.E. were seen as part of a larger pattern. Those happenings were transformed into the paradigm of loss of the land of Israel and restoration to that land—exile and return—that would characterize Judaisms as they would take shape for the next two and a half millennia, and as competing Judaic religious systems continue to thrive today. That is why the analogy—the condemned man reprieved for no clear reason and at risk still of being hanged—captures the situation of Israel after the return to Zion in 538 B.C.E. prior to the formation of the Torah-book. The Pentateuch transformed inchoate traditions into a cogent, rational system capable of solving a critical problem of Israel's existence in the mid-fifth century B.C.E.

Consider the crisis of hope faced by those who returned to Zion from 538 B.C.E. forward: What now? For since the land of Israel had once been lost, could it not be lost again? Holding the land and losing it (again) was a possibility scarcely thinkable before 586 B.C.E. (except by the pre-exilic prophets, and then perhaps after the fact) that became entirely plausible from 538 B.C.E. The return, like the condemned man's reprieve, carried with it no terms or conditions other than those set by the pagan Persian king of kings, Cyrus. Anything could happen, and no one knew why. Accordingly, the critical issue was: how shall we act so as never again to lose the land? Is this reprieve only so that the executioner can get a longer rope, or has he, indeed, been pardoned? The Pentateuch came to closure to answer the questions Israel needed to ask: for how long would Israel retain Zion, and what were the conditions of its reprieve?

For Israel, therefore, the return to Zion raised a question that turned a chronic complaint into an acute crisis. The prophets had long insisted that Israel's history tracks its moral condition. God punishes Israel for sin. Why Israel, elect of God, suffers defeat and disaster at the hands of idolaters was thus a question long ago answered. The prophets' explanation of the defeat, destruction, and exile as a consequence of Israel's sin had now to extend to the return to Zion. Then, more to the point, how long could Israel hope to possess the land once lost and then recovered—therefore forever after held in an uncertain grasp, with open arms? It is that uncertainty, that crisis of an uncertain future, that defines the context in which Judaism made its initial—and definitive—statement in the Pentateuch. There Israel was afforded the answer to the urgent question of exile and return. In the Five Books of Moses, therefore, Judaism reorganized records of the past to face the crisis of an uncertain future.

What was the Pentateuch's response to the crisis of the return to Zion and the uncertainty that accompanied the return? The Pentateuch, formed through the amalgamation of a variety of received narratives, laws, prophecies, and other written and oral traditions, explicitly answered the question: God has bound himself to a covenant with Israel. Israel was commanded to form an abode worthy of God's presence, in the land that had vomited forth prior, unworthy inhabitants and had been set aside by God for Israel. If Israel observes the conditions of the covenant as set forth in this Torah, it will retain the land and prosper in it. If, as Leviticus 26 and Deuteronomy 28 and other passages state in so many words, Israel violates the terms of the agreement, God will punish the people by sending them into exile from the land. But with repentance and atonement comes the possibility of restoration.

The Torah thus set forth the terms and conditions of the covenant between Israel and God concerning the land. This it did by organizing the received writings of pre-exilic Israel into a sustained, continuous narrative of Israel's corporate life and history—all of them recast to take account of current events and shaped to the governing paradigm. In this exemplary pattern of Israel's relationship to its land, Israel's past was reorganized to face the crisis of an uncertain future. Specifically, the rules that are shown to govern from Creation forward would set forth the terms and conditions of holding the land. So the key was to discern the pattern exhibited by unfolding events. Then with the past teaching lessons, the future would present no crisis, only opportunity.

What was this pattern? Judaism treated the tales of Adam and Israel as corresponding. Specifically, the paradigm encompassed the genus, humanity, and the species, Israel and non-Israel. Each of the species conformed to the same pattern, one of sin and exile. Both were shown to have undergone the same experience of exile by reason of sin. But Israel now had the opportunity of return: the Torah and its laws made all the difference. Adam did not know about the power of repentance to overcome sin and bring about reconciliation and restoration. Through the Torah, Israel did. So by fulfilling the Torah, Israel would retain the land that it held on the Torah's conditions and stipulations.

We see this construction of matters through the formulation of the later rabbinic sages. They not only mastered the details of Scripture but also grasped the pattern and possessed a conception of the whole. They in so many words compared Israel's experience of loss of the land to Adam's experience of loss of Eden. They found in the Pentateuch two corresponding stories: the prologue representing humanity in the person of Adam, and the main narrative concerning Israel, Adam's surrogate. Here is how they read the loss of the land in the context of the loss of Eden, Israel's story in the setting of Adam's:

Genesis Rabbah XIX:ix.2

A. R. Abbahu in the name of R. Yosé bar Haninah: "It is written, 'But they [Israel] are like a Man [Adam], they have transgressed the covenant' (Hos. 6:7).

B. "'They are like a Man,' specifically, like the first Man. [We shall now compare the story of the first Man in Eden with the story of Israel in its land.]

C. "'In the case of the first Man, I brought him into the garden of Eden, I commanded him, he violated my commandment, I judged him to be sent away and driven out, but I mourned for him, saying "How . . ." [which begins the book of Lamentations, hence stands for a lament, but which, as we just saw, also is written with the consonants that also yield, 'Where are you'].

D. "'I brought him into the garden of Eden,' as it is written, 'And the Lord God took the Man and put him into the garden of Eden' (Gen. 2:15).

E. "'I commanded him,' as it is written, 'And the Lord God commanded . . .' (Gen. 2:16).

F. "'And he violated my commandment,' as it is written, 'Did you eat from the tree concerning which I commanded you' (Gen. 3:11).

G. "'I judged him to be sent away,' as it is written, 'And the Lord God sent him from the garden of Eden' (Gen. 3:23).

H. "'And I judged him to be driven out.' 'And he drove out the Man' (Gen. 3:24).

I. "'But I mourned for him, saying, "How . . . "' 'And he said to him, "Where are you"' (Gen. 3:9), and the word for 'where are you' is written, 'How . . .'

J. "'So too in the case of his descendants [God continues to speak], I brought them into the land of Israel, I commanded them, they violated my commandment, I judged them to be sent out and driven away but I mourned for them, saying, "How . . . "'

K. "'I brought them into the land of Israel.' 'And I brought you into the land of Carmel' (Jer. 2:7).

L. "'I commanded them.' 'And you, command the children of Israel' (Ex. 27:20). 'Command the children of Israel' (Lev. 24:2).

M. "'They violated my commandment.' 'And all Israel have violated your Torah' (Dan. 9:11).

N. "'I judged them to be sent out.' 'Send them away, out of my sight and let them go forth' (Jer 15:1).

O. "' . . . and driven away.' 'From my house I shall drive them' (Hos. 9:15).

P. "'But I mourned for them, saying, "How . . ." How has the city sat solitary, that was full of people' (Lam. 1:1)."

This view of the whole then asks us to read the Pentateuch not as a collection of laws and stories, poems and prophecies, but as a coherent and accessible paradigm, a patterned account of what it means to be "Israel." And it invites reflection on the difference between Adam and Israel—that is to say, how Israel can recover the land in a way that Adam could never recover Eden.

The rabbinic sages later on would take up the narrative of the Torah and recast it into an account of the norms of Israel's social order. Their recapitulation of the Torah's story regulates relationships between Israelites and corporate Israel, among Israelites in their units of propagation and production, and between corporate Israel and the ever-present, always-sentient God. The details coalesce to yield a clear picture of an entire social order, its relationships and its points of stability and order. Rabbinic Judaism undertakes to realize in the everyday and here and now of the

Jews' communal existence the imperatives set forth in the Torah for the formation of God's abode on earth.

Their perspicacity in the reading of Scripture identifies for us how in the Judaic context the Pentateuch forms a coherent reply to the acutely urgent question facing the generation to whom in 450 B.C.E. the Pentateuch was addressed. The answer of the Pentateuch to that question is: Israel holds the land *conditionally*. God in the Torah has stipulated the conditions under which Israel can keep the land, and, he has specified the reasons that explain why those that were there before Israel lost it. These are made explicit in Leviticus 26. And the rabbinic sages, reading the story whole and complete, formed of the Pentateuch a design for Israel's social order, detailing the ways in which the kingdom of priests and holy people could form an abode worthy of God's presence in its midst. That is how the past was reorganized to meet the crisis of an uncertain future. The paradigm of exile and return began in the mind of the priestly sector of Israel and did not arise from, and merely describe the facts of, a perfectly secular experience of going into exile and returning home. The whole was a reconstruction and act of imagination.

But I have gotten ahead of my story. As we shall now see, what happened in 586 B.C.E. and after, and what the paradigm fabricated out of what happened, do not correspond entirely. Scripture said, in both the Torah and the prophetic-historical books, that Israel suffered, atoned, attained reconciliation, and renewed the covenant with God. What the Pentateuch added was the idea that the renewal of the covenant of the Torah, the covenant of Sinai, is signified by the return to Zion. Now, as I shall explain, only a minority of the people, Israel, in fact had undergone these experiences. But the Israelite system of the Torah made normative that experience of exile and return as the realization of Israel's alienation and reconciliation.

The Israelite system expressed by the Five Books of Moses as well as some of the prophetic books selected as events only a narrow sample of what had happened, and imparted to that selection of events meanings actually pertinent to the experience of only a few. In its original statement, the system of the Torah after 586 B.C.E. did not merely describe things that had actually happened, normal events so to speak, but selected among events. In actuality some Israelites went into exile, some did not; some of the exiles would return to Zion, but many did not. The selected events were thus rendered normative and mythic. The Pentateuch then turned an experience of part of the people into the only paradigm of experience.

Let me spell out how the first crisis and consequent response created Judaism—the Judaism that would privilege Scripture, and within Scripture, the Pentateuch and the social experience raised to the norm in that writing.

The Turning Point of 538–450 B.C.E.

The way of life of the Judaism that set the norm for the Second Temple period was that holy way of life depicted in the Five Books of Moses, the Pentateuch. The Pentateuch encompasses four originally distinct sources. Three—J (the Yahwist, where "the Lord" is God's name), E (the Elohist, where "God" is God's name), and D (the Deuteronomist, the account in the model of Deuteronomy)—derive from the period before 586 B.C.E. One, P (the priestly strand) came to closure in the period afterward. From our perspective, the Judaic system represented by the Pentateuch came into being when the several sources became one—that is, the Five Books of Moses as we now know them. And that work was accomplished by priestly redactors in the time of Ezra.

While, as I have emphasized, the Judaism represented by the Pentateuch of ca. 450 B.C.E. drew abundant materials from the period before 586 B.C.E., such as the Yahwist's and Deuteronomist's writings, the statement that the Torah of Moses made all together derived from and expressed the viewpoint, both in proportion and emphasis, of the priesthood. That is why a large portion of the Pentateuch devotes time and attention to the matter of the cult, that is to say, the centrality of sacrifice, the founding of the priesthood and its rules, and the importance of the temple in Jerusalem. That further explains why many of the texts in the Torah are aimed at explaining the origin, in the patriarchal period, of the locations of various cultic centers prior to the centralization of the cult in Jerusalem, the beginnings of the priesthood, the care and feeding of priests, the beginnings and rules of the sacrificial system, the contention between priestly castes, e.g., Levites and priests, and other matters. The Pentateuch in this way laid emphasis upon the service of God through sacrifice in the temple, conducted by the priests, and upon Israel's living of a holy way of life as a "kingdom of priests and a holy people"—all in accord with God's message to Moses at Sinai. But, of course, "God's message to Moses at Sinai" has effectively come to mean "the priestly redactors' message to Israel in Babylonia." There the priests drew together the elements of the received picture and reshaped them into the fairly coherent set of rules and narratives we now know as the Pentateuch.

Although making ample use of ancient texts, the framers of the Pentateuch as we now have it flourished in Babylonia after 586 B.C.E. and conceived as their systemic teleology the return to Zion and the rebuilding of the temple—hence the centrality of the tabernacle and its cult in the wilderness-narratives. So the Judaism of the priests imparts to the scripture of that first setting its ultimate meaning: response to historical disaster followed by (to the priests' mind) unprecedented triumph. Their vision is characterized as follows by Humphreys.

In the priests' narrative the chosen people are last seen as pilgrims moving through alien land toward a goal to be fulfilled in another time and place, and this is the vision, drawn from the ancient story of their past, that the priests now hold out to the scattered sons and daughters of old Israel. They too are exiles encamped for a time in an alien land, and they too must focus their hopes on the promise ahead. Like the Israelites in the Sinai wilderness, they must avoid setting roots in the land through which they pass, for Diaspora is not to become their permanent condition, and regulations must be adopted to facilitate this. They must resist assimilation into the world into which they are now dispersed, because hope and heart and fundamental identity lay in the future. Thus, the priestly document not only affirms Yahweh's continuing authority and action in the lives of his people but offers them a pattern for life that will ensure them a distinct identity.[1]

The net effect of the priests' pentateuchal vision of Israel, that is, its worldview seen in the aggregate, lays stress on the separateness and the holiness of Israel, all the while pointing to dangers of pollution by the other, the outsider. The way of life stresses distinguishing traits of an Israel that is distinct from, and threatened by, the outsider. The fate of the nation, moreover, depends upon the loyalty of the people in their everyday life to the requirements of their covenant with God, so history forms the barometer of the health of the nation. In these ways the several segments of the earlier traditions of Israel were drawn together so as to make the point peculiarly pertinent to Israel in exile, in that very same place from which Abram had departed in his quest for the promised land at the very beginning of the family-people that became Israel. It follows that the original Judaic system, the one set forth by the Pentateuch, answered the urgent issue of exile with the self-evident response of return. The question was not to be avoided, nor was the answer to be doubted. The center of the system, then, lay in the covenant, the contract that told Israel the rules that would govern: Keep these rules and you will not again suffer as you have suffered; violate them and you will. At the heart of the covenant was the call for Israel to form a kingdom of priests and a holy people.

If we ask ourselves for a single passage to express the priests' Judaism, we look to the book of Leviticus, which concerns the priesthood above all, and its version of the covenant, which is at Lev 19:1–18 (RSV translation):

> And the Lord said to Moses, "Say to all the congregation of the people of Israel, You shall be holy, for I the Lord your God am holy.
>
> "Every one of you shall revere his mother and his father and you shall keep my Sabbaths; I am the Lord your God.

---

[1] Lee H. Humphreys, *Crisis and Story: Introduction to the Old Testament* (Palo Alto: Mayfield, 1979), 217.

"Do not turn to idols or make for yourselves molten gods; I am the Lord your God.

"When you offer a sacrifice of peace offerings to the Lord, you shall offer it so that you may be accepted. It shall be eaten the same day you offer it or on the morrow, and anything left over until the third day shall be burned with fire. If it is eaten at all on the third day, it is an abomination, it will not be accepted, and every one who eats it shall bear his iniquity, because he has profaned a holy thing of the Lord; and that person shall be cut off from his people.

"When you reap the harvest of your land, you shall not reap your field to its very border, neither shall you gather the gleanings after your harvest. And you shall not strip your vineyard bare, neither shall you gather the fallen grapes of your vineyard; you shall leave them for the poor and for the sojourner. I am the Lord your God.

"You shall not steal, nor deal falsely, nor lie to one another. And you shall not swear by my name falsely and so profane the name of your God; I am the Lord. You shall not oppress your neighbor or rob him. The wages of a hired servant shall not remain with you all night until the morning. You shall not curse the deaf or put a stumbling block before the blind, but you shall fear your God; I am the Lord.

"You shall do no injustice in judgment; you shall not be partial to the poor or defer to the great, but in righteousness shall you judge your neighbor. You shall not go up and down as a slanderer among your people, and you shall not stand forth against the life of your neighbor; I am the Lord.

"You shall not hate your brother in your heart, but you shall reason with your neighbor, lest you bear sin because of him. You shall not take vengeance or bear any grudge against the sons of your own people, but you shall love your neighbor as yourself; I am the Lord."

This mixture of rules we should regard as cultic, as to sacrifice; moral, as to support of the poor; ethical, as to right-dealing; and above all religious, as to "being holy for I the Lord your God am holy." The pastiche all together portrays a complete and whole society: its worldview, holiness in the likeness of God; its way of life, an everyday life of sanctification through the making of distinctions; its Israel, a people distinct from all others and called *Israel*. But, as we know from other writings of the time, the Priestly Code conceived of a very special *Israel*, an Israel characterized by genealogical "purity." That meant, in this postexilic context, separation from not only the nations but also from those Israelites who had not undergone the experience of exile and return to Zion.

The definition of who is Israel lay at the foundation of the system, which was shaped to answer that urgent question of social explanation. For along with the revelation of the Torah of "Moses," Ezra insisted that the Israelites divorce the wives they had taken from the "peoples of the land." Now, as a matter of fact, the peoples of the land were none other than descendants of those Israelites who had not gone off into exile in Babylonia. They had remained behind, and had not undergone the paradigmatic experience of exile and return. *Israel* was comprised, in the priests' version, only by those who had gone into exile.

The book of Leviticus contains a clear statement of the consequence of violating the covenant, and that is geared to the events of the recent past:

> "If you walk in my statutes and observe my commandments and do them, then I will give you your rains in their season. . . . But if you will not hearken to me and will not do all these commandments . . . I will do this to you: I will appoint over you sudden terror . . . and you shall sow your seed in vain for your enemies shall eat it. . . . Then the land shall enjoy its Sabbaths as long as it lies desolate while you are in your enemies' land. . . ." (Lev 26:3, 34).

The Judaism of the priests therefore defined as its generative question the loss of the land—and its eventual restoration. It ignored the Jews in Babylonia. It failed to acknowledge the Jews in Egypt, settled for some time in a large community. It positively rejected the inhabitants of the land, who had no reason to answer the question of how to prevent the events of the recent past from happening ever again. That Judaism gave as its answer the formation of a separate and holy society, *Israel*, a people *Israel* returned to the land of Israel. The Judaic system of the Pentateuch, forming the normative system throughout the Second Temple period— from the return to Zion ca. 538 B.C.E. through Ezra's proclamation of the Torah about 450 B.C.E., to the destruction of the temple in 70 C.E.— therefore responded to the loss of the land *and* its restoration to the Israelites' possession. Israel must obey the rules of holiness, because by keeping its half of the covenant, it could make certain God would uphold the other half: "And I will give peace in the land, and you shall lie down and none shall make you afraid" (Lev 26:6 RSV). For the next five hundred years, the Judaic system of the Pentateuch predominated.

What we learn from the crisis and response is that religion does not merely respond to random events. Rather, it selects as normative happenings that it recognizes as enormously consequential. Religion—in the case of Judaism in its formative age and writings—does not describe and ratify in sacred terms the secular events understood in a worldly way. The generative logic and paradigmatic forms of religion, in the case of Judaism, take shape within the interiority of imagination. They only then, having taken shape, impart their pattern upon the social order. In the case of Judaism, the Torah's religion imparts its pattern upon the social world and polity of Jews. The Torah does not merely *record* history; the Torah *creates* history. Stated in more general terms: a particular experience, transformed by a religious system into a paradigm of the life of the social group, becomes normative and therefore generative for culture and society.

Let us stand back and see matters whole: the Pentateuch made its statement through a protracted narrative. Setting out its story as "the Torah of Moses," it delivered its message through its account of events of a long-ago past. Specifically: a single, continuous story begins with the creation of the world and proceeds to the making of man and woman; the fall of humanity through disobedience; the flood that wiped out nearly all of humanity except for Noah, progenitor of all subsequent humanity; the decline of humanity from Noah to Abraham, followed by the rise of humanity through Abraham, Isaac, Jacob (also called Israel); the twelve sons of Jacob; to exile in Egypt, and, ultimately, Sinai. There, in the wilderness, before Israel's entry into the land, the scriptural narrative continues, God revealed the Torah to Moses, and that revelation contained the terms of the covenant that God then made with Israel, the family of Abraham, Isaac, and Jacob.

In the Pentateuch we deal with a composite of materials. It was only after the destruction of the first temple in 586 B.C.E., followed by the return to Zion, that these diverse and free-standing materials—two versions of Creation, two versions of the Noah-story, for example—were joined into a single, composite account. Then the Torah, to be privileged as the earliest statement of a religious system and structure that the world calls "Judaism," came into being. It transcended its origins as a pastiche of received stories, some old and some new. All were now revised for the purposes of the final authorship. By the term "authorship" I mean those who brought it into being as redactor-authors, those who took older material and restructured and rearranged it, but who also brought into that material some of their own work. It was not in the aftermath of the loss of Zion but in consequence of its restoration that the pentateuchal redactors wrote the origins of Israel, the Jewish people: beginnings shed light on the ending, the ultimate restoration of Israel to Zion, Adam to Eden, that would be eternal.

How so? In light of Israel's ultimate destiny, which the redactors took to be Israel's loss of *and restoration to* the land, the origins of the people in its land took on their cogent meaning. Israel thus began with its acquisition of the land, through God's promise to and covenant with Abraham, and attained its identity as a people through the promise of the land, in the covenant of Sinai, and the entry into the land, under Joshua. Had Israel not sinned, the story would have concluded then. But Scripture proceeds, in the prophetical books, to record what happened next, which was one sinful event after another. The story from the entry into the land to the loss of the land recorded the descent of Israel from its climactic moment, with the entry into the land comparable to the entry of Adam into Eden on the eve of the first

Sabbath. That, at any rate, is how Judaism would read matters, in line with the implications of the Pentateuch.

Israel's history thus forms the story of how, because of its conduct in the land, Israel lost its land, first in the north, then in the south—and that despite the prophets' persistent warnings. From the exile in Babylonia, the authorship of the Torah recast Israel's history into the story of the conditional existence of the people, with their existence measured by their possession of the land upon the stipulation of God's favor. Everything depended on carrying out a contract: do this, get that; do not do this, do not get that—and nothing formed a given, beyond all stipulation. The task of that authorship was to interpret the condition of the present, and their response to the uncertainty of Israel's life beyond exile and restoration underlined the uncertainty of that life.

The formation of the Pentateuch and its explanation of history made two important points. First, the pentateuchal traditions specified that Israel stood in a contractual relationship with God. God had revealed the Torah to Israel, and the Torah contained God's will for Israel. If Israel kept the Torah, God would bless the people, and if not, God would exact punishment, in the form of loss of the land, for violation of this covenant. Second, the prophetic writings emphasized that God shaped history—those particular things that happened that made a difference—in a pattern that bore deep meaning. Not only so, but whatever happened reflected God's will, which the prophets (beginning with Moses) conveyed. Ultimately organized so that the prophetic writings appear to foretell the destruction that would come, the prophets' warnings therefore contained a message entirely harmonious with the basic message of the Pentateuch.

As a result of the events of 586–450 B.C.E., the loss of the land and the return to Zion, with the subsequent rebuilding of the temple, Judaism in all its forms began. The religion commenced with the formation of the Pentateuch. We may therefore say that, while the (genealogical) Israel of the Torah of "Moses" traces its origins back to Abraham, Isaac, and Jacob, and while historians tell the story of Israel from remote antiquity, that continuous and unfolding religious tradition we know as Judaism—in all its forms—begins with Scripture. And Scripture as we have it commences with the destruction of the first temple by the Babylonians in 586 B.C.E. The Torah as we know it came to its literary formation in response to the destruction of the first temple by the Babylonians and the subsequent return to Zion, with the critical uncertainty precipitated by those events. That is, the generative question to which the Pentateuch (and prophetic collections) responds becomes acute with the recovery of the land in full knowledge that the land was lost and can be lost again— that restoration, not the loss alone, precipitated the purposeful work of reconstructing the past as guide to the uncertain future.

The Torah in Context: Exile and Return

Accordingly, the Torah represents an act of selection, construction, and imagination, not a mere writing down of things that happened and *post facto* interpretation thereof. That becomes self-evident when we realize that the actual experience of exile and return affected very few Israelites, excluding both those who never went into exile and those who never came back, on the other—certainly by far the greater part of the people, Israel. The books of Ezra and Nehemiah, not to mention the post-exilic prophets, attest to the complaints of the minority that returned to Zion against the majority of those who remained in the land and never left, on the one side, and the majority of the descendants of the exiles of Babylonia, who stayed where they were, on the other. Then to whom, first of all, did the Pentateuch speak? Not many. Few Israelites actually underwent the experience of exile and return that the Pentateuch treats as normative for all Israel.

But it was the corresponding and joined experiences—its exile, then return—on which the pentateuchal narrative focused and attained coherence. So the process of selection and revision of the past in light of the issue of the future represented an act of fabrication and imagination, not of mere description and interpretation of social facts of palpable experience. That fact—I cannot overstress—shows us the true character of the Pentateuch's Judaic religious system, the one that would predominate and be realized in the Mishnah and the Talmuds and midrash of rabbinic Judaism. It began by making a selection of facts to be deemed consequential, and hence represented as historical: those that made history, embodied its structure and pattern. It further succeeded by ignoring, in making that selection, the experiences of others who had a quite different perception of what had happened—and, for all we know, a different appreciation of the message.

But even among those who returned to Zion, the Pentateuch framed matters in accord with the acute concerns of only a minority. For who among the returned exiles made all the difference? They are those who saw the restoration of the temple as critical, its destruction as definitive of Israel's condition, its rites as paramount in Israel's existence. Then who stands behind the ultimate composition of the Pentateuch? It is—as we have already noted—a document given its final character by the priesthood, the caste in the Israelite social order comprised of those most affected by the destruction in 586 B.C.E., and by those most motivated to return from 539 B.C.E. onward. The fact that the ones who came back, and, by definition, many who were taken away, were priests made all the difference, as the books of Ezra and Nehemiah indicate. For to the priests, what mattered in 586 B.C.E. was the destruction of the temple, and what made a difference was the restoration of Zion and the rebuilding of the temple. To them the cult was the key, with the temple the nexus between heaven and earth.

What attitude flowed from the normative experiences of the elect? The nation—as seen by the priests, as defined by the priests, its components as hierarchized by the priests at the apex—restored to its land may be compared, as I said at the outset, to a condemned man reprieved from the scaffold. The comparison fails, to be sure, because we are dealing with a public, communal event: a small group of people offering the entirety of the community a vision to be shared collectively and realized corporately. While the consciousness of life as a gift of grace changes things for the survivor alone, the return to Zion—cast as it was into the encompassing language of the Five Books of Moses—imposed upon the entire nation's imagination and inner consciousness the unsettling encounter with annihilation avoided, extinction postponed, life renewed—temple restored as portrayed in the priestly books of Leviticus and Numbers.

What defined the issue as framed by the pentateuchal compilers? The events selected as paradigmatic, exile then return, were interpreted as a paradigm of death and resurrection. But the events did not concern the individual—centuries would pass before corporate restoration formed the model for individual resurrection from the grave. Rather they concerned corporate Israel, and the death of Israel was understood as its ceasing to be different from all the nations. From the encounter with the destruction of the temple in 586 B.C.E. followed by the return to Zion beginning in 538 B.C.E., the issue was, and would remain, a simple one. It was: Who is Israel, what does it mean to be Israel, and what are the rules that define Israel as a social and political entity? The unstated premise throughout is that the answers to these questions make all the difference in the world.

First Comes the System with its Inner Logic

The consequence of this account of the recognition of the crisis and the formulation of the response cannot be overstated: the entire Judaic system of the social, religious, cultural, and political orders set forth by the Pentateuch constitutes an act of imagination and invention. It is a generative logic that is autonomous of the social order but definitive of the social order come to expression in writing. First comes the system with its inner logic, then follows the identification of the crisis and the formulation of the response. The principal givens of the Torah's paradigm, in fact, speak out of the inner structure of the system. They express its logic, which is not a logic intrinsic to or dictated by, events—even events selected and reworked. The systemic data—the givens—apply its premises, not the mere facts, the random data of Israel's common life in either Babylonia or the land of Israel. Again from the perspective of a vast population of Israel—Jews in Egypt, Jews who remained in the land, and Jews who never left Babylonia—the system spoke of events that exercised no special claim, no privilege in the formation of the social order. The sense of exile came from the corporate myth—Israel belonging to the land, with Israel's possession of the land indicating its moral condition—and the aspiration to return contradicted the facts of the successful migration to the new loci of Babylonia, Egypt, and elsewhere.

Reconsider, then, the perspective of the Jews who remained in the land after 586 B.C.E., or of those who remained in Babylonia after 538 B.C.E. For both groups, for different reasons, there was no alienation, and consequently, no yearning for reconciliation. Then the normative corresponded to the merely normal: life like any other nation, wherever it happened to locate itself. True enough, treating exile and return as normative imparted to the exile the critical and definitive position. It marked Israel as special, elect, subject to the rules of the covenant and its stipulations. But, as we now realize, for much of Israel some other system must have existed, and not the system of the normative alienation constructed by the Judaism of the Torah by the (priestly) exiles returning to the land.

For to those who stayed put, the urgent questions of exile and return, the self-evidently valid response of election and covenant, bore slight relevance, asked no questions worth asking, provided no answers worth believing. That is why, when we want an example of a religious system creating the social order of culture and imagination, we can find few better instances than the power of the conception of Israel expressed by the Pentateuch to construct a system in imagination, then to realize it in the social order. That is to say, here is a system invoking its inner logic, its moral calculus, to tell people not only the *meaning* of what had happened but also *what had actually happened*. That is why I earlier claimed that the system begins whole, fabricated out of its inner logic, only then to create for Israelite society a picture of what it must be and therefore had to have been. That sense of heightened reality, that intense focus on the identification of the nation as extraordinary, represented only one possible picture of the meaning of events from 586 B.C.E. onward. But we do not have access, so far as I know, to any other but the system of the Torah and the prophetic and historical writings as framed by the priests and given definitive statement under the auspices of the Persian's Jewish viceroy in Jerusalem, namely, Nehemiah, with Ezra as counselor.

The central issue is this. The paradigm embodied in the Pentateuch of possession, sin, dispossession, repentance, and return began as a paradigm alone and not as a set of actual events that later redactors transformed into a normative pattern or paradigm. The conclusions generated by the paradigm designed by these redactors, it must follow, derived not from their reflection on things that actually happened but from the logic of their own paradigm—and that alone. That paradigm, however, would come to create expectations that could not be met by the paradigm's immediate, assumed answer. From this failure of the existing paradigm to meet expectations from the then existing paradigm, the resentment captured by the myth of exile would be renewed, while at the same time the paradigm set the conditions for resolution of this resentment and thus would resolve the crisis of exile with the promise of (yet another new) return. This self-generating, self-renewing paradigm formed a self-fulfilling prophecy that all Judaisms since have offered as the both generative tension and central structure of their systems.

To summarize: the paradigm that imparted its imprint on the history of the day did not emerge from and was not generated by the events of the age. First came the system, its worldview and way of life formed whole most likely by the priestly caste. Then came the selection, by the system, of consequential events and their patterning into systemic propositions. And finally, at a third stage (of indeterminate length of time) came the formation and composition of the canon that would express the logic of the system and state those "events" that the system would select or invent for its own expression. Since chief among the propositions of the system as defined by the Torah of Moses is the notion of the election of Israel effected in the covenant, we may say that Israel—the Israel of the Torah and historical-prophetic books of the sixth and fifth centuries—selected itself. The system created the paradigm of the society that had gone into exile and come back home—and, by the way, the system also cut its own orders, that contract or covenant that certified not election but self-selection.

How the Pentateuch Met the Challenge of 538–450 B.C.E.: Why Did Pentateuchal Judaism Endure?

Here then is the upshot. Judaism is formed out of the encounters with crisis and response. At both of these moments facts are formed out of acts of social imagination. Neither moment embodies the given, records the mere facts of the matter, or writes down an account of how things are—the ordinary human condition. At the very foundations of the original and generative Judaic paradigm is the Torah's reformation, the paradigmatic explanation it could give to the sequence of events from 586 B.C.E. when the Israelites were exiled to Babylonia to about 450 B.C.E. when they had returned to Zion and proclaimed the Torah as God's explanation of Israel's existence. And there we find not history—what is compelling in events viewed as givens. Rather, it is history systemically selected, therefore by definition invented, and not described. That would make slight difference—everyone understands the mythopoeic power of belief—except for one thing.

It is the fact that a particular experience, transformed by a religious system into a paradigm of the life of the social group, has become—been made—normative and therefore generative. That particular experience itself happened, to begin with, in the minds and imaginations of the authorship of the Pentateuch, and not in the concrete life or in the politics and society of Israel in its land and in exile. No one of course imagined that the temple lay in ruins; that was a fact. But people clearly differed about its restoration and reconstruction as the incessant complaints of the post-exilic prophets about the neglected condition of the altar attest. No one denied that some of Israel had stayed home while others had gone into exile. Again, opinion surely differed as to the exclusion of those who had not undergone the normative experience of alienation and return, opinion surely differed. That is proved by a simple fact. It was only by force that Ezra and Nehemiah effected the dissolution of families of Judeans—those who had gone into exile and now returned—married to locals.

The same is so for a long list of systemic givens. All of them represent acts of choice. None of them, as a matter of fact, constitute matters of self-evidence—except to those to whom by reason of systemic logic they were self-evident. It follows that it is the Pentateuch—and the Pentateuch alone—that says that Israel died and was reborn. It is the Pentateuch alone that imposed its selective paradigm upon events, insisting Israel was punished through exile and then forgiven. Those who had not gone into exile had not atoned. Those who did not return could not enjoy the full merit of forgiveness embodied in the rebuilt temple and its restored atonement-rites. And the upshot, as the Pentateuch portrayed matters, was this: To be Israel is to have gone into exile and returned to Zion—in not an individual but rather a familial or a genealogical sense. The very normative standing of that experience defined what was at issue in the time of Ezra and Nehemiah, who imposed upon the Judaean society of the fifth century the norm of exile and return—that is to say, of death and resurrection. Only with the conception of return do the stories of Adam and Israel correspond.

Now the question presents itself: Why did pentateuchal Judaism endure, and how has the original paradigm survived from then to now? For it is one thing to explain how a system took shape, another to account for its long-term effect. One reason covers the near-term; another allows us to explain its long-term power of self-evidence.

The Near-term Explanation

Pentateuchal Judaism survived because the institutions of politics and government established by Israel restored to the land lay in the hands of the priests. Ezra enjoyed the support of Nehemiah, satrap of Jerusalem for the Persian government, supported by troops when force was needed, sustained by the priesthood when persuasion sufficed. Not only so, but the written-out revelation of Sinai, the Torah, enjoyed the status of God's word to Israel and enjoyed the privilege of self-evident truth. So the pentateuchal system in its original, fifth-century context—the Judaism that (speaking descriptively) constituted the normative system through the Second Temple period—flourished because the priests had the power to make it stick.

The reason for this is clear. First, the priests were the ones who organized and set forth the Torah revealed by God to Moses at Sinai, as the Jews would revere it. They furthermore controlled the political institutions of the country as the Persian government established them. Consequently their perspective, with its emphasis on the temple cult and its critical role in sustaining the life of the land and the nation, predominated in defining public policy. And the temple government had the necessary political support to sustain its authority. It furthermore laid forth the Torah as its political myth, so not having constantly to resort to force. Since the Torah of Moses at Sinai defined the faith, explained what had happened, and set forth the rules for God's continuing favor to Israel, the final shape and system of the Torah would make a deep impact on the consciousness and attitude of the people as a whole.

The Long-term Explanation: From System to Paradigm

But the social and political arrangements of the restored Zion themselves underwent change over time. So why did the system persist beyond its initial context, becoming paradigmatic even in other times and places and circumstances? The more important question is why its structure proved definitive long after the political facts had shifted dramatically—indeed, had ceased to pertain at all.

The pentateuchal Torah formed a self-sustaining paradigm, both asking its question as it was declaimed in worship from week to week and answering it with the force of self-evidence: this is the Torah of Moses at Sinai. Speaking in psychological terms, the Pentateuch both precipitated tension, with its insistence on life as a gift and not a given, and resolved the tension. It recapitulated the reasons for resentment but also restored repose. This process of resentment and remission formed a self-validating experience at once intellectual and psychological for the Israel for whom, and to whom, the Torah spoke as God's word. And that was the larger part of the Jews as an ethnic body, though—as the social evidence shows—not all Jews at any one time, and not all Jews everywhere.

With the continuing authority of the Torah in Israel, the experience to which it originally constituted a profound and systematic response was recapitulated, age after age, through the reading and authoritative exegesis of the original Scripture that preserved and portrayed it: "Your descendants will be aliens living in a land that is not theirs . . . but I will punish that nation whose slaves they are, and after that they shall come out with great possessions" (Gen 15:13–14). The long-term reason for the persistence of the priests' Judaism as the self-evidently valid explanation of Israel's life therefore derives from two facts, only one of which matters.

True, the institutional consideration introduced above should not be forgotten. The Scriptures themselves would retain their authority. As the Torah became the primary document for Israel beyond Jerusalem with its temple, priesthood, and offerings, Scripture gained its own authority, independent of the circumstance of society. The priests' paradigm therefore imposed itself even in situations in which its fundamental premises hardly pertained. Accordingly, when the world imposed upon Jewry questions of a different order, the Jews would then go in search of more answers—an additional Torah (hence the "Oral Torah" of rabbinic Judaism)—and even different answers. But even then, a great many Jews continued to envision the world through that original perspective created in the aftermath of destruction and restoration—that is, to see the world as a gift instead of a given and themselves as chosen for a life of special suffering but also special reward.

But that explanation on its own begs the question. For the reason does not account for the continuing assent to, and acknowledgement as authoritative of, those Scriptures. Something within the scriptural message itself must serve to account for the persistence of the pentateuchal system.

The second reason is that that system in its basic structure not only addressed, *but also created,* a continuing and chronic fact of Israel's inner life. Israel was taught to see itself—to repeat my favored formulation—not as a given, a social order by its historical nature, but as a gift subject to conditions and stipulations. Israel could cease to exist, and therefore now endured by God's grace. The sense of uncertainty about the future, the dependence on God's blessing and intervention for the maintenance of its social order, marked Israel as the ever-dying people from the complaint of Abraham:

> Some time later, the word of the Lord came to Abram in a vision. He said, "Fear not, Abram; I am a shield to you; your reward shall be very great." But Abram said, "O Lord, God, what can you give me, seeing that I shall die childless, and the one in charge of my household is Dammesek Eliezer!" Abram said further, "Since You have granted me no offspring, my steward shall be my heir."
>
> Genesis 15:1–3 (NJPS translation)

Scripture captures at the very outset of Israel's existence the uncertainty of a small, defeated nation, exiled from its land and therefore challenged to sustain itself in a situation of cultural adversity. There is nothing natural, nothing given, about Israel's existence. But—so the generative myth insists—under certain conditions, Israel will endure, becoming as numerous as the stars in the heaven. To state now the long-term explanation with emphasis: *the pentateuchal system sustained itself by creating unmet expectations and then explaining why they were not met but might yet be.*

In simple language, the system both provoked resentment and afforded remission from the consequent distress. It both identified the urgent question that it answered and created the conditions in which that question would be recapitulated, generation by generation. So long as the people perceived the world in such a way as to make urgent the question that Scripture framed and to make self-evidently valid the answer Scripture gave, Scripture enjoyed that power of persuasion beyond all need for argument that imparted to it self-evident status. The myth of the Pentateuch as God's revealed will to Israel retold itself because the Pentateuch both selected and accounted for the condition of the Israel to which it spoke. And that interval of self-evidence—Israel elect but in exile until certain conditions be met, Israel of an uncertain future but master of its own fate through keeping the covenant—lasted for a very long time, even to today. Most, though not all, Judaic systems of the social order recapitulate the paradigm of exile and return, resentment and remission.

I therefore see two reasons for the perennial power of the priests' system and perspective. One was the persistence of the generative tension, precipitated by the interpretation of the Jews' life as exile and return, that had formed the critical center of the Torah of Moses. Therefore the urgent question answered by the Torah retained its original character and definition, and the self-evidently valid answer—read in the synagogue every week—retained its relevance. With the persistent problem renewing, generation after generation, that same resentment, the product of a memory of loss and restoration joined to the present recognition of the danger of a further loss, the priests' authoritative answer would not lose its power to persist and to persuade. But the other was that people saw what was not always there, because through the Torah of Moses they were taught to. To state the matter simply: religion (the particular Judaism at hand) did more than merely recapitulate resentment.

Sacred Persistence

That is why the second of the two reasons—the one explaining the long-term power of the Judaic system of the priests to shape Israel's worldview and way of life—is the more important: the question answered by the Five Books of Moses persisted at the center of national life and remained, if chronic, also urgent. The answer provided by the Pentateuch therefore retained its self-evident importance. The question persisted, to be sure, because Scripture kept reminding people to ask that question, to see the world as the world was described, in Scripture's mythic terms, out of the perception of the experience of exile and return: the stipulative character of Israel's corporate existence. But the penta-teuchal Israel's social world matched the governing myth. Israel was few, weak, and uncertain of itself and subject to the will of others, incorporated as it was in world-empires from 586 B.C.E. onward. So if its existence depended on God's favor, the theology matched the sociology of the group.

To those troubled by the question of exile and return—that is, the chronic allegation that Israel's group-life did not constitute a given but formed a gift accorded on conditions and stipulations—then, the answer enjoyed the status of (mere) fact. Keep the Torah and all will go well. And the Torah extended the range of the covenant to even humble matters of ordinary, everyday life: sanctification of the here and now. The human condition takes on heightened intensity when God cares what you eat for lunch, on the one hand, but will reward you for having suitable food, on the other. For a small, uncertain people, captured by a vision of distant horizons behind and before, a mere speck on the crowded plain of humanity, such a message bore its powerful and immediate message as a map of meaning. Israel's death and resurrection—as the Torah portrayed matters—therefore left nothing as it had been and changed everything for all time. But the matter—central to the history of Judaism—demands yet another angle of analysis. We have to ask what was at stake, and so penetrate into the deepest layers of the structure to state the issues at their most abstract and general. For the sacred persistence in the end rested on judgments found self-evidently valid in circumstances remote from the original world subject to those judgments.

Not only did the systemic theory of Israel correspond to social reality, but the way of life realized the system in everyday activities. The reason for that obsession—that is to say, the persistence of the exegesis of the everyday as a sequence of acts of sanctification—was the Torah's encapsulation of the experience of the loss and recovery of the land and of political sovereignty as normative and recurrent. Israel, because of its amazing experience, had attained a self-consciousness that continuous existence in a single place under a long-term government denied others.

And this worldview reinforced and explained the social facts. There was nothing given, nothing to be merely taken for granted in the life of a nation that had ceased to be a nation on its own land and then once more had regained that (once-normal, now tenuous) condition. Transforming received traditions into a coherent statement of its own, pentateuchal Judaism took shape as the system that accounted for the death and resurrection of the Jewish people and pointed for the source of renewed life toward sanctification now, and salvation at the end of time.

The codification and closure of the law under Ezra produced the Torah as a law code that laid heavy emphasis on the exclusivist character of the Israelite God and cult. "Judaism"—that is to say, the priestly Judaism of the Pentateuch—gained the character of a cultically centered way of life and worldview. Both rite and myth aimed at the continuing self-definition of Israel by separation from and exclusion of the rest of the world. Order against chaos meant holiness over uncleanness, life over death. The purpose was to define Israel against the background of the other peoples of the Near and Middle East with whom Israel had much in common, and, especially, to differentiate Israel from its near-relations and neighbors, e.g., the Samaritans, in the same land. The issue of who is the other persisted, extending beyond the nearest frontier in the definition of the other: the woman, the slave, and the minor to the near-Israelite; the Gentile; and later on, to the Christian (sharing common Scriptures) as a special kind of non-gentile-Gentile; and on and on.

Acute differentiation was required because the social and cultural facts were precisely to the contrary: common traits hardly bespeaking clear-cut points of difference, except of idiom. The mode of differentiation taken by the Torah literature in general, and the priestly sector of that literature in particular, was cultic. The meaning, however, also was social. The power of the Torah composed in this time lay in its control of the temple which it made pivotal and focal. The Torah literature—with its concerned God, who cares what people do about rather curious matters, and the temple cult, with its total exclusion of the non-Israelite from participation, and (all the more so) from cultic commensality—raised high those walls of separation and underlined such distinctiveness as already existed. The life of Israel flowed from the altar; what made Israel *Israel* was the center, the altar.

A Successful System for this Israel's Social Order

The reason that the pentateuchal system retained self-evidence is now clear. The social forces that lent urgency to the issue of who is Israel would endure. It is hardly an exaggeration to say that this ongoing confusion about the distinctive identification to be assigned to Israel would define the very framework of the social and imaginative ecology of Jews who formed communities. So long as memory remained, the conflicting claims of exclusivist Torah literature and prophecy of a people living in utopia, located in no particular place, while framing its vision of itself in the deeply locative symbols of cult and center, would make vivid the abiding issue of self-definition. At issue was, and is, life, its source and its sustenance. For if we ask why the temple with its cult proved enduringly central in the imagination of the Israelites living in the land, as indeed it did, we have only to repeat the statements made by the priests of the temple. These explain the critical importance of cult and rite.

If we reread the priestly viewpoint as it is contained throughout the Torah—especially in the books of Leviticus and Numbers—this is the picture we derive. The altar was the center of life, the conduit both from heaven to earth and from earth to heaven. Therefore, all things are to be arrayed in relationship to the altar. The movement of the heavens demarcated and celebrated at the cult marked out the divisions of time in relationship to the altar. The spatial dimension of the land was likewise demarcated and celebrated in relationship to the altar. The natural life of Israel's fields and corrals, the social life of its hierarchical caste-system and the political life (this was not only in theory by any means) all centered on the temple as the locus of ongoing government—all things in order and in place expressed the single message. The natural order of the world corresponded to, reinforced, and was reinforced by, the social order of Israel. Both were fully realized in the cult, the nexus between the opposite and corresponding forces of heaven and earth.

The lines of structure emanated from the altar. And these lines of structure constituted high and impenetrable frontiers to separate Israel from the Gentiles. Israel, which was holy, ate holy food, reproduced itself in accord with the laws of holiness, and conducted all of its affairs—both affairs of state and the business of the table and the bed—in accord with the demands of holiness. So the cult prescribed and defined holiness. Holiness meant separateness. Separateness meant life. Why? Because outside the Land of Israel, the realm of the holy, lay the domain of death. The "lands" are unclean. The Land of Israel is holy. For the scriptural vocabulary, one antonym for "holy" is "unclean," and one opposite of "unclean" is "holy." The synonym of "holy" is "life." The principal force and symbol of uncleanness and its highest expression are death. Thus the Torah stood for life, the covenant with the Lord would guarantee life, and the way of life required sanctification in the here and now of the natural world.

To conclude: the Pentateuch, the Torah of Moses, created the world that it revealed, which in no way corresponded either to the world out of which it emerged or to the one to which, for the following centuries, it spoke. And how to account for the persistence of the paradigm? The life of the group is uncertain, subject to conditions and stipulations. Nothing is set and given, but all things—land and life itself— are a gift. But what actually did happen in that uncertain world—exile and then restoration—marked the group as special, different, select. The condition for the continuing power of the Judaic system of the Torah not only required the recapitulation or renewal of resentment, but also what was required to restore hope. That condition was the constant renewal of the resentment precipitated and provoked by the discrepancy ever present in the Torah's own system. The Torah of Moses therefore did more than recapitulate resentment. In age succeeding age, the Torah generated that resentment which powered the system.

Since the Pentateuch's formative pattern imposed that perpetual, self-conscious uncertainty, treating the life of the group as conditional and discontinuous, Jews have asked themselves who they are, and from then to now they have invented Judaisms to answer that question. Accordingly, on account of the definitive paradigm affecting their group-life in various contexts, no circumstances—not in the land, all the more so not in the Diaspora—have permitted Jews to take for granted their existence as a group. Looking back on Scripture and its message, Jews have ordinarily treated as special, subject to conditions, and therefore uncertain, what (in their view) other groups enjoyed as unconditional and simply given. Why the paradigm renewed itself is clear: this particular view of matters generated expectations that could not be met, hence created resentment—and then provided comfort and hope that made it possible to cope with that resentment. To state my thesis with appropriate emphasis:

> *Promising what could not be delivered, then providing solace for the consequent disappointment, the system at hand—the Pentateuch read whole and complete and in sequence—precipitated in age succeeding age the very conditions necessary for its own replication, its own persistence.*

To be "an Israel" within any given Judaism from the Pentateuch to now—where "Israel" is the social component of a Judaism—has meant to ask what it means to be Israel. The original pattern meant that an Israel would be a social group whose existence had been called into question and affirmed—and therefore always would be called into question, and remained perpetually to be affirmed. Every future Judaism then would find as its task the recapitulation—and reaffirmation—of the original Judaism. Each successive Judaism made its own distinctive statement of the generative and critical resentment contained within the questioning of the given structure, a deep understanding of the uncertain character of the existence of the group in its normal location in the midst of the permanence that (so far as the Judaic group understood things) characterized the life of every other group but Israel.

What for everyone else was a given, for Israel was a conditional gift. What all the nations knew as certain, Israel understood as uncertain: exile and loss, alienation and resentment, but instead of annihilation, renewal, restoration, reconciliation, and (in theological language) redemption. So that paradigmatic experience, the one beginning in 586 B.C.E. and ending about 450 B.C.E. and written down in the Torah of Moses, made its mark. That pattern, permanently inscribed in the Torah of God to Moses at Sinai, would define for all Israels over all time the resentment that demanded recapitulation: leaving home, and coming home.

There have been many Judaisms, each with its indicative symbol and generative paradigm, each pronouncing its worldview and prescribing its way of life and identifying the particular Israel that, in its unique view, is Israel, bearer of the original promise of God. We begin with the one important augmentation of the Torah of Moses at Sinai—appropriately, the point at which the paradigm itself perished, and the pattern of exile and return would require renewal.

2

The Loss of the Jerusalem Temple and the Response of the Mishnah

From Disaster to Despair

The next transformation that yielded enduring consequences for Judaism from the formative age to the present day took place when the pentateuchal paradigm—exile, repentance, reconciliation and forgiveness, and return—broke down. That happened not after the temple was lost in 70 C.E., during the first rebellion against Rome, but during the second, a war aiming at the restoration of the temple, which was fought from 132–135 C.E. The consequent despair, from 135 C.E., formed the setting for the promulgation, about 200 C.E., of a document of renewal, the Mishnah, which, like the Pentateuch, rapidly would be given the status of the Torah of Moses at Sinai. The Mishnah represents the first document of rabbinic Judaism, the system that would prevail for close to two thousand years. All the other Judaic religious systems from 450 B.C.E. to 200 C.E. eventually passed from the Jewish scene; none of the canonical writings produced by them would be preserved and transmitted by Judaism or by Jews. We know about those other Judaic religious systems only because, for their own reasons, Christians preserved the writings, or because of accidents of preservation.

Let me start from the beginning, with the challenge to the pentateuchal paradigm. From the closure of the Pentateuch with its initial Judaism of 450 B.C.E. onward, Israel in the land of Israel had its good days and bad. Disaster was no stranger, foreign conquests not uncommon. But from the return to Zion in the sixth century B.C.E. and the restoration of Israelite polity in the land of Israel in the fifth century B.C.E., one disaster which began in 70 C.E. and came to its climax in 135 C.E. presented a crisis to the interior life of Judaism, the religious tradition. The beginning of the disaster—the destruction of the second temple—asked a familiar question; the climax of the disaster—the definitive defeat and closure of Jerusalem to the Jewish people—gave an unprecedented answer.

In 70 C.E., after four years of fighting, the Roman Army captured Jerusalem and burned the temple. That was a disaster. But the defeat provoked no crisis, for people knew what to expect. Scripture had told them about the exile of 586 B.C.E. and the return to Zion "three generations later," begun in ca. 538 B.C.E. and fully realized in the next century by Ezra and Nehemiah and the rebuilding of the temple. They therefore could explain what had happened and knew what to expect. Israel could look forward to the recapitulation of the earlier pattern, and understood the current disaster in that context. But that is not how matters turned out. After "three generations" (a period corresponding to the span from 586 to 538 B.C.E.) a second war against Rome broke out, in 132 C.E. Three years of a catastrophic war for Israel's freedom from Rome ended when Jerusalem fell once more. The Romans retook Jerusalem, this time ploughing over the temple site and forbidding Jews to enter the city. The upshot is self-evident: the loss of the temple was not followed by the possibility of recovery and restoration, but rather by utter and irreversible ruin. And that event violated the established pattern. It invited only despair. The first of the two events—the destruction that happened in 70—could find its place in the established pattern of exile and return. The temple had been destroyed before, but restored in the aftermath of Israel's suffering as punishment for its sin, repentance, atonement, and reconciliation with God. The restored temple represented that reconciliation. No wonder, three generations beyond 70, people fought to realize the ancient earlier pattern.

Now we may define how a disaster becomes a crisis. That transformation takes place when people no longer can make sense of what has happened and so can find no reason to take courage in the future. So what was to be said now, when the earlier pattern failed to repeat itself? The second destruction—definitive defeat, leaving no prospect of recovery—could find no explanation in the familiar pattern of exile and return. And that failure of the received Judaic account of Israel defined the crisis to which the Mishnah responded, by setting forth the terms of the new beginning. For the Mishnah responded to the failure of the established pattern with a message of restoration and reconstruction all its own: a statement of future-history.

The Mishnah's Response to Despair

The self-evident answer to the urgent question of the crisis of an earlier and now failed paradigm—who is Israel now? meaning, is Israel still holy now?—was simple. The Mishnah's system maintained that the holiness of the life of Israel, the people—a holiness that had formerly centered on the temple—could still endure. Sanctification transcended the physical destruction of the building and the cessation of sacrifices there. For beyond the locative sanctity of the temple, the utopian Israel, the people, was holy. Its eternal calling was to embody the instrument of God's sanctification of creation. The system then instructed Israel to create *occasions*, to succeed, at least for the interim—until the Messiah would come and rebuild the temple—the lost location of sanctification. The crisis of what might well be the permanent loss of Jerusalem and the temple shifted attention from what had been lost to what had endured: the holiness of the people itself.

Why the focus of attention turned to that people, Israel, is not a difficult question to answer. We recall the established conviction that Israel was special, and that what happened to Israel signified God's will. What was unpredictable in fact marked a recapitulation of the most typical and fundamental characteristic of the original, and generative, paradigm. That is, Israel because of its (in its mind) amazing experience of loss and restoration, death and resurrection, had attained remarkable self-consciousness. In the life of a nation that had ceased to be a nation on its own land and then once more had regained their former condition, the present calamity invoked once more the paradigm of death and resurrection, but with a difference. Before it was a pattern of temple destroyed, exile, return, temple reconstructed. Now Israel itself embodied the holiness formerly vested principally in the temple and its rites. Consequently, the truly fresh and definitive component of the new system, after the disaster of 70–135 C.E., in fact restated in contemporary terms the fixed and established doctrine with which the first Judaism, the pentateuchal system after 450 B.C.E., had commenced.

What makes the Mishnah's system for Israel's social order distinctive therefore is the conviction that the community now—for the interim, however protracted—forms the counterpart and surrogate of the temple. It was the genius of the Mishnah's system of sanctification to recognize that the holy people might, for the moment, reconstitute the temple in the sanctity of its own community life. Therefore the people had to be made holy, as the temple had been holy. The people's social life had to be sanctified as the surrogate for what had been lost. But how distant do we find ourselves from the counterpart convictions of the pentateuchal system? The category-formations endured, and the system formed was congruent with that of the Pentateuch in every detail. That is signaled when the rabbinic ideal for Judaism further maintained that the rabbi served as the new priest, the study of Torah substituted for the temple sacrifice, and deeds of lovingkindness were the social surrogate for the sin-offering. All things fit together to construct out of the old Judaism the worldview and way of life of the new and enduring system that ultimately became normative Judaism: a reworking of the pentateuchal system and its category-formations.

The Mishnah's Modes of Thought: Hierarchical Classification

Before we deal with the substance of the mishnaic system, let us consider its logic, the modes of thought that generate its propositions on any subject. The Mishnah primarily presents rules, and it treats stories (including history) as incidental and of merely taxonomic interest. Its logic is propositional, and its intellect does its work through a vast labor of classification, with comparison and contrast generating governing rules and generalizations. The following case shows us that the stakes are very high. For that purpose, let us turn to a document we know our authorship knew well—the written Torah.

The Pentateuch appeals to a different logic of cogent discourse from the Mishnah's. Its cogency is imparted by teleology—that is, a logic that provides an account of how things *were* in order to explain how things *are* and set forth how they *should be*—with the tabernacle in the wilderness the model for (and modeled after) the temple in the Jerusalem building. In contrast to this, the Mishnah speaks in a continuing present tense, saying only how things are, indifferent to the past and the future. The Pentateuch focuses upon self-conscious "Israel," saying who they were and what they must become to overcome what they now are. The Mishnah understands by "Israel" as much the individual as the nation; it identifies as its principal actors, the heroes of its narrative, not the family become a nation, but the priest and the householder, the woman and the slave, the adult and the child, and other castes and categories of person within an inward-looking, established, fully landed community. Given the Mishnah's interest in classifications and categories—therefore in systematic hierarchization of an orderly world—one can hardly find odd its (re)definition of the subject-matter and the systemic social entity.

We may briefly dwell on this matter of difference in the prevailing logic, because the contrast allows us to see how one document will appeal to one logic, another to a different logic. While the Pentateuch appeals to the logic of teleology to make sense of facts, making connections by appeal to the end and drawing conclusions concerning the purpose of things, the Mishnah knows only the philosophical logic of syllogism, the rule-making logic of lists. The pentateuchal logic reached concrete expression in narrative, which served to point to the direction and goal of matters, hence, in the nature of things, of history. Accordingly, those authors, when putting together diverse materials, shaped everything so as to form of it all as continuous a narrative as they could construct, and through that "history" that they made up, they delivered their message and also portrayed that message as cogent and compelling. If the pentateuchal writers were theologians of history, the Mishnah's aimed at composing a natural philosophy for supernatural, holy Israel. The Mishnah's logic of cogent discourse establishes propositions that rest upon philosophical bases, e.g., through the proposal of a thesis and the composition of a list of facts that (e.g., through shared traits of a taxonomic order) prove the thesis. In other words, we deal with a document of natural philosophy, natural history, engaged in the taxonomic analysis of things. Like good Aristotelians, the Mishnah's authors would uncover the components of the rules by comparison and contrast, showing the rule for one thing by finding out how it compared with like things and contrasted with the unlike. Then, in their view, the unknown would become known, conforming to the rule of the like thing and also to the opposite of the rule governing the unlike thing.

That purpose is accomplished, in particular, though list-making, which places on display the data of the like and the unlike and then implicitly (ordinarily, not explicitly) conveys the rule. It is this resort to list-making that accounts for the rhetorical stress on groups of examples of a common principle (three or five, for instance). Once a series is established, the authorship assumes, the governing rule will be perceived. That explains why, in exposing the interior logic of its authorship's intellect, the Mishnah had to be a book of lists, with the implicit order, the nomothetic traits of a monotheistic order, dictating the ordinarily unstated general and encompassing rule.

And all this why? It is in order to make a single statement, endless times over, and to repeat in a mass of tangled detail precisely the same fundamental judgment. The Mishnah in its way is as blatantly repetitious in its fundamental statement as is the Pentateuch. But the power of the pentateuchal authorship, denied to that of the Mishnah, lies in their capacity always to be heard, to create sound by resonance of the surfaces of things. The Pentateuch is a fundamentally popular and accessible piece of writing. In contrast, the Mishnah's writers spoke into the depths, anticipating a more eager hearing than they ever would receive. So the repetitions of Scripture reinforce the message, while the endlessly repeated paradigm of the Mishnah sits too deep in the structure of the system to gain hearing from the untrained ear or to attain visibility to the untutored eye. So much for the logic. What of the systemic message? Given the intellectual subtlety of the Mishnah's authorship, we cannot find surprising that the message speaks not only in what is said, but in what is omitted.

The framers of the Mishnah appeal solely to the traits of things. The logical basis of coherent speech and discourse in the Mishnah then derives from *Listenwissenschaft*. That mode of thought defines classification as the way of proving propositions establishing a set of shared traits that form a rule that compels us to reach a given conclusion. A catalogue of facts, for example, may be so composed that, through the regularities and indicative traits of the entries, the catalogue yields a proposition. A list of parallel items all together point to a simple conclusion; the conclusion may or may not be given at the end of the catalogue, but the catalogue—by definition—is pointed, bearing meaning and pointing through the weight of evidence to an inescapable conclusion. This mode of classification of facts leads to an identification of what the facts have in common and—it goes without saying, an explanation of their meaning.

The Mishnah's Six Components

Everyone knows Scripture. Far fewer know the Mishnah. So some simple words of description are required. What, precisely, do we find in the Mishnah? Before we interpret the contents in context, as we must, let us survey the main outlines of the writing.

The Mishnah is comprised of six large divisions, which deal with issues of sanctification in Agriculture (Zera'im), Appointed Times (Mo'ed), Family Life (a.k.a., "Women") (Našim), Civil Society (a.k.a., "Damages") (Neziqin), Holy Things (Qodašim), and Purities (Teharot). A brief sketch of the foci—theological and social—of each of those divisions reveals the way the system takes shape and makes its coherent statement. Let me first present an overview of the six components of the Mishnah's whole, closed system, then review the contents in detail.

The first division deals with the critical issue in the economic life, namely farming; three matters are involved here. First, Israel, as tenant on God's holy land, maintains the property in the ways God requires, keeping the rules which mark the land and its crops as holy. Next, the hour at which the sanctification of the land comes to form a critical mass—namely, in the ripened crops—is the moment ponderous with danger and heightened holiness. Lastly, Israel's will so affects the crops as to mark a part of them as holy and the rest of them as available for common use. The human will is determinative in the process of sanctification.

In the second division, what happens in the land at certain appointed times marks off spaces of the land as holy in yet another way. The center of the land and the focus of its sanctification is the temple. There the produce of the land is received and given back to God, who created and sanctified the land. At these moments of sanctification, the inhabitants of the land enter a state of spatial sanctification, in which the village or town boundaries mark off holy space, within which one must remain during the holy time. This is expressed in two ways. First, the temple itself observes and expresses the special, recurring holy time. Second, the villages and towns of the land are brought into alignment with the temple, forming a complement and completion to the temple's sacred being. The advent of the appointed times precipitates a spatial reordering of the land, so that the boundaries of the sacred are matched and mirrored in both town and in temple. At the heightened holiness marked by these moments of appointed times, therefore, the occasion for an affective sanctification is worked out. Like the harvest, the advent of an appointed time, such as a pilgrim festival, is made to express that regular, orderly, and predictable sort of sanctification for Israel which the system as a whole seeks.

If for a moment we now leap over the next two divisions, the third and fourth, we come to the counterpart of the divisions of Agriculture and Appointed Times. These are the fifth and sixth divisions, namely Holy Things and Purities, which deal with the everyday and the ordinary, as against the special moments of harvest and special times or seasons. The fifth division is about the temple on ordinary days. The temple, the locus of sanctification, is conducted in a wholly routine and trustworthy, punctilious manner. The one thing which may unsettle matters is the intention and will of the human actor. This is therefore subjected to carefully prescribed limitations and remedies. The division of Holy Things generates its companion, Purities, dealing with cultic cleanness. The relationship between the two is like that between Agriculture and Appointed Times: the former locative, dealing with the fields; the latter utopian dealing with the interplay between fields and altar.

Here too, in the sixth division, once we speak of the one place of the temple, we address, too, the cleanness which pertains to every place. This system takes into account what imparts uncleanness and how this is done, what is subject to uncleanness, and how that state is overcome—and the system is fully expressed, once more, in response to the participation of the human will. Without the wish and act of a human being, the system does not function. It is inert. Sources of uncleanness (which come naturally and not by volition), and modes of purification (which work naturally, and not by human intervention), remain inert until the human will has imparted susceptibility to uncleanness—that is, introduced, food and drink, bed, pot, chair, and pan into the system, which begin to form the focus of the system. The movement from sanctification to uncleanness takes place only when human will and work precipitate it.

This now brings us back to the middle divisions, the third and fourth, on Women and Damages. They take their place in the structure of the whole by showing the congruence, within the larger framework of regularity and order, of human concerns of family and farm, politics and workaday transactions, among ordinary people. For without attending to these matters, the Mishnah's system does not encompass what, at its foundations, it is meant to comprehend and order. In the case of Women, the third division, attention focuses upon the point of disorder marked by the transfer of that disordering entity, woman, from the regular status provided by one man to the equally trustworthy status provided by another. That is the point at which the Mishnah's interests are aroused: predictably, at the moment of disorder. In the case of Damages, the fourth division, there are two important concerns. First, there is the paramount interest in preventing, so far as possible, the disorderly rise of one person and fall of another, and in sustaining the status quo of the economy, the house and household, of Israel, the holy society in eternal stasis. Second, there is the necessary concomitant in the provision of a system of political institutions to carry out the laws that preserve the balance and steady state of persons.

Now let us return to the divisions and address the details: the governing category-formations or tractates organized around topics which comprise the construction as a whole.

Agriculture (Zera'im)

The theology of the division of Agriculture (literally, "Seeds"), with its focus on the tithing laws, is conveniently expressed by Richard S. Sarason in the following language:[1]

> The Mishnah's primary concern is with the process of sanctification of the various agricultural offerings and, particularly, in the part that man plays in the process of sanctification.
>
> The tractates on tithing give us a kind of geometry or logic of the sacred and sanctification in the realm of agricultural produce. . . . The Mishnah's theory of the holiness of produce that grows from the soil of the land of Israel is transactional. That is to say, holiness does not naturally inhere in produce. Rather, God and man are the agents of sanctification. God, as owner of the land, has a prior claim on its produce. But man must acknowledge God's ownership, and validate God's claim through actively designating and separating God's portion. Additionally, holiness is to be understood primarily in functional rather than substantive terms, i.e., that which is deemed holy belongs to God (and frequently is allotted by God to his priests), and must not be used by ordinary Israelites. Sacrilege thus is conceived as a violation of God's property rights.
>
> The authorities behind the Mishnah primarily are interested in spelling out the role of human action and, particularly, intention in the process of sanctification. That role is determinative throughout the process. To begin with, the locus of susceptibility to sanctification is determined with reference to man's actions and intentions (cf. Tractate Ma'aserot). Not everything that grows in the soil of the land of Israel is liable to the separation of heave-offering and tithes. Liability falls only on produce that is cultivated for

---

[1] Richard S. Sarason, "Mishnah and Scripture: Preliminary Observations on the Law of Tithing in Seder Zeraim," published in *Approaches to Ancient Judaism,* edited by William Scott Green (Chico, Calif.: Scholars Press for Brown Judaic Studies, 1980), II:86–87.

human food (M. Ma. 1:1). This notion, of course, begins in Scripture, which requires Israelite farmers to offer to God, as owner of the land, the best part of their grain, wine, and oil, and to feed the priests and Levites, who do not farm the land. The Mishnah expands the liability to include all edible produce. The tithing laws, then, are food laws. Only produce that can be human food enters the system of tithing and sanctification. Similarly, the point at which produce becomes liable to the separation of terumah and tithes (i.e., becomes tebel; see below) is the point at which it becomes edible (M. Ma. 1:2).

But man's actions and intentions further determine liability at this juncture. For before edible produce has been fully harvested or processed, it may be eaten randomly without incurring liability to tithing. Only if a man eats the produce as a regular meal before it is harvested must he tithe it. Furthermore, the point at which produce is considered to be fully harvested and liable to tithing also is determined by human intention regarding its ultimate disposition. If the farmer intends to bring his produce to market, it becomes liable to tithing when it is in that condition in which it will be brought to market—sifted, stacked, tied in bundles. If, on the other hand, he intends to bring the produce home to be eaten by his household, it does not become liable to tithing until it enters his private domain—the house or the courtyard. Finally, produce becomes holy (i.e., God's property) only through man's act of consecration.

Nothing is inherently sacred. The land of Israel is sanctified through its relationship to God. The produce of the Lord is sanctified by man, acting under God's commandment, through verbal designation and separation of the various offerings. Man, through his action and intention, additionally determines what is susceptible to sanctification (i.e., liable to tithing as human food), and the point at which it is susceptible (i.e., edible, at the point of completion of processing or harvesting, or the point of intention to make a fixed meal). The Mishnah's primary concern . . . is that man should separate properly that which is due to God, so that non-priests will not inadvertently eat produce bonded to God or consecrated to him. The Mishnah's authorities further wish to examine in detail man's role in the process of sanctification, and to specify the power of his will, word, and deed.

This account of the main issues of the division of Agriculture correlates with what we see when we turn to the succeeding divisions.

Appointed Times (Mo‘ed)

The division of Appointed Times forms a system in which the advent of a holy day, like the Sabbath, sanctifies the life of the Israelite village by imposing on the village rules modeled on those of the temple. The purpose of the system, therefore, is to bring the sanctification of the village and the household into alignment with the condition of sanctification of the temple on those same occasions of appointed times, Sabbath and festival alike. The underlying and generative theory of the system is that the village is the mirror image of the temple. If things are done in one way in the temple, they will be done in the opposite way in the village. Thus the village and the temple together on the occasion of the holy day form a single continuum, a completed creation, awaiting sanctification.

How does this set of correspondences and contrasts work itself out? The boundary lines prevent free entry into the temple, so they restrict free egress from the town. On the holy day, what one may do in the temple is precisely what one may not do in the village. So the advent of the holy day affects the village or town by bringing it into sacred symmetry in such wise as to effect a system of opposites; each realm is holy in a way precisely the opposite of the other. Because of the underlying conception of perfection attained through the union of opposites, the village is not represented as conforming to the model of the temple cult, but of constituting its antithesis. This moment of perfection renders the events of ordinary time, of "history," essentially irrelevant. For what really matters in time are those moments in which sacred time intervenes and effects the perfection formed of the union of heaven and earth, of temple, in the model of the former, and Israel, its complement. It is not a return to a perfect time but a recovery of perfect being, a fulfillment of creation, which explains the essentially ahistorical character of the Mishnah's division of Appointed Times. Sanctification constitutes an ontological category and is effected by the creator, and the sanctified people Israel can likewise effect sanctification in time by the proper marking and observance of the festivals.

This explains why the division in its rich detail is composed of two quite distinct sets of materials. First, it addresses what one does in the sacred space of the temple on the occasion of sacred time, as distinct from what one does in that same sacred space on ordinary, undifferentiated days, which is a subject worked out in the division of Holy Things (see below). Second, the division defines how for the occasion of the holy day one creates a corresponding space in one's own non-temple circumstance, and what one does, within that space, during sacred time. The issue of the temple and cult on festivals is treated in tractates *Pesaḥim, Šeqalim, Yoma, Sukkah,* and *Ḥagigah.* Three further tractates, *Roš Haššanah, Taʿanit,* and *Megillah,* are necessary to complete the discussion. The matter of the rigid definition of the outlines of a sacred space in the village, delineated by the limits within which one may move on the Sabbath and festival, and of the specification of those things which one may not do within that space in sacred time, is found in *Šabbat, ʿErubin, Beṣah,* and *Moʿed Qaṭan.*

While the twelve tractates of the division appear to fall into two distinct groups, joined merely by a common theme, in fact they relate through a shared, generative metaphor. It is the comparison, in the context of sacred time, of the spatial life of the temple to the spatial life of the village or town, with activities and restrictions to be specified for each, upon the common occasion of the Sabbath or festival. The Mishnah's purpose therefore is to correlate the sanctity of the temple with the restrictions of space and of action that make the life of the village different and holy, as defined in each locale by the holy day.

The Division of Families (Našim)

The division of Families situates women in the social economy of Israel's supernatural and natural reality. Women acquire definition wholly in relationship to men, who impart form to the Israelite social economy. The status of women is effected through both supernatural and natural, this-worldly action. What man and woman do on earth provokes a corresponding response in heaven. So women are defined and secured both in heaven and here on earth, and that position is always and invariably relative to men. The principal interest for the Mishnah are the points at which a woman becomes and ceases to be holy to a particular man—that is, when she enters and leaves the marital union. These transfers of women are the dangerous and disorderly points in the relationship of woman to man—and therefore, the Mishnah states, to society as well.

Five of the seven tractates of the division of Women are devoted to the formation and dissolution of the marital bond. Of them, three treat what is done by man here on earth—that is, formation of a marital bond through betrothal and marriage contract, and dissolution through divorce and its consequences: *Qiddušin, Ketubbot,* and *Giṭṭin.* One of them is devoted to what is done by woman here on earth: *Soṭah.* And *Yebamot,* greatest of the seven in size and in formal and substantive brilliance, deals with the corresponding heavenly intervention into the formation and end of a marriage: the effect of death upon both forming the marital bond and dissolving it through death. *Yebamot* states that supernature sanctifies a woman to a man (under the conditions of the levirate connection). What it says by indirection is that man sanctifies too: man, like God, can sanctify the relationship between a man and a woman, and can also effect the cessation of the sanctity of that same relationship.

The other two tractates in this division, *Nedarim* and *Nazir,* draw into one the two realms of reality, heaven and earth, as they work out the effects of vows, perhaps because vows taken by women and subject to the confirmation or abrogation of the father or husband make a deep impact upon the marital life of the woman who has taken them. Other important overall issues are the transfer of property, along with women (covered in *Ketubbot* and to some measure in *Qiddušin*), and the proper documentation of the transfer of women and property (treated in *Ketubbot* and *Giṭṭin*). The critical issues therefore turn upon legal documents—writs of divorce, for example—and legal recognition of changes in the ownership of property, e.g., through the collection of the settlement of a marriage contract by a widow, through the provision of a dowry, or through the disposition of the property of a woman during the period in which she is married. The system of Women thus focuses upon the two crucial stages in the transfer of women and of property from one domain to another: the leaving of the father's house in the formation of a marriage, and the return to the father's house at its dissolution through divorce or the husband's death. There is yet a third point of interest, though, as is clear, it is much less important than these first two stages: the duration of the marriage.

The division and its system delineate the natural and supernatural character of the woman's role in the social economy framed by man: the beginning, end, and middle of the marital relationship. The whole constitutes a significant part of the Mishnah's encompassing system of sanctification, for the reason that heaven confirms what humans do on earth. A correctly prepared writ of divorce on earth changes the status of the woman to whom it is given, so that in heaven she is available for sanctification to some other man, while, without that same writ, in heaven's view, should she go to some other man, she would be liable to be put to death. The earthly deed and the heavenly perspective correlate. That is indeed very much part of larger system, which says the same thing over and over again.

The Division of Civil Law (Neziqin)

The division of Civil Law comprises two subsystems, which fit together in a logical way. One part presents rules for the normal conduct of civil society. These cover commerce, trade, real estate, and other matters of everyday intercourse, as well as mishaps, such as damages by chattels and persons, fraud, overcharge, interest, and the like, in that same context of everyday social life. The other part describes the institutions governing the normal conduct of civil society, that is, courts of administration, and the penalties at the disposal of the government for the enforcement of the law. The two subjects form a single tight and systematic dissertation on the nature of Israelite society and its economic, social, and political relationships, as the Mishnah envisages them.

The first part of the division expresses the task of society in maintaining perfect stasis, preserving the prevailing situation, and securing the stability of all relationships, and this is found in the three Babas: *Baba Qamma, Baba Meṣiʿa,* and *Baba Batra.* These tractates deal with the interchanges of buying and selling, giving and taking, borrowing and lending, in which it is important that there be an essential equality of interchange. An appropriate appendix to the Babas is ʿ*Abodah Zarah,* which deals with the orderly governance of transactions and relationships between Israelite society and the outside world—namely, the realm of idolatry. Ordinary everyday relationships with the gentile world, with special reference to trade and commerce, conclude the Mishnah's discourse about all those matters of civil and criminal law that together define everyday relationships both within the Israelite nation and also between that nation and all others in the world among whom they lived side by side.

The other part of the division describes the institutions of Israelite government and politics in the tractates. This is laid out in two main aspects, *Sanhedrin* and *Makkot*. First, the description of the institutions and their jurisdiction, with reference to courts—conceived as both judicial and administrative agencies—is provided and, second, an extensive discussion of criminal penalties, including the death penalty, is set forth. *Sanhedrin* further describes the way in which trials are conducted in both monetary and capital cases, and pays attention to the possibilities of perjury.

These matters are supplemented in the tractates *Šebuʿot* and *Horayot*, which deal with various oaths that apply in courts as well as with errors of judgment inadvertently made and carried out by the courts. This material emerges from Scripture, at Leviticus 5–6 and 4, respectively. But the Mishnah approaches it from the viewpoint of the oath or erroneous instruction, rather than the cultic penalty emphasized in the Pentateuch. In *Šebuʿot* the discussion is intellectually imaginative and thorough; in *Horayot*, routine. The relevance of both to the issues of *Sanhedrin* and *Makkot* is obvious: the matter of oaths enriches the discussion of the conduct of the courts, since the possibility of error is principally in the courts and other political institutions. Thus the four tractates on institutions and their functioning form a remarkable unified and cogent set.

The character and interests of the division of Damages present probative evidence of the larger program of those who wrote and compiled the Mishnah, the philosophers of the Mishnah. Their intention is to create in legal theory—and in some measure in practice as well, so far as is possible—nothing less than a full-scale Israelite government, subject to the administration of sages. This government is fully supplied with a constitution and bylaws *(Sanhedrin, Makkot)*. It makes provision for a court system and procedures *(Šebuʿot, Sanhedrin, Makkot)*, as well as a full set of laws governing civil society *(Baba Qamma, Baba Meṣiʿa, Baba Batra)* and criminal justice *(Sanhedrin, Makkot)*. This government, moreover, mediates between its own community and the outside ("pagan") world. Through its system of laws it expresses its judgment of others and at the same time defines, protects, and defends its own society and social frontiers *(ʿAbodah Zarah)*. It even makes provision for procedures of remission, to expiate its own errors *(Horayot)*.

I earlier referred to the Mishnah as a work of future history, a design for the social order of an Israel restored to its authentic being. Here is an example of what I mean. The (then non-existent) Israelite government imagined by the second-century philosophers centers upon the (then non-existent) temple and the (then forbidden) city, Jerusalem. The temple is a principal focus because there the highest court is in session and there the high priest reigns. The penalties for law infringement sometimes involve sacrifice in the temple, since the basic conception of punishment is that unintentional infringement of the rules of society, whether "religious" or otherwise, is expiated through an offering in the temple. So offerings in the temple are made to appease heaven and restore a whole bond between heaven and Israel, specifically on those occasions on which without malice or ill will an Israelite has disturbed the relationship. Israelite civil society without a temple is not stable or normal, and not to be imagined. And the Mishnah is above all an act of imagination in defiance of reality.

The plan for the government involves a clear-cut philosophy of society, a philosophy that defines the purpose of the government and ensures that its task is not merely to perpetuate its own power. What the Israelite government, within the mishnaic fantasy, is supposed to do is to preserve that state of perfection which, within the same fantasy, the society to begin everywhere attains. The law expresses its obsession with the perfect stasis of Israelite society. Its paramount purpose is in preserving and ensuring that that perfection of the division of this world is kept inviolate or restored to its true status when violated.

The Division of Holy Things (Qodašim)

The division of Holy Things presents a system of sanctification pertaining to matters of sacrifice and sanctuary: the praxis of the altar and maintenance of the (then inaccessible, destroyed) temple building. The praxis of the altar, specifically, involves sacrifice and things set aside for sacrifice and so deemed consecrated. The topic is covered among these tractates of the present division: *Zebaḥim* and part of *Ḥullin, Menaḥot, Temurah, Kerithot,* part of *Meʿilah, Tamid,* and *Qinnim.* The maintenance of the sanctuary (inclusive of the personnel) is dealt with in *Bekorot, ʿArakin,* part of *Meʿilah, Middot,* and part of *Ḥullin.* Viewed from a distance, therefore, the Mishnah's tractates divide themselves up into the following groups (in parentheses are tractates containing relevant materials): (1) Rules for the altar and the praxis of the cult—*Zebaḥim, Menaḥot, Ḥullin, Kerithot, Tamid, Qinnim (Bekorot, Meʿilah);* (2) Rules for the altar and the animals set aside for the cult—*ʿArakin, Temurah, Meʿilah (Bekorot);* and (3) Rules for the altar and support of the temple staff and buildings—*Bekorot, Middot (Ḥullin, ʿArakin, Meʿilah, Tamid).* In a word, this division speaks of the sacrificial cult and the sanctuary in which the cult is conducted. The law pays special attention to the status of the property of the altar and of the sanctuary, both materials to be utilized in the actual sacrificial rites and property the value of which supports the cult and sanctuary in general. Both are deemed to be sanctified, that is: "holy things."

The division of Holy Things centers upon the everyday and rules always applicable to the cult: the daily whole offering; the sin offering and guilt offering that one may bring any time under ordinary circumstances; the right sequence of diverse offerings; the way in which the rites of the whole, sin, and guilt offerings are carried out; what sorts of animals are acceptable; the accompanying cereal offerings; the support and provision of animals for the cult and of meat for the priesthood; the support and material maintenance of the cult and its building. We have before us the system of the cult of the Jerusalem temple, seen as an ordinary and everyday affair, a continuing and routine operation. That is why special rules for the cult, both in respect to the altar and in regard to the maintenance of the buildings, personnel, and even the holy city, will be elsewhere—in Appointed Times and Agriculture. But from the perspective of Holy Things, those divisions intersect by supplying special rules and raising extraordinary (Agriculture: land-bound; Appointed Times: time-bound) considerations for that theme which Holy Things claims to set forth in its most general and unexceptional way: the cult as something permanent and everyday.

The division of Holy Things in a concrete way maps out the cosmology of the sanctuary and its sacrificial system—that is, the world of the temple—which had been the cosmic center of Israelite life. A saying in a medieval compilation states matters as follows:

> "Just as the navel is found at the center of a human being, so the land of Israel is found at the center of the world . . . and it is the foundation of the world. Jerusalem is at the center of the land of Israel, the temple is at the center of Jerusalem, the Holy of Holies is at the center of the temple, the Ark is at the center of the Holy of Holies, and the Foundation Stone is in front of the Ark, which spot is the foundation of the world."
>
> (*Tanhuma Qedoshim* 10)

The Division of Purities (Teharot)

The division of Purities presents a very simple system of cultic purity in three principal parts: sources of uncleanness, objects and substances susceptible to uncleanness, and modes of purification from uncleanness. So it tells the story of what makes a given sort of object unclean and what makes it clean. The tractates on these several topics are as follows: (1) sources of uncleanness—*Ohalot, Negaʿim, Niddah, Makširin, Zabim, Tebul Yom;* (2) objects and substances susceptible to uncleanness—*Kelim, Teharot, ʿUqsin;* and (3) modes of purification—*Parah, Miqwaʾot, Yadayim.*

Viewed as a whole, the division of Purities treats the interplay of persons, food, and liquids. Dry inanimate objects or food are not susceptible to uncleanness. What is wet is susceptible, so liquids activate the system. What is unclean, moreover, emerges from uncleanness through the operation of liquids—specifically, through immersion in fit water of requisite volume and in natural condition. Liquids thus also deactivate the system, since water in its natural condition is what concludes the process by removing uncleanness. Water in its unnatural condition—that is, deliberately affected by human agency—is what imparts susceptibility to uncleanness to begin with. The uncleanness of persons, furthermore, is signified by body liquids or flux in the case of the menstruating woman *(Niddah)* and the *zab (Zabim)*. Corpse uncleanness is conceived to be a kind of effluent, a viscous gas, which flows like liquid. Utensils for their part receive uncleanness when they form receptacles able to contain liquid. In sum, we have a system in which the invisible flow of fluid-like substances or powers serve to put food, drink, and receptacles into the status of uncleanness and to remove those things from that status. Whether or not we call the system "metaphysical," it certainly has no material base but is conditioned upon highly abstract notions. Thus in material terms, the effect of liquid is upon food, drink, utensils. The consequence has to do with who may eat and drink what food and liquid, and what food and drink may be consumed in which pots and pans. These loci are specified by tractates on utensils *(Kelim)* and on food and drink *(Teharot* and *'Uqsin)*.

The human being is ambivalent. Persons fall in the middle, between sources and loci of uncleanness, because they are both. They serve as sources of uncleanness and they also become unclean. The *zab*, suffering the uncleanness described in Leviticus 15; the menstruating woman; the woman after childbirth; and the person afflicted with the skin ailment described in Leviticus 13 and 14 all are sources of uncleanness. But being unclean, they fall within the system's loci, its program of consequences. So they make other things unclean and are subject to penalties because they are unclean. Unambiguous sources of uncleanness never also constitute loci affected by uncleanness. They always are unclean and never can become clean: the corpse, the dead creeping thing, and things like them. Inanimate sources of uncleanness and inanimate objects are affected by uncleanness. Systemically unique, man and liquids have the capacity to inaugurate the processes of uncleanness (as sources) and also are subject to those same processes (as objects of uncleanness). The division of Purities, which presents the basically simple system just now described, is not only the oldest in the Mishnah. It also is the largest and contains by far the most complex laws and ideas. The main point of the system of uncleanness and purification concerns death and life. Death is the principal source of uncleanness, and the system of laws aims at removing its residue and preserving from contamination the food and drink, persons and possessions, of Israelites, especially in the setting of the Temple and its offerings, the source of life.

So much for the details of the Mishnah's legal category-formations. Let us now stand back and characterize the system as a whole.

The Mishnah's System Seen Whole

The system centers upon sanctification, understood as the correct arrangement of all things, each in its proper category, each called by its rightful name, just as at the creation: Everything having been given its

proper name, God called the natural world "very good" and God sanctified it. Then to restore the world to its Creator's conception, all things
would have to be made worthy of a counterpart act of sanctification. For
the Mishnah makes a statement of philosophy, concerning the ordering of
the natural world in its correspondence with the supernatural world.
Sanctification means two things, first, distinguishing Israel in all its dimensions from the world in all its ways; second, establishing the stability,
order, regularity, predictability, and reliability of Israel in the world of nature and supernature in particular at moments and in contexts of danger.
Danger—as our initial survey showed—means instability, disorder, irregularity, uncertainty, and betrayal. Each topic of the system as a whole
takes up a critical and indispensable moment or context of social being.
Through what is said in regard to each of the Mishnah's principal topics,
what the halakic system as a whole wishes to declare is fully expressed.
Yet if the parts severally and jointly give the message of the whole, the
whole cannot exist without all of the parts, so well joined and carefully
crafted are they all.

It is one thing to state the system as a whole. It is quite another to address the issue of the circumstance addressed by the authorship of the
Mishnah. I represent the document as a response to a crisis, a moment in
historical time. But the Mishnah's authorship does not think it urgent to
speak to a particular time or place. They provide no account of the occasion, history, or authority of their code. They rarely refer to specific circumstances subject to legislation. They speak in the language of general,
descriptive rules, implicitly applicable everywhere and any time. From
the first line to the last, discourse takes up questions internal to a system
that is never introduced. The Mishnah provides information without establishing context. It presents disputes about facts hardly urgent outside
of a circle of faceless disputants. Consequently, we start with the impression that we join a conversation already long under way about topics we
can never grasp anyhow. The Mishnah does not identify its authors. That
is to say, while the document cites the opinions of many authorities, it
does not identify who wrote it, why, and in what context. It is a collective
statement, the anonymous voice speaking on behalf of the consensus of
authorities. Many of these authorities who are named in the Mishnah are
cited in tractate *'Abot*, The Fathers, a list of names of sages extending backward from the second-century C.E. rabbis to Moses at Sinai. So on behalf of
the sages of the Mishnah is set forth the claim of tradition from God to
Moses and onward to the Mishnah. But the document itself is silent on
whom it represents and for whom it speaks. The attribution to R. Judah
the Patriarch, the head of the Jewish community on the land of Israel
recognized by the Roman government, is not sustained by the internal
evidence of the Mishnah. The Mishnah permits only slight variations, if
any, in its authorities' patterns of language and speech, so there is no
place for individual characteristics of expression. It nowhere tells us when

it speaks. It does not address a particular place or time and rarely speaks of events in its own day. It never identifies its prospective audience. There is scarcely a "you" in the entire mass of sayings and rules. The Mishnah begins nowhere, with a rule out of all context. It ends abruptly, with another such rule. There is no predicting where it will commence or explaining why it is done. Where, when, why the document is laid out and set forth are questions not deemed urgent and not answered.

Indeed, the Mishnah contains not a hint about what its authors conceive their work to be. Is it a law code? Is it a school book? Since it makes statements describing what people should and should not do—or rather, in its language, do and do not do—we might suppose it is a law code. Since, as we shall see in a moment, it covers topics of both practical and theoretical interest, we might suppose it is a school book. But the Mishnah never expresses a hint about its authors' intent. The reason is that the authors do what they must to efface all traces not only of individuality but even of their own participation in the formation of the document. So it is not only a "letter" from utopia to whom it may concern. It also is a "letter" written by no one person—but not by a committee, either.

Nor should we fail to notice, even at the outset, that while the Mishnah clearly addresses Israel, the Jewish people, it is remarkably different from the Hebrew Scriptures. The Mishnah makes no effort at imitating the Hebrew of the Hebrew Bible, as do the writers of the Dead Sea Scrolls. The Mishnah does not attribute its sayings to biblical heroes, prophets or holy men, as do the writings of the pseudepigraphs of the Hebrew Scriptures. The Mishnah does not claim to emerge from a fresh encounter with God through revelation, as is not uncommon in Israelite writings of the preceding five hundred years; the Holy Spirit is not alleged to speak here. All the devices by which other Israelite writers gain credence for their messages are ignored. Perhaps the authority of the Mishnah was self-evident to its authors. But, self-evident or not, they in no way take the trouble to explain to their document's audience why people should conform to the descriptive statements contained in their holy book.

If then we turn to the contents of the document, we are helped not at all in determining the place of the Mishnah's origination, the purpose of its formation, the reasons for its anonymous and collective plane of discourse and monotonous tone of voice. The Mishnah covers a carefully defined program of topics. But it never tells us why one topic is introduced and another is omitted, or what the agglutination of these particular topics in the formation of a system or imaginative construction is meant to accomplish. Nor is there any predicting how a given topic will be treated, why a given set of issues will be explored in close detail, and another set of possible issues ignored. Discourse on a theme begins and ends as if all things are self-evident—including, as I said, the reason for beginning at one point and ending at some other. In all one might readily imagine, upon first glance at this strange and curious book, that what we have is a

rulebook. It appears on the surface to be a book lacking all traces of elo-
quence and style, revealing no evidence of system and reflection, and
serving no important purpose. First glance might indicate that in hand is
yet another shard from remote antiquity—no different from the king-lists
inscribed on the ancient shards, the random catalogue of (to us) useless,
meaningless facts: a scrapbook, a cookbook, a placard of posted tariffs, de-
tritus of random information, accidentally thrown up on the currents of
historical time. Who would have wanted to make such a thing? Who
would now want to refer to it?

The answer to that question is deceptively straight-forward: The
Mishnah is important because it has become a principal component of the
canon of Judaism. Indeed, that answer begs the question: Why should
some of the ancient Jews of the land of Israel have brought together these
particular facts and rules into a book and set them forth for the Israelite
people? Why should the Mishnah have been received, as much later on it
certainly was received, as a half of the "whole Torah of Moses at Sinai"?
The Mishnah was represented, after it was compiled, as the part of the
"whole Torah of Moses, our rabbi," which had been formulated and transmitted orally, so it bore the status of divine revelation right alongside the
Pentateuch. Yet it is already entirely obvious that little in the actual contents of the document evoked the character or the moral authority of the
written Torah of Moses. None pretended otherwise.

Indeed, since most of the authorities named in the Mishnah lived in
the century and a half prior to the promulgation of the document, the
claim that their statements in fact derived from Moses at Sinai through a
long chain of oral tradition contradicted the well-known facts of the matter, e.g., *m. 'Abot* 1:1. So this claim presents a paradox even on the surface:
How can the Mishnah be deemed a book of religion, a program for consecration, a mode of sanctification? Why should Jews from the end of the
second century to our own day have deemed the study of the Mishnah to
be a holy act, a deed of service to God through the study of an important
constituent of God's Torah, God's will for Israel, the Jewish people?

Drawing Nourishment from the Past, Thinking about the Future—Always in the Here and Now: The Mishnah's Eternal Present-tense Paradigm

We can derive no answers from the world in which the document
emerged. The world addressed by the Mishnah is hardly congruent to the
worldview presented within the Mishnah. On the contrary, point by
point, the Mishnah portrays the opposite of the world its framers confronted. Consider: there was no sacrificial or blood cult, no temple, no
holy city to which, at this time, the description of the mishnaic laws

applied. We observe at the very outset, therefore, that a sizable proportion of the Mishnah deals with matters to which the sages had no material
access or practical knowledge at the time of their work. For we have seen
that the Mishnah contains a division on the conduct of the cult (namely,
Holy Things, the fifth) as well as one on the conduct of matters so as to
preserve the cultic purity of the sacrificial system (the sixth, Purities). In
fact, a fair part of the second division (Appointed Times) takes up the conduct of the cult on special days (e.g., the sacrifices offered on the Day of
Atonement, Passover, and the like). Indeed, what the Mishnah wants to
know about appointed seasons concerns the cult far more than it does
that of the synagogue.

Then notice: the fourth division, on civil law (Damages), for its part,
presents an elaborate account of a political structure and system of Israelite self-government in tractates *Sanhedrin* and *Makkot*, not to mention
Šebu ͑ot and *Horayot*. This system speaks of king, priest, temple, and court.
But so far as Jews exercised legitimate political authority over other
Jews and so constituted a Jewish politic, it was through the instrument of
the patriarchate, the Roman-sponsored ethnarchy of Jewry. For such a
political contraption, the Mishnah makes no provision in its design of Israelite politics.

So it would appear that well over half of the document before us
speaks of a world out of the past in a design for an indeterminate future.
That judgment covers much of the second division, most of the fifth and
sixth divisions, as well as large segments of the fourth division. Then
there are entire tractates elsewhere that legislate for some world other
than that of second-century Israel: for instance, tractate *Soṭah*, on the wife
accused of adultery and the temple ordeal that pertains, in the division of
Family/Women. When we consider that, in the very time in which the authorities before us did their work, the temple lay in ruins, the city of Jerusalem was prohibited to all Israelites, and the Jewish government and
administration that had centered on the temple and based its authority on
the holy life lived there were in ruins, the fantastic character of the Mishnah's address to its own catastrophic day becomes clear.

What is the upshot of the contrast between the Mishnah's fantasy
and Israel's dismal reality? The Mishnah stands in contrast to the world to
which it speaks. In the age of crisis, the problem is to reorder a world off
course and adrift, to gain reorientation for an age in which the sun will
come out after the night and the fog. The Mishnah is a document of imagination and fantasy, describing out of the shards and remnants of reality
how things are, but also, in larger measure, building social being out of
beams of hope. Stated simply: the Mishnah tells us something about how
things were when the Mishnah was finally compiled, but everything
about how a small group of men wanted things to be. The document is orderly, repetitious, and careful in both language and message. It is pica-
yune, obvious, dull, routine—everything its age was not. The Mishnah's

message treats of small achievements and modest hope, defying a world of immodest demands. The heirs of heroes define affairs for an unheroic folk, for an ordinary age.

What is the point? With its stress on the critical role of attitude and intentionality, the Mishnah's message is that what a person wants matters in important ways. It speaks to an Israelite world that can shape affairs in no important ways and speaks to people who by no means will the way things now are. The Mishnah therefore lays down a practical judgment upon, and in favor of, the imagination and will to reshape reality, regain a system, and reestablish that order upon which trustworthy existence is to be built.

How the Mishnah Resolved the Crisis of 135 and Defined Normative Judaism: Israel and Adam Once More

Yet the Mishnah matched its occasion, and for those who received it, the document's system responded to the crisis of 135. And the circumstances of the Israel to which the document spoke persisted, so that the mishnaic transformation of the pentateuchal system would continue to pertain. Who was that Israel encompassed by the pentateuchal-mishnaic system? The document addressed all Israel but a handful of exceptions— that is, its Israel encompassed all those destined to rise from the grave at the resurrection of the dead, stand in judgment, and enter eternal life. The system of the Mishnah would be modified, revised, and transformed over time but would be left forever unimpaired. The Mishnah defined what became normative Judaism because it compellingly addressed the very enduring condition of that same Israel—that is to say, those who conceived they had been promised and given a land but lost it, had served God in a temple prescribed by him that was now in ruins, and had been told to perform rites now suspended. The pentateuchal paradigm therefore was extended to a new chapter in its unfolding, with the Mishnah addressing the question opened by the caesura in the paradigm represented by the situation of 135.

So—in more secular language—because of its adaptation of the pentateuchal system to the Israelite condition beyond 135, the Judaic system of the social order put forth by the Mishnah would be realized in the life of most of the Jewish people from antiquity to the present. The Mishnah would define that single Judaism, the normative system, for the vast majority of those that would practice any Judaism—any religious system that privileged the Pentateuch and articulated its paradigm—from antiquity to the present day.

A more general reprise of the mishnaic system will now show us how the document marked a turning point, responding not only to a

particular crisis but to an on-going condition defining the social order of
Israel, the Jewish people. The transformation it effected refracted the
pentateuchal pattern through the prism of the loss, for the interim, of the
pentateuchal realization in offerings, temple, Jerusalem. The contrast between the Mishnah's emphases in its recapitulation of the pentateuchal
system and the contrary qualities of the Israelite condition tells why.
Stated simply: the Mishnah found a way for Israel to realize the pentateuchal plan even without the institutional and political media set forth
by the Pentateuch. It laid out a Judaism focused on the Land of Israel,
yet not limited by the land's boundaries—it was a system Ezra could have
sent out to Babylonia and to Egypt, not limited to Jerusalem and Judea. It
provided for the continued but now utopian sanctification of Israel
through Israel's very being. What was then lacking from the system—a
clear promise of its realization in the restoration of cult, buildings, and
city—would come to the fore at the next turning point.

The Pentateuch aimed at the sanctification of Israel in the Land
through the realization of the revealed program for sanctification: setting
all things in their proper place under their rightful name, as at creation.
The Judaism shaped by the Mishnah sets forth a heightened and deep-
ened perception of the sanctification of Israel in deed and in deliberation.
Sanctification now means two things, realized both in the model of the
pentateuchal construction and also abstracted from the pentateuchal particularities. This was done by, first, distinguishing Israel in all its dimensions from the world in all its ways; second, establishing the stability,
order, regularity, predictability, and reliability of Israel at moments and in
contexts of danger. The former—reaffirming the sanctification of Israel by
separation from the gentiles—obviously flowed from the pentateuchal
system. The latter, the recapitulation of creation through the hierarchical
ordering of Israelite being, requires a word of clarification. What was at
stake in the Mishnah's system of hierarchical classification was the establishing of order amidst disorder. A society was in ruins, a social order in
utter devastation. Danger means instability, disorder, irregularity, uncertainty, and betrayal. Each topic of the system as a whole took up a critical
and indispensable moment or context of social being subject to disorder,
and orders what is disorderly and on that account dangerous. Through
what is said in regard to each of the Mishnah's principal topics, what the
system as a whole wishes to declare is fully expressed. It is a message for
Israel in crisis.

The crisis precipitated by the permanent destruction of the second
temple that the collapse of the paradigm signaled affected both the nation
and the individual, since, in the nature of things, what happened in
the metropolis inevitably touched affairs of home and family. What con-
nected the individual fate to the national destiny was the long-established
Israelite conviction that the fate of the individual and the destiny of the
Jewish nation depended upon the moral character of both. Disaster came

about because of the people's sin, so went the message of biblical history and prophecy. The sins of individuals and of nation alike ran against the revealed will of God, the Torah. So reflection upon the meaning of the recent catastrophe inexorably followed paths laid out long ago, trod from one generation to the next. Then the pentateuchal paradigm still served. That claim found reinforcement in the very topical program seemingly so out of phase with the social world addressed by the Mishnah. A structure coming in the aftermath of the temple's destruction which doggedly restated rules governing the temple so reaffirmed, in the most obvious possible way, the cult and the created world celebrated therein. When a document emerges rich in discourse on these matters and doggedly repetitive of precisely what Scripture says about exactly the same things, the meaning in context is clear.

According to the pentateuchal account, Israel had originally become Israel and sustained its perpetual vocation through its living on the holy land and organizing all aspects of its life in relationship to the conduct of the holy temple, eating as priests and farming in accord with the cultic taboos and obsessions with order and form, dividing up time between profane and holy in relationship to the cult's calendar and temporal division of its own rites. Now Israel remained Israel, loyal to its calling, through continuing to live in the mirror and under the aspect of that same cult. The turning point represented by the permanent destruction of the temple and closure of Jerusalem to Israel marked not a transformation of the pentateuchal system but a realization of its inner logic.

That old, reliable, priestly way of life and worldview from the temple mountain came to be subsumed by, and transformed into, a social vision framed on the plane of Israel, who would share in the world to come, in restored Eden. Then, just as the pentateuchal system said through its parallel narratives of Adam and Israel, Eden and the land, rebellion through sin, Israel is the other, the new Adam.

The Mishnah's principal message, which makes the Judaism of this document and of its social components distinctive and cogent, is precisely the message of the Priests' Genesis story. It is that man is at the center of creation, the head of all creatures upon earth, corresponding to God in heaven, in whose image man is made. The Mishnah makes this simple and fundamental statement by imputing power to man to inaugurate and initiate those corresponding processes, sanctification and uncleanness, which play so critical a role in the Mishnah's account of reality. The will of man, expressed through the deed of man, is the active power in the world. Will and deed constitute those actors of creation that work upon neutral realms, subject to either sanctification or uncleanness: the temple and table, the field and family, the altar and hearth, woman, time, space, transactions in the material world and in the world above as well. An object, a substance, a transaction—even a phrase or a sentence—is inert, but may be made holy when the interplay of the will and deed of man arouses or generates its potential to be sanctified. Each may be treated as ordinary or (where relevant) made unclean by the neglect of the will and inattentive act of man. Just as the entire system of uncleanness and holiness awaits the intervention of man, which imparts the capacity to become unclean upon what was formerly inert, or which removes the capacity to impart cleanness from what was formerly in its natural and puissant condition— so in the other ranges of reality, man is at the center on earth, just as is God in heaven. Man is counterpart and partner and creation in that, like God, he has power over the status and condition of creation, putting everything in its proper place and calling everything by its rightful name.

So, stated briefly, the question taken up by the Mishnah and answered by Judaism is: What can a man of Israel do? And the answer laid down by the Mishnah is: Man, through will and deed, is master of this world, the measure of all things. Since when the Mishnah thinks of man, it means the Israelite, who is the subject and actor of its system, the statement is clear. This man is Israel, who can do what he wills and whose actions have tremendous ramifications in the world around him. In the aftermath of the two wars, the message of the Mishnah cannot have proved more pertinent—or more poignant.

Judaism without Christianity

Before leaving the second century and the way in which the Mishnah addressed the crisis of the failure of the received pentateuchal paradigm, let us stand back and gain perspective on the character of the Judaism without a temple that emerged in a world in which, so far as the rabbinic sages were concerned, there was no Christianity. Nothing in the mishnaic system focuses on issues made vivid and urgent by the challenge of Christianity. Here therefore we see the Judaism that flowed only from the destruction of the temple and the despair following the permanent loss of Jerusalem. Given the later paramount importance of Christianity, we find it natural to wonder where and how the system of the Mishnah responded to the competition represented by Christianity for hegemony over Scripture, which both Judaism and Christianity affirmed as God's will and word.

The Mishnah presents a Judaism that answered a single encompassing question concerning the enduring sanctification of Israel: What, in the aftermath of the destruction of the holy place and holy cult, remained of the sanctity of the holy caste, the priesthood; the holy land; and, above all, the holy people and its holy way of life? The answer was that sanctity persists, indelibly, in Israel, the people; in its way of life; in its land; in its priesthood; in its food, its mode of sustaining life; and in its manner of procreating and so sustaining the nation. That holiness would endure. And the Mishnah then laid out the structures of sanctification: what does it mean to live a holy life? But that answer found itself absorbed, in time to come, within a successor-system, with its own points of stress and emphasis. That successor-system, both continuous with and asymmetrical to the Mishnah, would take over the Mishnah and turn it into the one whole Torah of Moses, our rabbi, that became Judaism. The indicative marks of the transformation are, first, the formation of a doctrine of history, a theology that encompassed a variety of historical events and category-formations; and, second, the figure of Messiah as sage, as we shall see.

In the second-century document, we are hard put to identify points at which the mishnaic system addressed issues important to Christianity of the same age. For example, the system of the Mishnah—a Judaism for a world in which Christianity played no considerable role—took slight interest in the Messiah and presented a teleology lacking all eschatological, and therefore messianic, focus. It laid no considerable stress on the symbol of the Torah, though, of course, the Torah as a scroll—as a matter of status, and as revelation of God's will at Sinai—enjoyed prominence. And it produced a document, the Mishnah, so independent of Scripture that, when the authors wished to say what Scripture said, they almost always chose to do so in their own words and in their own way. Whatever their intent, it clearly did not encompass explaining to a competing Israel, heirs of the same Scriptures of Sinai, just what authority validated the document, and how the document related to Scripture. However, the Mishnah spawned a successor-system, with its own points of stress and emphasis. So let us now turn to the Judaism that took shape beyond 70 but before Constantine's rise to power in the fourth century. Having now seen where Christianity made no difference, we shall notice when Christianity made all the difference in the world. It was then that the pentateuchal system, as transformed by the Mishnah, would address those still-unanswered questions: how long? by whom?

3

Asymmetries: Gaps in the Pentateuchal-Mishnaic System

Systemic Silences: Gaps between the Systems

The mishnaic system recapitulates the pentateuchal one, stating as a design for the Israelite social order the implicit program of God's Instruction to Moses at Sinai for the kingdom of priests and holy people. What sages in the Mishnah (and beyond) contributed is the perspective on the unfolding story of Scripture that is afforded by their knowledge of how things came out: the recapitulation of Scripture's paradigm in Israel's future history. From beginning to end, the rabbinic Midrash-compilations build their structure out of a reading of Scripture that is both retrospective—from the twin-calamities of 586 B.C.E. and 70–135 C.E.—and prospective. Sages read from Scripture forward and produced the systemic outcome, then read Scripture backward, from the system to the narratives, laws, and prophecies, toward the restoration of the perfection of creation and the sanctification of all things by God, pleased with creation. That is because any outline of Scripture's account begins with creation and tells about the passage from Eden via Sinai and Jerusalem to Babylon—*and back.*

But the pentateuchal-mishnaic system—that is, the Mishnah's reworking of the Pentateuch's laws, narratives, and prophecies—into a coherent set of rules for the sanctification of Israel's social order processes scriptural data of all kinds but two. These are (1) historical (including apocalyptic) and (2) eschatological. That system finds a place in its governing category-formations for everything but pentateuchal facts out of the past and the counterpart assertions facing the future. In this respect, the mishnaic categorical reworking of the Pentateuch proves asymmetrical to the received pentateuchal system.

At issue in particular is the construction of category-formations—topics deemed systemically urgent, requiring incorporation within the large structure. Concerning history and eschatology, the Mishnah preserves silence in its systemic category-formations. That is not because history and eschatology were absent from the foundation-document. On the contrary, the pentateuchal system had in part made its statement through the medium of historical narratives about one-time, sequential events. Not only so, but that statement had encompassed the end of days as envisioned by Jacob and then by Moses. So the pentateuchal statement on its own had explicitly invoked historical and eschatological events as systemic indicators, with times of peace and prosperity signifying Israel's oneness with God, and war and disaster indicating rebellion against God.

The pentateuchal-mishnaic system for its part looked to the past for evidence of regularity and order. In so doing, it invoked the model of creation and took as its task the restoration of the world to its original perfection at creation—the realization of perpetual Sabbath. Consequently, the system both acknowledged and ignored considerations of time and of change, such as we call history, for which the Mishnah found little use. True, the Mishnah encompassed in its system important happenings, to which it made reference. But, as we shall see, that was on the terms defined by the Mishnah's own system. When the Mishnah afforded recognition to axial events, such as the destruction of the temple, which marked a considerable turning in Israel's history and demanded accommodation within the system, it reduced those events to components of a paradigm of an ahistorical character.

Why the asymmetry between the pentateuchal foundations and the mishnaic system built thereon? Because the Mishnah's recapitulation of the Pentateuch aimed at identifying *regularities* in the building of Israel's social order. To these, one-time events proved disruptive—and, worse still, inconsequential. The stories, laws, and prophecies of the Pentateuch set forth the original system in historical form, speaking of past, present, and future as a linear and unitary account of Israel's social order. Subsequently retrospectively systematized and regularized by the Mishnah, these stories, laws, and prophecies were reformed into an eternal present tense. The past is forever embodied in the present, the present in the past, and the future is now too. That represents a judgment upon what counts, which is, the patterns to be discerned out of discrete data. The consequent system, finding singular happenings uninformative, either bypassed in silence or treated casually the particular, one-time meaning of singular events and their goal for the end of time.

In more abstract language, the pentateuchal-mishnaic structure of category-formations did not encompass a doctrine of history as singular, linear, and purposive. And, consequently, while the system bore an implicit teleology—the restoration of Israel to the land, the temple to Zion, and the offerings to the holy altar—no effort was made to match past and future. That is, the pentateuchal-mishnaic system was remarkably uninterested in adapting the Messiah theme to its teleology, which was not framed eschatologically at all. There is no category-formation built out of, or in relationship to, the Messiah-theme. Hence the systemic gap; the pentateuchal-mishnaic system had no interest in history, and therefore defined a teleology lacking an eschatological dimension.

Because the generative logic that animated the pentateuchal-mishnaic system dealt in eternities, the massive presences of the ancient Israelite literary culture, history, and eschatology proved asymmetrical to the systemic construction produced by the Mishnah out of Scripture. That logic conceived a pattern by which to realize the perfection of the world. It derived from the model of the stasis achieved, with all things in place and properly categorized, with the divine act of sanctification at the advent of the first Sabbath. That systemic logic left no space for the data of history and eschatology, even when read propositionally and systematically, in category-formations. Events had to be subsumed under ahistorical, timeless rubrics, signifiers of patterns. Accordingly, the Messiah-theme gave way to the Messiah as a systemic indicator, another piece of data pertinent to hierarchical classification, in particular of generals and priests.

Scripture read all together at the end, as the rabbinic sages construed matters, accounts for the matter. Comparing Adam and Israel and promising to restore Adam to Eden through Israel's recovery of the land, the pentateuchal-mishnaic system aimed at the regularization, the right ordering, of the everyday. One-time events, whether catastrophic or redemptive, past or future, presented obstacles to the realization of that goal. After all, one-time events could not accommodate themselves to the quest for paradigm, the timeless rules that transcend history brought together in the Mishnah. The Pentateuch's urgent question—how Israel is to retain the land held on the stipulations of a covenant—produced the answer: by an everyday, enduring life of sanctification. The pentateuchal way of life and worldview then defined the details of that life to be lived by the kingdom of priests and holy people. Continuing the pentateuchal system, the Mishnah responded to a different question: What remains of Israel's sanctification, when the places and rites that embodied sanctification lay in ruins? Its answer was that holiness inheres in Israel, the people—specifically, in its social order.

The whole complex—the pentateuchal structure taken over and systematized in the categorical recapitulation after 135 C.E.—then merged in the halakic system set forth by the Mishnah's category-formations. That powerful, detailed account covered the routinized requirements of holiness. It pertained, as we saw in chapter two, to the timeless world of the everyday: the fields and farms of the holy land (Agriculture), marking holy time (Appointed Seasons), preserving the sanctification of woman to man in the household and family (Women), and the holy offerings at the holy temple (Holy Things, Purities). Through the civil code (Damages), the whole was formed into a community of stasis and balance, with all things in order and in place. These traits of the social order enabled the realization of sanctification, in line with the initial act of sanctification and blessing at the moment of the Sabbath of Creation. The Pentateuch provided most (though not all) of the details; the Mishnah, the category-formations that generalized and ordered the details into a coherent design for Israel's sacred order in its realization in society.

Although the generative logic of the pentateuchal-mishnaic construction yielded a coherent system, the whole failed to respond to its own context—namely, the age of despair that had overtaken Israel. The pentateuchal-mishnaic system did not address concerns that the recent wars certainly rendered vivid: the meaning of one-time events such as the destruction of the temple and the massive military defeat Israel had suffered. Nor did it address the perfectly natural yearning for the resolution of history in the Messiah's coming, which other Judaisms, if not this Judaism, expressed. Indeed, the pentateuchal-mishnaic system pointedly avoided the two-part critical question confronting quotidian Israel: (1) how long, and (2) by whom? To Scripture viewed whole and read forward, these were perfectly legitimate questions, with answers supplied both by prophecy in times of old and also by prophets who presented themselves in this period. But to Scripture read backward from the perspective of 135 C.E., these questions precipitated precisely that condition of chaos that the rabbinic sages meant to remedy through their labor of social regularization. "How long?" was in a precise sense simply unthinkable, and "by whom?" self-evidently answered: by corporate Israel.

So the pentateuchal-mishnaic system provided in detail for enduring institutions and relationships, showing how these nurtured and embodied the requirements of the kingdom of priests and holy people. But, with its stress on paradigms of conduct, it could accommodate only with difficulty the un-patterned, one-time turnings that comprise history. Although the Pentateuch posited a prophet to bring salvation, and the Pentateuch and the prophetic books told of anointing this leader, the Messiah-theme in the Mishnah formed merely a taxic indicator for the priesthood—a mere detail of a chapter in the Mishnah's program of hierarchical classification. The Mishnah occasionally acknowledges the Messiah-theme in its eschatological expression (at *m. Soṭah* 9:15, cited presently, for example), but in no way treats that theme as the foundation for a systematic, halakic exposition in one of its generative category-formations. Stated simply: the Messiah-theme in the Mishnah in no way forms a principal part of the document's working system for the social order.

To recapitulate: the temple lay in ruins—but for how long? The restored paradigm insisted it would be restored—but by whom? The pentateuchal narratives lend plausibility to these questions, but the Mishnah does not answer them or even recognize them as requiring answers. The Mishnah and the Pentateuch here reveal their asymmetry. The Pentateuch had made its statement through a narrative history, the story of the formation of Israel and its pilgrimage through history to the promised land. The prophets for their part, had deemed great events to convey God's judgment, which they made explicit. So the generality of Israelites had good reason to anticipate in a pentateuchal-mishnaic formulation doctrines of not only sanctification and atonement, restoration and renewal, but salvation and redemption, set forth in a doctrine of history and its goal, eschatology.

The Contrast between the Pentateuch's and the Mishnah's Media of Expression

The Pentateuch makes its statement through narrative, both continuous, historical narrative concerning the entire people of Israel (e.g., the entirety of Deuteronomy) and also episodic biographical narrative set within the larger historical framework (e.g., much of Genesis). Rich in law, Exodus, Leviticus, Numbers, and Deuteronomy frame all law within a narrative-historical framework, whether elaborate, as in Deuteronomy, or casual, as in the repeated priestly historical mythologumenon, "The Lord spoke to Moses saying, Speak to the children of Israel and say to them." Less broadly recognized is that when the Mishnah recapitulates pentateuchal law (or presents non-pentateuchal law) it homogenizes the whole within a single medium of expression. That is done by the persistently present-tense, descriptive statement of how things are done. The prose is formalized and uniform throughout, not shaped to topical context let alone to a particular occasion. The Mishnah's presentation of law, unlike Scripture's counterpart, is never contextual, never episodic, and never historical. The Pentateuch's invitation to history through narrative and the Mishnah's exclusion of history thus come to concrete realization in the very language and style that serve each of the respective documents. And that contrast underscores the gap between the pentateuchal and the mishnaic systems, a gap that would become a chasm when the explicit confrontation with Scripture would present the only medium for coping with events beyond the scope of the pentateuchal-mishnaic system (as we shall see in chapter four).

Since the Mishnah's homogenization of the diversities of everyday life within a single language-system is unlikely to prove familiar to readers beyond narrow circles of Judaic learning, a few words of amplification are in order. The Mishnah makes its statement principally by describing the commonplace facts of life, which stand for nothing beyond themselves and their consequences, e.g., clean unclean, or liability and exemption from liability. The rhetoric is readily recognized: all is balanced, explicit in detail, but reticent about the whole. The meaning of what is said emerges through the balance of facts as set forth in patterned language.

The Mishnah generally avoids explicit statement of a generalization, but prefers to implicitly communicate its generalizations through grouped examples of a common rule (which itself is rarely articulated). It is indeed a subtle mode of discourse indeed to convey principles through details. How, precisely, does the Mishnah formalize language to its own purposes? Let me summarize the two criteria of linguistic formalization and organization of the Mishnah.

The first criterion derives from the nature of the principal divisions themselves: theme. The redactors organized vast corpora of materials into principal divisions and tractates along thematic lines. These fundamental themes were then subdivided into smaller conceptual units. The principal divisions treat their themes in units indicated by the sequential unfolding of their inner logical structure. Accordingly, one established criterion for the deliberation of an aggregate of materials from some other will be a shift in the theme, or predominant and characteristic concern, of a sequence of materials.

The second fundamental criterion is the syntactical and grammatical pattern, which differentiates and characterizes a sequence of primitive (that is, undifferentiable or indivisible) units of thought. A single pattern will govern the formalization of discourse for a single unit of thought. Normally, when the subject changes, the mode of expression, the formal or formulary character, the patterning of language, will change as well.

From the basic traits of large-scale organization, which devolve from the subject-matter, we turn to the way in which sentences and paragraphs are put together. "Paragraph" means a completed exposition of thought, the setting forth of a proposition whole and complete, without regard to the larger function (e.g., in a sustained discourse of argument or proposition) served by that thought. Two or more lapidary statements (e.g., allegations as to fact) will make up such a sustained cognitive unit. The cognitive units in the Mishnah in particular resort to a remarkably limited repertoire of formulary patterns, and the document as a whole exhibits remarkable formal linguistic and stylistic uniformity. The authorship of the Mishnah manages to say whatever it wants in one of the following ways, with special reference to the division of Purities (here representative of the traits of formalization of the document as a whole):

1. a sequence of matched, simple declarative sentences, in which the subject and predicate are syntactically tightly joined to one another, e.g., "He who does so and so is such and such";

2. the duplicated subject, in which the subject of the sentence is stated twice, e.g., "He who does so and so, lo, he is such and such";

3. mild apocopation, in which the subject of the sentence is cut off from the verb, which refers to its own subject, and not the one with which the sentence commences, e.g., "He who does so and so . . . , it [the thing he has done] is such and such";

4. extreme apocopation, in which a series of clauses is presented, none of them tightly joined to what precedes or follows, and all of them cut off from the predicate of the sentence, e.g., "He who does so and so . . . , it [the thing he has done] is such and such . . . , it is a matter of doubt whether . . . or whether . . . lo, it [referring to nothing in the antecedent, apocopated clauses of the subject of the sentence] is so and so . . .";

5. rather than effecting the distinctive formulary traits through variations in the relationship between the subject and the predicate of the sentence, this fifth one has a contrastive complex predicate. We may have two sentences, independent of one another, yet clearly formulated so as to stand in acute balance with one another in the predicate, thus, "He who does . . . is unclean, and he who does not . . . is clean."

There will be a natural objection to entry number one: is it possible that a simple declarative sentence may serve as a formulary pattern, alongside the rather distinctive and unusual constructions which follow? True, by itself, a tightly constructed sentence consisting of subject, verb, and complement, in which the verb refers to the subject, and the complement to the verb, hardly exhibits traits of particular formal interest. Yet a sequence of such sentences, built along the same gross grammatical lines, does exhibit a clear-cut and distinctive pattern.

And here the mnemonics of the document meant to be memorized enter into consideration. The Mishnah is not a generalizing document; it makes its points by repeating several cases that yield the same, ordinarily unarticulated, general principle. Accordingly, the Mishnah repeats sets of three or five cases to make a single point, with groupings of three or five (or multiples thereof) matched sentences predominating. Now when three or five "simple declarative sentences" take up one principle or problem, and then, when the principle or problem shifts, a quite distinctive formal pattern will be utilized. The "simple declarative sentence" has thus served the formulator of the unit of thought as aptly as did apocopation, a dispute, or another more obviously distinctive form or formal pattern. The contrastive predicate (#5 above) is but one example; the Mishnah contains many more.

The important point of differentiation, particularly for the simple declarative sentence, therefore appears in the intermediate or the whole cognitive unit, thus in the interplay between theme and form. It is there that we see a single pattern recurring in a long sequence of sentences. For example, "The X which has lost its Y is unclean because of its Z. The Z which has lost its Y is unclean because of its X." Another example will be a long sequence of highly developed sentences, laden with relative clauses and other explanatory matter, in which a single syntactical pattern will govern the articulation of three (or six or nine) exempla. That sequence will be followed by one repeated terse sentence pattern, e.g., "X is so and so, Y is such and such, Z is thus and so." The former group will treat one principle or theme, the latter some other. There can be no doubt, there-fore, that the declarative sentence in recurrent patterns is, in its way, just as carefully formalized as a sequence of severely apocopated sentences or of contrastive predicates or duplicated subjects. None of the Mishnah's secondary and amplificatory companions (e.g., the Tosefta, the Yeru-shalmi, or Bavli) exhibits the same tight and rigidly-adhered-to rhetorical cogency.

The Mishnah's formal traits of rhetoric indicate that the document has been formulated all at once, and not in an incremental, linear process extending into a remote (mythic) past (e.g., to Sinai). These traits, com-mon to a series of distinct cognitive units, are redactional, imposed at that point at which someone intended to join together discrete (finished) units on a given theme. The varieties of traits particular to the discrete units and the diversity of authorities cited therein—including masters of two or three or even four strata from the turn of the first century to the end of the second—make it highly improbable that the several units were for-mulated in a common pattern and preserved, until, later on, further units were composed on the same theme and in the same pattern, and added. The entire indifference to the historical order of authorities, as well as the concentration on the logical unfolding of a given theme or problem with-out reference to the sequence of authorities, confirm the supposition that the work of formulation and of redaction went forward together.

The upshot is simple. The principal framework of formulation and formalization in the Mishnah is the intermediate division rather than the cognitive unit—in our terms, the paragraph and not the sentence. The least-formalized formulary pattern, the simple declarative sentence, turns out in aggregates to yield many examples of acute formalization, in which a single distinctive pattern is imposed upon two or more (very commonly, groups of three or groups of five) cognitive units. While an in-termediate division of a tractate may be composed of several such con-glomerates of cognitive units, it is rare indeed for cognitive units formally to stand wholly by themselves. Normally, cognitive units share formal or formulary traits with others with the same theme to which they are juxtaposed. The form-analysis of the Mishnah thus yields a document rhetorically out of phase with Scripture. That makes all the more acute the problem of how the pentateuchal paradigm is recast by the mishnaic recapitulation, and the asymmetries that resulted. And that brings us to the two points of asymmetry between the pentateuchal and the pentateuchal-mishnaic systems: history and eschatology.

The Mishnah's Systemization of Singular Historical Events into Components of a Paradigm

By "history" I mean the conglomeration of a sequence of one-time events, each of them singular, all of them meaningful on their own and in relationship to one another. These events move from a beginning somewhere to an end at a foreordained goal. History aims at a goal, an end in two senses: a purpose and a denouement. In Scripture, the teleology of Israel's life finds its definition in eschatological fulfillment. Eschatology therefore constitutes not a choice within, but the definition of, teleology. A theory of the goal and purpose of things (teleology) is shaped solely by appeal to the account of the end of times (eschatology). History in this sense then sits enthroned as the queen of theological science. Events do not conform to patterns; they *form* patterns. What happens matters because events bear meaning and constitute history.

Clearly, such a conception of mythic and apocalyptic history comes to realization in the writing of history in the prophetic pattern or in the apocalyptic framework, both of which are mythic modes of selecting (even inventing) and organizing events. We have every right to expect such a view of matters to lead people to write books of one sort, rather than of some other. In the case of Judaism from the time of the Pentateuch and forward, obviously, we should expect people to write history books that teach lessons or apocalyptic books that, through pregnant imagery, predict the future and record the direction and end of time. In antiquity, that kind of writing proved commonplace among all kinds of groups and characteristic of all sorts of Judaisms but one: the system of the Mishnah.

That is not because the past is ignored in the Mishnah. Nor does the character of the Mishnah as a law book explain the systemic disposition of history. The Mishnah *does* deal with events, but not in the manner of the Pentateuch, the prophets, or the apocalyptic writers of the Hebrew Bible. The Mishnah cannot be said to omit historical narratives because these occur elsewhere; the Mishnah, as we shall see, selects historical events and finds a systemic location for them. Which events are selected and how they are accommodated, then, form the key to the Mishnah's systematization of all data it chooses for processing. What the Mishnah has to say about history is quite different from what the Pentateuch, prophets, and apocalyptic writings have to say, and, consequently, the Mishnah does not conform in any way to the scriptural pattern of representing, and sorting out, events into history, myth, and apocalypse.

The first difference between the pentateuchal and the pentateuchal-mishnaic systems appears right at the surface. The Mishnah contains no sustained narrative whatsoever, very few tales, and no large-scale conception of history. As explained in chapter two, it organizes and sets forth its system in non-historical terms. Rarely does anyone set any of the laws of the Mishnah into a historical context, such as a particular time, place, or circumstance defined by important events. (Narratives of how in a given circumstance the sages voted on this or that, as at *m. Šabbat* 2:6, do not change the picture.) The Mishnah's system is set forth out of all historical framework, and such a medium has no precedent in prior systems of Judaism or in prior kinds of Jewish literature. The law codes of Exodus and Deuteronomy, for example, are set forth in a narrative framework, and the priestly code of Leviticus, for its part, appeals to God's revelation to Moses and Aaron at specific times and places and contexts. In the Mishnah we have neither narrative nor setting for the representation of law.

Instead of narrative which, as in Exodus, spills over into case-law, the Mishnah gives description of how things are done in general and universally, that is, descriptive laws. Instead of reflecting on the meaning and end of history, it constructs a world in which history plays little part. Instead of narratives full of didactic meaning, the Mishnah provides lists of events, so as to expose the traits that they share and thus the rules to which they conform. The definitive components of a historical-eschatological system of Judaism—description of events as one-time happenings, analysis of the meaning and end of events, and interpretation of the end and future of singular events—are all commonplace constituents of Scripture as well as of all other systems of ancient Judaism (including nascent Christianity), but find no place in the Mishnah's system of Judaism. In form, the Mishnah represents its system as outside of all historical framework. Yet, to say that the Mishnah's system is ahistorical could not be more wrong. The Mishnah presents a different kind of history. In our terms and categories, we might call it history as social science, and not history as exemplary narrative; generalizing history, and not hortatory history. How does this work?

The framers of the Mishnah refer to very few events explicitly. Those they do mention are treated within a particular focus, in a context quite separate from—the actual unfolding of the events themselves. Narratives are rarely created or used. Historical events do not supply organizing categories or taxonomic classifications. We find no tractate devoted to the destruction of the temple, nor a complete chapter detailing the events of Bar Kokhba, nor even a sustained celebration of the events of the sages' own biographies. When things that have happened are mentioned, it is neither to narrate nor to interpret and draw lessons from the event. Rather, it is either to illustrate a point of law or to pose a problem of the law—always *en passant,* never in a pointed way. So when sages refer to what has happened, it is casual and tangential to the main thrust of discourse. Famous events, or those of enduring meaning, such as the return to Zion from Babylonia in the time of Ezra and Nehemiah, gain entry into the Mishnah's discourse only because of the genealogical divisions of Israelite society into castes among the immigrants (*m. Qiddušin* 4:1). Where the Mishnah provides little tales or narratives, moreover, they more often treat how things in the cult are done in general than what, in particular, happened on some one day. It is sufficient to refer casually to well-known incidents. Narrative, in the Mishnah's limited rhetorical repertoire, is reserved for the narrow framework of what priests and others do on recurrent occasions and around the temple. Stories about dramatic events and important deeds provide little nourishment in the minds of the Mishnah's jurisprudents. Events, if they appear at all, are treated as trivial. They may be well-known, but are consequential in some way other than is revealed in the detailed account of what actually happened.

The sages' treatment of events determines what in the Mishnah is important about what happens. Since the greatest event in the century and a half during which the Mishnah's materials came into being (ca. 50 C.E. to ca. 200 C.E.) was not the destruction of the temple in 70 C.E. but its definitive closure in 135 C.E., we must expect the Mishnah's treatment of the matter to illustrate the document's larger theory of history: what is important and unimportant about what happens. The treatment of the destruction of 70 C.E. and its permanent closure in 135 C.E. occurs in this way. First, the destruction of the temple constitutes a noteworthy fact in the history of the law. Why? Because various laws about rite and cult had to undergo revision on account of the destruction. The following provides a stunningly apt example of how the Mishnah's authors regard what actually happened as being simply changes in the law. We begin with Mishnah-tractate *Roš Haššanah,* chapter four.

Mishnah-tractate *Roš Haššanah* 4:1–3

1. A. The festival day of the New Year which coincided with the Sabbath—

   B. in the temple they would sound the *shofar.*

   C. But not in the provinces.

   D. When the Temple was destroyed, Rabban Yohanan ben Zakkai made the rule that they should sound the *shofar* in every locale in which there was a court.

   E. Said R. Eleazar, "Rabban Yohanan ben Zakkai made that rule only in the case of Yabneh alone."

F. They said to him, "All the same are Yabneh and every locale in which there is a court."

2. A. And in this regard also was Jerusalem ahead of Yabneh:

B. in every town which is within sight and sound [of Jerusalem], and nearby and able to come up to Jerusalem, they sound the *shofar*.

C. But as to Yabneh, they sound the *shofar* only in the court alone.

3. A. In olden times the *lulab* was taken up in the Temple for seven days, and in the provinces, for one day.

B. When the Temple was destroyed, Rabban Yohanan ben Zakkai made the rule that in the provinces the *lulab* should be taken up for seven days, as a memorial to the Temple;

C. and that the day [the sixteenth of Nisan] on which the *omer* is waved should be wholly prohibited [in regard to the eating of new produce] [*m. Sukkah* 3:12].

First, let us examine the passage in its own terms, and then point to its consequence for the argument about history. The rules of sounding the *shofar* run to the special case of the New Year which coincides with the Sabbath, *m. Roš Haš.* 4:1A–C. Clearly, we have some diverse materials here since *m. Roš Haš.* 4:1A–D (+ E–F), are formally different from *m. Roš Haš.* 4:3. The point of difference, however, is clear, since *m. Roš Haš.* 4:3A has no counterpart at *m. Roš Haš.* 4:1A–C, and this is for redactional reasons. That is, to connect his materials with what has preceded in the tractate, the redactor could not introduce the issue of *shofar* in *m. Roš Haš.* 4:1A–C with the formulary, "*In olden times . . . When the Temple was destroyed . . .*" Consequently, he has used the more common, mild apocopation to announce his topic, and then (in 4:3) reverted to the expected formulary pattern—which, I think, characterized *m. Roš Haš.* 4:1A–C as much as *m. Roš Haš.* 4:3. The middle section, *m. Roš Haš.* 4:2A assumes a different antecedent construction from the one we have, a formulary which lists ways in which Jerusalem is ahead of Yabneh (and, perhaps, ways in which Yabneh is ahead of Jerusalem). But *m. Roš Haš.* 4:2 clearly responds to *m. Roš Haš.* 4:1E's view. The meaning of the several entries is clear and requires no comment.

But the point as to the use and meaning of history does. What we see is that the destruction of the temple is recognized and treated as consequential—but only for the hierarchical classification of rules. The event effects division between one time and some other, and, in consequence, we sort out rules pertaining to the temple and synagogue in one way rather than in another. The destruction of the temple, then, is significant only insofar as it serves as an indicator in the organization of rules. The one-time meaning of events is inconsequential but their all-time significance in the making of rules is paramount. Events are now treated not as irregular and intrinsically consequential but as regular and merely instrumental.

Mishnah-tractate *Roš Haššanah* 4:4

A. At first they would receive testimony about the new moon all day long.

B. One time the witnesses came late, and the Levites consequently were mixed up as to [what] song [they should sing].

C. They made the rule that they should receive testimony [about the new moon] only up to the afternoon offering.

D. Then, if witnesses came after the afternoon-offering, they would treat that entire day as holy, and the next day as holy too.

E. When the Temple was destroyed, Rabban Yohanan b. Zakkai made the rule that they should [once more] receive testimony about the new moon all day long.

F. Said R. Joshua b. Qorha, "This rule too did Rabban Yohanan b. Zakkai make:

G. "Even if the head of the court is located somewhere else, the witnesses should come only to the location of the council [to give testimony, and not to the location of the head of the court]."

A–D form a complete unit. E is distinctly secondary. The long antecedent narrative, A–D, is formally out of phase with *m. Roš Haš.* 4:3. The appendix supplied at F–G is thematically appropriate.

The passages before us leave no doubt about what sages emphasized as critical about the destruction: it produced changes in synagogue rites. The sages surely mourned for the destruction and the loss of Israel's principal mode of worship. However, as we shall see, they recorded the historical events of both 70 and 135 as items in a catalogue of similar things that therefore demand the same response. The destruction of 70 and the calamity of 135 then no longer appear as unique events; they are absorbed into a pattern of like disasters, all exhibiting similar taxonomic traits—events to which the people, now well-schooled in tragedy, knows full well the appropriate response. So it is in demonstrating regularity that sages reveal their way of coping. When the uniqueness of an event fades away, its mundane character is emphasized. The power of taxonomy in imposing order upon chaos once more does its healing work: the consequence was reassurance that historical events obeyed discoverable laws. Israel's ongoing life would override disruptive, one-time happenings.

Catalogues of events thus served as brilliant apologetic by providing reassurance that nothing lies beyond the range and power of ordering system and stabilizing pattern. Let us examine the Mishnah's catalogue of catastrophe, to bring the taxonomic effect into full view:

Mishnah-tractate *Ta'anit* 4:6–7

6. A. Five events took place for our fathers on the seventeenth of Tammuz, and five on the ninth of Ab.

   B. On the seventeenth of Tammuz

      (1) the tablets [of the Torah] were broken,
      (2) the daily whole offering was cancelled,
      (3) the city wall was breached,
      (4) Apostemos burned the Torah, and
      (5) he set up an idol in the Temple.

   C. On the ninth of Ab

      (1) the decree was made against our forefathers that they should not enter the land,
      (2) the first Temple,
      (3) the second [Temple] were destroyed,
      (4) Betar was taken,
      (5) the city was ploughed up [after the war of Hadrian].

   D. When Ab comes, rejoicing diminishes.

7. A. In the week in which the ninth of Ab occurs it is prohibited to get a haircut and to wash one's clothes.

   B. But on Thursday of that week these are permitted,

   C. because of the honor due to the Sabbath.

   D. On the eve of the ninth of Ab a person should not eat two prepared dishes, nor should one eat meat or drink wine.

   E. Rabban Simeon b. Gamaliel says, "He should make some change from ordinary procedures."

   F. R. Judah declares people obligated to turn over beds.

   G. But sages did not concur with him.

My reading of the critical event as 135, not 70, is confirmed at *m. Ta'an.* 4:6C, which adds that item as the climax. I include *m. Ta'an.* 4:7 to show the context in which the list of *m. Ta'an.* 4:6 stands. The stunning calamities catalogued at *m. Ta'an.* 4:6 form groups revealing common traits, so are subject to classification. Then the laws of *m. Ta'an.* 4:7 provide regular rules for responding to, and coping with, these untimely catastrophes, all (fortuitously) in a single classification. So the raw materials of history are absorbed into the ahistorical, supernatural system of the Mishnah. The process of absorption and regularization of the unique and one-time moment is illustrated in the passage at hand.

A still more striking example of the reordering of one-time events into all-time patterns derives from the effort to put together in a coherent way the rather haphazard history of the cult as the facts of that history were inherited from Scripture, with sacrifices made here and there, following this procedure or that, and finally in Jerusalem. Now, the entire history of the cult—so critical in the larger system created by the Mishnah's sages—produced a patterned, therefore sensible and intelligible, picture. Everything that happened turned out to be susceptible to classification, once the taxonomic traits were specified. A monothetic exercise, sorting out periods and their characteristics, took the place of narrative, to explain things in its own way: first this, and then that, and, in consequence, the other. So in the neutral turf of holy ground everything was absorbed into one thing, all classified in its proper place and by its appropriate rule. Indeed, so far as the sages proposed to write history at all, they wrote it into their picture of the way in which Israel served God: the places in which the sacrificial labor was carried on, the people who did it, the places where the priests ate their portion of the meat after God's portion was set aside and burned up. This "historical" account forthwith generated precisely that problem of locating the regular and orderly, which the philosophers loved to investigate: the intersection of conflicting but equally correct taxonomic rules, as we see at *m. Zebaḥim* 14:9, below. The passage that follows therefore is history so far as the Mishnah's creators proposed to write history: the reduction of events to rules forming compositions of regularity, therefore meaning.

Mishnah-tractate *Zebaḥim* 14:4–8

4. A. Before the tabernacle was set up, (*1) the high places were permitted, and (2) [the sacrificial] service [was done by] the first born [Num. 3:12–15, 8:16–18].

   B. When the tabernacle was set up, (1) the high places were prohibited, and (2) the [sacrificial] service [was done by] priests.

   C. Most Holy Things were eaten within the veils, Lesser Holy Things [were eaten] throughout the camp of Israel.

5. A. They came to Gilgal.

   B. The high places were permitted.

C. Most Holy Things were eaten within the veils, Lesser Holy Things, anywhere.

6. A. They came to Shiloh.

B. The high places were prohibited.

C. (1) There was no roof-beam there, but below was a house of stone, and hangings above it, and (2) it was 'the resting place' [Deut. 12:9].

D. Most Holy Things were eaten within the veils, Lesser Holy Things and second-tithe [were eaten] in any place within sight [of Shiloh].

7. A. They came to Nob and Gibeon.

B. The high places were permitted.

C. Most Holy Things were eaten within the veils, Lesser Holy Things, in all the towns of Israel.

8. A. They came to Jerusalem.

B. The high places were prohibited.

C. And they never again were permitted.

D. And it was 'the inheritance' [Deut. 12:9].

E. Most Holy Things were eaten within the veils, Lesser Holy Things and second-tithe within the wall.

Let us rapidly review the formal traits of this lovely composition, because those traits justify my insistence that we are dealing with a patterning of events. This set of five formally balanced items bears remarkably few glosses. The form is best revealed at *m. Zebaḥ.* 14:5, 7. The only significant gloss is *m. Zebaḥ.* 14:6C. *M. Zebaḥ.* 14:4 sets up a fine introduction, integral to the whole despite its interpolated and extraneous information at *m. Zebaḥ.* A2, B2. The information at *m. Zebaḥ.* 14:8C is essential; D is a gloss, parallel to *m. Zebaḥ.* 14:6C(2). The unitary construction is self-explanatory. At some points it was permitted to sacrifice on high places, at others it was not—a neat way of harmonizing Scripture's numerous contradictions on the subject. *M. Zebaḥ.* 14:4B depends upon Lev 17:5; *m. Zebaḥ.* 14:5 refers to Josh 4:19ff.; and *m. Zebaḥ.* 14:6 refers to Josh 18:1. The 'resting place' of Deut 12:9 is identified with Shiloh. At this point the obligation to separate second tithe is incurred, which accounts for the conclusion of *m. Zebaḥ.* 14:4D. *M. Zebaḥ.* 14:7 refers to 1 Sam 21:2, 7, after the destruction of Shiloh, and to 1 Kgs 3:4. *M. Zebaḥ.* 14:8 then identifies the 'inheritance' of Deut 12:9 with Jerusalem. The 'veils' are familiar at *m. Zebaḥ.* 5:3, 5, and the walls of Jerusalem, *m. Zebaḥ.* 5:6–8. I see not a single flaw in the entire composition, which is coherent start to finish.

Mishnah-tractate *Zebaḥim* 14:9

A. All the Holy Things which one sanctified at the time of the prohibition of the high places and offered at the time of the prohibition of
high places outside –

B. lo, these are subject to the transgression of a positive commandment and a negative commandment, and they are liable on their
account to extirpation [for sacrificing outside the designated place,
Lev. 17:8–9, *m. Zebaḥ.* 13:1A].

C. [If] one sanctified them at the time of the permission of high places
and offered them up at the time of the prohibition of high places,

D. lo, these are subject to transgression of a positive commandment
and to a negative commandment, but they are not liable on their
account to extirpation [since if the offerings had been sacrificed
when they were sanctified, there should have been no violation].

E. [If] one sanctified them at the time of the prohibition of high places
and offered them up at the time of the permission of high places,

F. lo, these are subject to transgression of a positive commandment,
but they are not subject to a negative commandment at all.

Now we see how the Mishnah's sages turn events into rules and
show the orderly nature of history. The secondary expansion of *m. Zebaḥ.*
14:4–8 in 14:9 is in three parts, A–B, C–D, and E–F, all in close verbal balance. The upshot is to cover all sorts of circumstances within a single well-
composed pattern. This is easy to represent by simple symbols. We deal
with two circumstances and two sets of actions: the circumstance of the
prohibition of high places (-) and that of their permission (+), and the act
of sanctification of a sacrifice (A) and offering it up (B), thus:

A–B: -A -B = positive, negative, extirpation

C–D: +A +B = positive, negative

E–F: -A +B = positive only

There is no reason to prohibit or to punish the one who sanctifies
and offers up a sacrifice on a high place when it is permitted to do so. Accordingly, all possible cases are dealt with. In the first case, both sanctification and offering up take place at the time that prohibition of high places
applies. There is transgression of both a negative commandment (Deut
12:13) and a positive commandment (Deut 12:14): "Take heed that you do
not offer your burnt-offerings at every place that you see; but at the place
which the Lord will choose in one of your tribes, there you shall offer
your burnt-offerings."

The second and third, C and E, then go over the same ground. If sanctification takes place when it is permitted to sanctify animals for use in high places, but the offering up takes place when it is not allowed to do so (e.g., the former for *m. Zebaḥ.* 14:4, the latter, *m. Zebaḥ.* 14:6), extirpation does not apply (Lev. 17:5–7). When we then reverse the order (e.g., *m. Zebaḥ.* 14:6, and 14:7), there is no transgression of a negative (Deut. 12:13), but the positive commandment (Deut. 12:14) has been transgressed.

Mishnah-tractate *Zebaḥim* 14:10

A. These are the Holy Things offered in the tabernacle [of Gilgal, Nob, and Gibeon]:

B. Holy Things which were sanctified for the tabernacle.

C. Offerings of the congregation are offered in the tabernacle.

D. Offerings of the individual [are offered] on a high place.

E. Offerings of the individual which were sanctified for the tabernacle are to be offered in the tabernacle.

F. And if one offered them up on a high place, he is free.

G. What is the difference between the high place of an individual and the high place of the community?

H. (1) Laying on of hands, and (2) slaughtering at the north [of the altar], and (3) placing [of the blood] round about [the altar], and (4) waving, and (5) bring near.

I. R. Judah says, "there is no meal-offering on a high place [but there is in the tabernacle]" —

J. and (1) the priestly service, and (2) the wearing of garments of ministry, and (3) the use of utensils of ministry, and (4) the sweet-smelling savor and (5) the dividing line for the [tossing of various kinds of] blood, and (6) the rule concerning the washing of hands and feet.

K. But the matters of time, and remnant, and uncleanness are applicable both here and there.

When *m. Zebaḥ.* 14:4–8 refer to a high place which was permitted, and refer also to the presence of veils, it is assumed that there were both a tabernacle (hence the veils) and also high places. This must mean Gilgal, *m. Zebaḥ.* 14:5 and Nob and Gibeon, *m. Zebaḥ.* 14:7. Now the issue is: if there are both a tabernacle and high places, which sorts of offerings belong to which kind of altar? It follows that the pericope treats the situations specified at *m. Zebaḥ.* 14:5, 7, a secondary expansion. In *m. Zebaḥ.* 14:10, A is answered by B while C–F go on to work out their own interests, and cannot be constructed to answer A, because they specify "are offered in the tabernacle" as a complete apodosis, which A does not require and B clearly does not want. B tells us that even though it is permitted to offer a sacrifice on a high place, a sacrifice which is set aside for the tabernacle (obviously) is to be offered in the tabernacle. Then C–F work the matter out. Holy Things that are sanctified for the tabernacle are offerings of the congregation (C). It is taken for granted that they are meant for the tabernacle, even when not so designated as specified (B). Individuals' sacrifices are assumed to be for high places unless specified otherwise (D). Obviously, if they are sanctified for the tabernacle (E), they are sacrificed there. But there is no reason to inflict liability if they are offered on a high place (F). The whole is carefully worked out, leaving no unanswered questions.

G then asks what difference there is between a high place that serves an individual, and "the high place"—the tabernacle—which serves the congregation, that is, those at Gilgal, Nob, and Gibeon. H specifies five items, J, six more, and Judah brings the list up to twelve (I). K completes the matter. Time at *m. Zebaḥ.* 14:8K refers to a somewhat complex set of rules. They concern when the meat of the offering is to be eaten. The meat must be eaten in a brief span of time—two days and the intervening night. Now if the priest before he kills the sacrificial beast forms the intention to dispose of the meat beyond the required time limit, he spoils the offering. And that is without regard to what the priest actually does. This is what is referred to as "a matter of time," meaning, the intent of the priest to eat his portion of the sacrificial meat beyond the time limit that pertains to it. His improper intentionality assigns the sacrifice to the category of "refuse," and the sacrifice is null as a result. The word-choice is unexpected. The inclusion of *m. Zebaḥ.* 14:9, structurally matching *m. Taʿan.* 4:7, shows us the goal of the historical composition. It is to set forth rules that intersect and produce confusion, so that we may sort out confusion and make sense of all the data. The authorship had the option of narrative, but chose the way of philosophy: generalization through hierarchical classification, comparison, and contrast.

To summarize, the Mishnah absorbs into its encompassing system all events, small and large. The sages organize these events into their vast labor of taxonomy, an immense construction of the order and rules governing the classification of everything on earth and in heaven. The disruptive character of history—one-time events of ineluctable significance—scarcely impresses the sages. They have no difficulty in showing that what appears unique and beyond classification has in fact happened before and so falls within the range of trustworthy rules and known procedures.

So lessons and rules come from sorting things out and classifying them, that is, from the procedures and modes of thought of the philosopher seeking regularity. To this labor of taxonomy, the historian's way of selecting data and arranging them into patterns of meaning to teach lessons, proves inconsequential. One-time events are not what matters. The world is composed of nature and supernature. The repetitious laws that count are those to be discovered in heaven and, in heaven's creation and counterpart, on earth. Keep those laws and things will work out. Break them, and the result is predictable: calamity will supervene in accordance with the rules. Because it is predictable, a catastrophic happening testifies to what has always been and must always be, in accordance with reliable rules and within categories already discovered and well explained. That is why the sages of the second century produced the Mishnah—to explain how things are. Within the framework of well-classified rules, there could be messiahs, but no single Messiah, as we shall now see.

The Mishnah's Teleology without Eschatology

In the Mishnah the Messiah-theme plays no formidable role. "Messiah" supplies a categorical indicator for the Mishnah's system of hierarchical classification, a higher status for a priest, for example. The Messiah-myth plays no role in the construction of a teleology for the system. Since the rabbinic sages certainly knew, and even alluded to, long-standing and widely held convictions on eschatological subjects, beginning with those in Scripture, in trivializing the Messiah-theme the framers thereby testified that, knowing the larger repertoire, they made choices different from those made by others before and after them.

That fact is surprising, for the pentateuchal (and prophetic) emphasis on historical narrative as a mode of theological explanation leads us to anticipate that Judaic systems will evolve as deeply messianic religious systems. With all prescribed actions pointed toward the coming of the Messiah at the end of time, and all interest focused upon answering the historical-salvific questions ("how long?"), rabbinic Judaism from late antiquity to the present day, for its part, presents no surprises. Its liturgy evokes historical events to prefigure salvation, prayers of petition repeatedly turn to the speedy coming of the Messiah, and the experience of worship invariably leaves the devotee expectant and hopeful. Just as rabbinic Judaism is a deeply messianic religion, secular extensions of Judaism, such as Zionism, have commonly proposed secularized versions of the focus upon history and have shown interest in the purpose and denouement of events. Teleology again appears as an eschatology embodied in messianic symbols.

How does the mishnaic system differ? Messiahs do play a part in the system, but these "anointed men"—a priest anointed for war (*m. Soṭah* 7:1)— had no historical role. They undertook a task quite different from that assigned to Jesus by the framers of the Gospels. They were merely a species of priest, falling into one classification rather than another. For the Mishnah, "Messiah" is a category of priest or general. The Mishnah finds little of consequence to say about the Messiah as savior of Israel, one particular person at one specific time. Indeed, it manages to set forth its system's teleology without appeal to eschatology in any form, because the Messiah-theme proved marginal to the system's program. As we shall see in chapter four, by ca. 400 C.E., by contrast, a system of Judaism would emerge fully documented in the pages of the Talmud of the Land of Israel and related Midrash-compilations (e.g., *Genesis Rabbah, Leviticus Rabbah,* and *Pesiqta deRab Kahana*) in which the Messiah-theme had a much more central role. The Mishnah as foundation document would be asked to support a structure continuous with, but in no way fully defined by, the outlines of the Mishnah itself. The ultimate, rabbinic system that would come to full articulation in the Talmuds and Midrash-compilations would prove symmetrical with the pentateuchal one, so we may speak of pentateuchal-rabbinic Judaism without identifying gaps between the joined systems.

So now we ask the Mishnah to answer the questions at hand. What of the Messiah? When will he come? To whom, in Israel, will he come? And what must, or can, we do while we wait to hasten his coming? If we now re-frame these questions and divest them of their mythic cloak, we ask about the Mishnah's theory of the history and destiny of Israel and the purpose of the Mishnah's own system in relationship to Israel's present and end: the implicit teleology of the law-system at hand.

Answering these questions out of the resources of the Mishnah is not possible. As we have now seen, the Mishnah presents no large view of history. It contains no reflection whatsoever on the nature and meaning of the destruction of the temple in 70, apart from some changes in the law explained as resulting from the end of the cult. The Mishnah pays no attention to the matter of the end time. The word "salvation"—whether as noun or verb—is rare, "sanctification"—as noun and verb—commonplace. More strikingly, the framers of the Mishnah are virtually silent on the teleology of the system; they never discuss why one should do what the Mishnah instructs, let alone explain what will happen to those who do. Events in the Mishnah are preserved either as narrative settings for the statement of the law, or, occasionally, as precedents (*maʿasim*). Historical events are classified and turned into entries on lists. But incidents in any case come few and far between. True, events do make an impact. But it always is for the Mishnah's own purpose and within its own taxonomic system and rule-seeking mode of thought. To be sure, the framers of the Mishnah may also have had a theory of the Messiah and of the meaning of Israel's history and destiny. But they kept it hidden, and their document manages to provide an immense account of Israel's life without explicitly telling us about such matters.

Is that to say the Mishnah utterly ignores the eschatological Messiah-theme? Not at all. The Mishnah sets forth the decline of generations, in which the destruction of the temple and the death of great sages mark the movement of time and impart to an age the general rules that govern life therein.

Mishnah-tractate *Soṭah* 9:15

A. When R. Meir died, makers of parables came to an end.

B. When Ben Azzai died, diligent students came to an end.

C. When Ben Zoma died, exegetes came to an end.

D. When R. Joshua died, goodness went away from the world.

E. When Rabban Simeon b. Gamaliel died, the locust came, and troubles multiplied.

F. When Eleazar b. Azariah died, wealth went away from the sages.

G. When R. Aqiba died, the glory of the Torah came to an end.

H. When R. Hanina b. Dosa died, wonder-workers came to an end.

I. When R. Yosé Qatnuta died, pietists went away.

J. (And why was he called Qatnuta? Because he was the least of the pietists.)

K. When Rabban Yohanan b. Zakkai died, the splendor of wisdom came to an end.

L. When Rabban Gamaliel the Elder died, the glory of the Torah came to an end, and cleanness and separateness perished.

M. When R. Ishmael b. Phabi died, the splendor of the priesthood came to an end.

N. When Rabbi died, modesty and fear of sin came to an end.

What follows is added in some MSS to the Mishnah, treated as external to the Mishnah by others:

O. R. Pinhas b. Yair says, "When the Temple was destroyed, associates became ashamed and so did free men, and they covered their heads.

P. "And wonder-workers became feeble. And violent men and big takers grew strong.

Q. "And none expounds and none seeks [learning] and none asks.

R. "Upon whom shall we depend? Upon our Father in heaven."

S. R. Eliezer the Great says, "From the day on which the Temple was destroyed, sages began to be like scribes, and scribes like ministers, and ministers like ordinary folk.

T. "And the ordinary folk have become feeble.

U. "And none seeks.

V. "Upon whom shall we depend? Upon our Father in heaven."

W. With the footprints of the Messiah: presuption increases, and dearth increases.

X. The Vine gives its fruit and wine at great cost.

Y. And the government turns to heresy.

Z. And there is no reproof.

AA. The gathering place will be for prostitution.

BB. And Galilee will be laid waste.

CC. And the Gablan will be made desolate.

DD. And the men of the frontier will go about from town to town, and none will take pity on them.

EE. And the wisdom of scribes will putrefy.

FF. And those who fear sin will be rejected.

GG. And the truth will be locked away.

HH. Children will shame elders, and elders will stand up before children.

II. "For the son dishonors the father and the daughter rises up against her mother, the daughter-in-law against her mother-in-law; a man's enemies are the men of his own house" (Mic. 7:6).

JJ. The face of the generation in the face of a dog.

KK. A son is not ashamed before his father.

LL. Upon whom shall we depend? Upon our Father in heaven.

MM. R. Pinhas b. Yair says, "Heedfulness leads to cleanliness, cleanliness leads to cleanness, cleanness leads to abstinence, abstinence leads to holiness, holiness leads to modesty, modesty leads to the fear of sin, the fear of sin leads to piety, piety leads to the Holy Spirit, the Holy Spirit leads to the resurrection of the dead, and the resurrection of the dead comes through Elijah, blessed be his memory, Amen."

Here is the Mishnah's one representation of the eschatological Messiah. The issues encapsulated in the myth and person of the Messiah are scarcely addressed. The framers of the Mishnah do not resort to speculation about the Messiah as a historical-supernatural figure. The Messiah's coming is not made contingent on Israelite behavior. On the contrary, Israelites are told to depend on God. Where are we heading? What can we do about it? The Mishnah does not say. Rather, in response, it sighs. That does not mean questions found urgent in the aftermath of the destruction of the temple and the disaster of Bar Kokhba failed to attract the attention of the Mishnah's sages. But they treated history in a different way, offering their own answers to its questions.

Some argue that the Mishnah limits itself to legal matters and cannot be expected to legislate about imponderables that God alone decides. They insist that *m. 'Abot* be included in any account of the Mishnah's system. Tractate *'Abot* deals with theological issues. It is not part of the Mishnah but came to closure about a half century later. Formally, topically, and logically it is a distinct document. But there too we find no systematic confrontation with the Messiah-theme. The teleology articulated by *m. 'Abot* is no more Messianic in focus than that of the Mishnah itself. So now we ask, what alternative teleology does the Mishnah's first apologetic, Tractate *'Abot*, provide? Only when we appreciate the clear answers given in that document, brought to closure at ca. 250 B.C.E., about a generation or two beyond the closure of the Mishnah, shall we grasp how remarkable is the shift evident in the fourth- and fifth-century documents, the Talmud of the Land of Israel and cognate Midrash-compilations, to a messianic framing of the issues of the Torah's ultimate purpose and value.

Let us see how the framers of *m. 'Abot*, in the aftermath of the creation of the Mishnah, explain the purpose and meaning of the Mishnah's ahistorical, non-messianic teleology. Whatever explicit teleology the Mishnah would ever acquire would derive from *m. 'Abot*, which presents statements expressing the ethos and ethic of the Mishnah. *M. 'Abot* agreed with the other sixty-two tractates: history proved no more important here than it had been before. With scarcely a word about history and no account of events at all, *m. 'Abot* manages to provide an ample account of how the Torah—written and oral, thus in later eyes, Scripture and Mishnah—was transmitted down to its own day. Accordingly, the passage of time as such plays no role in the explanation of the origins of the Mishnah, nor is the document presented as eschatological.

We note that "historical" occurrences of great weight are never invoked. How, then, does the tractate tell the story of Torah and narrate the history of God's revelation to Israel, encompassing both Scripture and Mishnah? M. ʾAbot's framers managed to do their work of explanation without telling a story or invoking history at all, but rather by exploiting a non-historical mode of thought and method of legitimation. That is the main point: teleology serves the purpose of legitimation, and hence is accomplished in ways other than explaining how things originated or assuming that historical fact explains anything. Here is the "history" of the Torah—hardly history at all, rather an exemplary story of masters and their disciples, a pattern of discipleship that renews itself, generation by generation. I cite only the beginning of the composition, consisting of the first three components of the chain of tradition and then the five pairs. These suffice to make the main point required for this argument.

Tractate ʾAbot 1:1–11

1. A. Moses received Torah at Sinai and handed it on to Joshua, Joshua to elders, and elders to prophets.

   B. And prophets handed it on to the men of the great assembly.

   C. They said three things:

      (1) "Be prudent in judgment.
      (2) "Raise up many disciples.
      (3) "Make a fence for the Torah."

2. A. Simeon the Righteous was one of the last survivors of the great assembly.

   B. He would say: "On three things does the world stand:

      (1) "On the Torah,
      (2) "and on the Temple service,
      (3) "and on deeds of loving kindness."

3. A. Antigonos of Sokho received [the Torah] from Simeon the Righteous.

   B. He would say,

      (1) "Do not be like servants who serve the master on condition of receiving a reward,
      (2) "but [be] like servants who serve the master not on condition of receiving a reward.
      (3) "And let the fear of Heaven be upon you."

4. A. Yosé b. Yoezer of Seredah and Yosé b. Yohanan of Jerusalem received [it] from them.

   B. Yosé b. Yoezer says,

      (1) "Let your house be a gathering place for sages.
      (2) "And wallow in the dust of their feet.
      (3) "And drink in their words with gusto."

5. A. Yosé b. Yohanan of Jerusalem says,

      (1) "Let your house be wide open.
      (2) "And seat the poor at your table ["make . . . members of your household"].
      (3) "And don't talk too much with women."

   B. (He spoke of a man's wife, all the more so is the rule to be applied to the wife of one's fellow. In this regard did sages say, "So long as a man talks too much with a woman,

      (1) "he brings trouble on himself,
      (2) wastes time better spent on studying Torah, and
      (3) ends up an heir of Gehenna.")

6. A. Joshua b. Perahiah and Nittai the Arbelite received [it] from them.

   B. Joshua b. Perahiah says,

      (1) "Set up a master for yourself.
      (2) "And get yourself a fellow disciple.
      (3) "And give everybody the benefit of the doubt."

7. A. Nittai the Arbelite says,

      (1) "Keep away from a bad neighbor.
      (2) "And don't get involved with a wicked man.
      (3) "And don't give up hope of retribution."

8. A. Judah b. Tabbai and Simeon b. Shatah received [it] from them.

   B. Judah b. Tabbai says,

      (1) "Don't make yourself like one of those who make advocacy before judges [while you yourself are judging a case].
      (2) "And when the litigants stand before you, regard them as guilty.
      (3) "And when they leave you, regard them as acquitted (when they have accepted your judgment)."

9. A. Simeon b. Shatah says,

      (1) "Examine the witnesses with great care.
      (2) "And watch what you say,
      (3) "lest they learn from what you say how to lie."

10. A. Shemaiah and Abtalion received [it] from them.

    B. Shemaiah says,

        (1) "Love work.

        (2) "Hate authority.

        (3) "Don't get friendly with the government."

11. A. Abtalion says, (1) "Sages, watch what you say, Lest you become liable to the punishment of exile, and go into exile to a place of bad water, and disciples who follow you drink [bad water] and die, and the name of heaven be thereby profaned."

The history of the Torah consists in the names of the masters and disciples, and well it should, since the opening entry, God and Moses, establishes what is at stake. What the sages leave as their exemplary sayings scarcely matters; the chain of tradition consists of the names of the sages themselves and their connections forward and aft, to Sinai. The history of the Torah from Sinai forward encompasses the oral tradition carried forward by the sages, from Moses to the masters of the Mishnah itself. It is a list of figures and their sayings, classified as components of the Torah revealed by God to Moses at Sinai. As tractate *m. ʾAbot* progresses, it states a systemic teleology: preparation in this world for the life of the world to come. That statement is accomplished without once resorting to the Messiah-theme or promising the advent of the Messiah. Indeed, we look in vain in the sayings of the Tractate *ʾAbot* for reference to that theme. In *t. ʾAbot* "this world" is when one is alive; "the world to come" corresponds to after a person dies. The point is a simple one: tractate *t. ʾAbot* succeeds in pointing the system toward its goal—of Torah study (which matters both in this world and in the world to come) without invoking the Messiah-theme, let alone the figure of the Messiah.

Asymmetries: A Different Kind of History

Here then we discern the gaps in the pentateuchal-mishnaic system set forth on the foundations of the Pentateuch by the Mishnah. The pentateuchal system makes its statement through historical narrative; the Mishnah's recapitulation of that system speaks otherwise, finding its patterns in the givens of the social order contemplated by the Pentateuch. Events are organized and narrated so as to teach lessons, reveal patterns, and set forth norms of behavior. In that context, some events contain richer lessons than others; for example, the destruction of the Jerusalem temple teaches more than a crop failure. Furthermore, lessons taught by events—"history" in the didactic sense—follow a progression from trivial and private to consequential and public.

The framers of the Mishnah thus present us with a kind of historical thinking quite different from the one that they, along with all Israel, had inherited in Scripture. The legacy of prophecy, apocalypse, and mythic-history handed on by the books of the Scriptures of ancient Israel exhibits a single and quite familiar conception of history. History, in this conception, refers to unfolding events seen whole. Events bear meaning, form a pattern, and, therefore, deliver God's message and judgment. The upshot is that every event, each one seen on its own, must be interpreted on its own terms, not as part of a pattern but as significant in itself.

If things do not happen randomly, they also do not form indifferent patterns of merely secular, social facts. What happens is important because of the meaning contained therein, which is to be discovered and revealed through the narrative of what has happened. So for all Judaisms until the Mishnah, as for rabbinic Judaism after the Mishnah, the writing of history serves as a form or medium of prophecy. Just as prophecy takes up the interpretation of historical events, so historians retell these events in the frame of prophetic theses. And out of the two—historiography as a mode of mythic reflection, prophecy as a means of mythic construction—emerges a picture of future history—that is, what is going to happen. That picture, framed in terms of visions and supernatural symbols, ultimately focuses on the here and now.

In the Mishnah, then, lessons and rules come from sorting things out and classifying them according to procedures and modes of thought of the philosopher seeking regularity. To this labor of taxonomy, the historian's way of selecting data and arranging them into patterns of meaning to teach lessons proves inconsequential. Onetime events are not important. The world is composed of nature and supernature. The laws that count are those to be discovered in heaven and, in heaven's creation and counterpart, on earth. Keep those laws and things will work out. Break them, and the result is predictable: calamity of whatever sort will supervene in accordance with the rules. But just because it is predictable, a catastrophic happening testifies to what has always been and must always be, in accordance with reliable rules and within categories already discovered and well explained. That is why the lawyer-philosophers of the mid-second century produced the Mishnah—to explain how things are. Within the framework of well-classified rules, there could be Messiahs, but no single Messiah.

Once history's components, onetime events, lose their distinctiveness, then history as a didactic intellectual construct, as a source of lessons and rules, also loses all pertinence. Theirs was a teleology without eschatology.

The framers of the Mishnah recognized the past-ness of the past and hence, by definition, laid out a conception of the past that constitutes a historical doctrine. But it is a different conception from the familiar one. For modern history-writing, it is important to describe what is unique and individual, not what is ongoing and unremarkable. History is the story of change, development, movement, not of stasis. For the thinkers of the Mishnah, historical patterning emerges as today scientific knowledge does: through classification, classifying the unique and individual, and organizing change and movement within unchanging categories. That is why the dichotomy between history and eternity, change and permanence, signals an un-nuanced exegesis of what was, in fact, a subtle and reflective doctrine of history. That doctrine proves entirely consistent with the large perspectives of scribes, from the ones who made omenseries in ancient Babylonia to the ones who made the Mishnah. That is why the category of salvation does not serve, but the one of sanctification fits admirably. But, as we anticipate, that is not how matters would emerge at the end of the formation of Judaism.

The Talmud of the Land of Israel and its cognate Midrash-compilations, *Genesis Rabbah* and *Leviticus Rabbah,* would not concur. The interior logic of the pentateuchal-mishnaic system would govern in the articulation of the rabbinic system that would emerge from the fourth century onward. But it would impart its imprint upon category-formations— history and the Messiah in eschatological context—completely foreign to its own formation. A near-term explanation and a long-term explanation—once more, from system to paradigm—would account for the remarkable systemic reform represented by the new documents, with their new media for expressing a new construction of matters.

4

Rabbinic Judaism and the Emergence of the Christian Empire

From 70–135 to 312–363: The Crisis of the Fourth Century C.E.

The Mishnah's paradigmatization of historical events within a system of timeless classification and hierarchization contradicts the emphasis of a thousand years of biblical thought. The biblical historians, the ancient prophets, and the apocalyptic visionaries had all testified that what happened mattered; singular events carried the message of the living God. To other non-rabbinic Judaic religious systems, events constituted history and they pointed toward, and so explained, Israel's destiny. Here, by contrast, an essentially ahistorical system aimed at the restoration of Eden, a timeless moment of sanctification, worked out by constructing an eternal rhythm centered on the movement of the sun and the moon and seasons. In the extant Judaic writings, this represented a choice hardly characteristic outside of the limited circles of the rabbinic sages and survivors of those of priestly descent.

Did the mass of Jews concur in the rabbinic sages' design of their "Israel"? The great wars against Rome hardly suggest so. Those wars testified to competition from a historical-eschatological theology, which certainly animated the lives of a great many Jews in the land of Israel. Furthermore, the claim of the mishnaic system—what *happens* matters less than what *is*—testified against palpable and remembered reality. In the fourth century as in the second, Israel once more had ample reason for despair and little grounds for hope. When defeat turns to despair, a Judaic system comes to a turning point. And with the response to despair, that Judaism is transformed. That pattern was realized in the movement from the disaster of 70 C.E., with the destruction of Jerusalem, to the catastrophe of 135 C.E., with the despair following the collapse of the pentateuchal paradigm of destruction, suffering, repentance and atonement, forgiveness and restoration. It recapitulated itself in the fourth century C.E, when a severe challenge to Israel's faith, in the events of 312, was then intensified by the heart-shattering disappointment of 362–363.

The former date—312—marked the turning point in the history of catholic, orthodox Christianity, which competed with Judaism for the patrimony of ancient Israel. That Christianity (unlike its Gnostic competition) possessed the same Israelite Scriptures as Judaism, and claimed to be the heir and successor of Israel after the flesh—the Jews in the here and now. For its first three centuries, Christianity constructed its indictment of "the Jews" (meaning, those who rejected its account of Israel's destiny in Christ) and its fabricated opposition, "Judaism" (meaning, the competition to Christianity). During this time, Christianity found no debating partner. Judaic voices spoke of other matters. Christianity rarely won the attention of rabbinic sages, and when they did, what they had to say was casual and unengaged. But in 312 the emperor Constantine declared Christianity licit, ending the long centuries of suppression. The Emperor treated Christianity as his most favored religion; he served as its patron (with his mother); and before dying he converted. His successors would declare Christianity the established, official religion of the Roman Empire. Judaism could no longer ignore Christianity, which claimed that the miracles of political success proved its truth and falsified the Jews' hope for a Messiah. But the Judaic sages hardly found themselves bound to interpret events in the way the Christians did.

We shall presently take up writings universally assigned to the late fourth or early fifth century, by which point Rome had turned definitively Christian. We will therefore do well first to examine a document that came to closure before 300, the Tosefta, to see how it speaks of Christianity. That document addressed the fact that others besides the rabbinic sages (and the Israel after the flesh responsive to their authority) claimed to interpret the Torah and represent Israel. To the first-century authority Tarfon, the Tosefta attributes the angry observation that there were people who knew the truth of the Torah but rejected it. The attribution may not be reliable and the opinion might not represent late first-century perspectives. But preserved in a document of ca. 300, the statement (and the halakic ruling to which it is attached) certainly reflects an authoritative opinion in the time before Christianity enjoyed state sponsorship and claimed political validation.

Tosefta *Šabbat* 13:5

A. The books of the Evangelists and the books of the *minim* they do not save from a fire [on the Sabbath]. But they are allowed to burn where they are,

B. they and [even] the references to the Divine Name that are in them.

D. Said R. Ṭarfon, "May I bury my sons, if such things come into my hands and I do not burn them, and even the references to the Divine Name which are in them.

E. "And if someone was running after me, I should go into a temple of idolatry, but I should not go into their houses [of worship].

F. "For idolators do not recognize the Divinity in denying him, but these recognize the Divinity and deny him.

G. "About them Scripture states, *Behind the door and the door-post you have set your symbol* [for deserting me, you have uncovered your bed] (Is. 57:8)."

This famous passage has long persuaded scholars that the rabbinic authority recognized the difference between pagans and the *minim* under discussion, in context assumed to be Christian. Given the context I see no reason to differ from the established consensus.

What we witness is a trivial dispute within the rabbinic community concerning heretics who should, but do not, know better. The text in no way considers the world-historical issues that would later face Israel. The reason, I maintain, is that, when the Tosefta was brought to closure, no one could imagine the ultimate conversion of the empire to Christianity and the triumph of Christianity on the stage of history. In the third century Christianity could still be ignored and dismissed: it was completely irrelevant to the sages. The upshot is simple: when the sources that came to closure by 300 C.E.—Mishnah, *m. ʾAbot*, Tosefta—discuss what may be Christians, they treat them with exasperation. More to the point as I shall show, in these documents Rome is represented casually and inconsequentially—simply another pagan empire, but not the very counterpart and opposite of Israel. Rome would eventually stand for the fourth and penultimate kingdom, antecedent to Israel's ultimate hegemony and salvation. But that representation takes place only in the documents that reached closure from the end of the fourth century onward, when the now-Christian empire would consistently be represented as Israel's rival for ruler of the world and as precursor to Israel's final triumph in history. In the Tosefta, we stand at a considerable distance from the deep thought about Israel and Rome, Jacob and Esau, this age and the coming one, that we find in the post-Constantinian documents (e.g., *Genesis Rabbah, Leviticus Rabbah,* and the Palestinian Talmud).

The politics of Israelite insouciance, its inner-turning to the construction of a holy community exempt from history, could no longer serve when an event having to do with rebuilding the Jerusalem temple struck at the very heart of the Judaic consciousness—destroying all hope and leaving in its wake despair. From 312 to 363, Judaism could continue to regard the victory of the competition as merely transient. Then, as we shall see in section D., in 361 the Emperor Julian came to the throne and brought about the restoration of paganism.

But Julian's was not a pagan moment alone. In 362–363 he undertook to humiliate Christianity by having the Jerusalem temple rebuilt. Alas, before much progress (if any) had been made, the pagan Emperor perished on the eastern battlefields. A Christian heir, and many to follow, decisively re-established Christianity and secured the permanent exclusion of paganism from the imperial throne. The project of rebuilding the temple thus perished with the last pagan emperor of Rome. For Judaism, this aborted rebuilding of the temple confirmed the previous ruin of the temple: the paradigm that failed in 135 failed again in 362–363. Now, not only "three generations," from 70 to 135, but three centuries from 70 to 363, confirmed that the temple would not be rebuilt any time soon and produced utter despair.

The events of the fourth century—the triumph of Christianity in 312, followed by the utter failure of hope and the onset of despair about a half-century later in 363—thus recapitulated and confirmed the pattern of destruction (in 70), followed by the complete ruin of the older order (in 135). Hopes were first raised then dashed, leaving nothing.

What of the inherited system, the Mishnah, with its apologia in tractate ʾAbot, and its rich and dense amplification in the Tosefta? It suffices to observe that the pentateuchal-mishnaic system had remarkably little to say about events of such tragic grandeur for Judaism. Its powerful mode of thought—classification of data, hierarchization of the classifications—could not accord recognition to the unique events represented by the dates 312 and 363. That is what I mean with the equation, the event of 70 is to the event of 135 as the event of 312 is to the event of 363.

The Basis for this Inquiry

To make sense of all that follows, we now have to turn aside for a moment to consider three problems of method. Those issues require attention before we proceed to the substantive inquiry into the post-Constantinian Judaic compilations produced by the late fourth- and fifth-century rabbinic sages. They concern the rational use of rabbinic writings for historical study, the rules for the description of a system out of those writings, and the disposition of variant readings of a given document, differing testimonies to the condition of said document deriving from diverse manuscript evidence.

The three distinct considerations that inform our approach are as follows. (1) How are we to deal with the attribution of sayings to named authorities, a universal trait in the rabbinic documents? In other words, who is represented by the documents? (2) How are we to evaluate the data found in documents that came to definitive closure at a determinate moment? On what basis do we localize our evidence and treat it as determinate for that time and place? (3) How are we to cope with the uncertain manuscript traditions for the rabbinic documents of late antiquity, and what shall we make of diverse versions of the documents treated here to begin with?

We do not know the state of opinion characteristic of Jews in the land of Israel, or even of "the rabbis" in general, but only of the rabbinic sages responsible for the writings in hand. So to answer the above questions:

(1) Clearly, our evidence represents those who made up and valued the documents in hand. The documents, then, afford access to ideas held when those documents reached closure, by those who valued and sponsored the compilations.

(2) Only that formulation of the history of ideas by the unfolding of documents—"the documentary history of ideas"—can show us how ideas coalesced into systemic statements, cogent constructions of the social order. Random ideas, circulating we know not where or when, tell us nothing beyond themselves; they do not show us how people fit them together into a whole that transcended the sum of the parts, a principle that cohered with other principles to extend beyond the case and constitute a rule or establish a principle.

(3) As to variant readings, we rely on the indicative traits characteristic of entire documents attested by the entire aggregate of manuscript evidence, so far as this is accessible in the standard editions. Indicative traits of rhetoric, logic of coherent discourse, and topical programs recur and define what is distinctive to, and representative of, the document. I do not build a conclusion on the foundation of a particular saying or story that does not conform to the documentary traits and program, or that is not common to all the manuscript evidence of the document that presents that saying or story.[1]

---

[1] I pursue these issues more fully in the following trilogy: *Extra- and Non-Documentary Writing in the Canon of Formative Judaism. I. The Pointless Parallel: Hans-Jürgen Becker and the Myth of the Autonomous Tradition in rabbinic Documents. II. Paltry Parallels. The Negligible Proportion and Peripheral Role of Free-Standing Compositions in Rabbinic Documents. III. Peripatetic Parallels* (Academic Studies in the History of Judaism Series: Binghamton, N.Y.: Global Publications, 2001). *The Peripatetic Saying: The Problem of the Thrice-Told Tale in Talmudic Literature* (2d ed.: Chico, Calif.: Scholars Press for Brown Judaic Studies, 1985).

The Documentary History of Ideas

The premise of my representation of Judaism in the late fourth and fifth centuries through the documents redacted at this time should be articulated.[2] I hold that documents testify to the ideas held in particular at the time they came to closure, by those responsible for the compilation and closure of the documents. I therefore have to explain the basis on which I maintain that the principal Judaic documents—*Genesis Rabbah*, the Talmud of the Land of Israel, and *Leviticus Rabbah*—tell us about rabbinic opinion held in the fourth century in particular. I work with what I know, not with what I do not know. The consensus of scholarship is that the three documents at hand reached closure at the end of the fourth century or shortly thereafter, between ca. 400 and 450 and I concur with the consensus. So I hold that the documents represent opinions held at that point, and, I assume, perhaps up to fifty years prior to that point. That does not strike me as uncritical, credulous, or gullible.

But what of sayings attributed to named authorities who flourished prior to the point of redaction? Do we disregard the allegation that a given opinion was held by a named authority long before that time? As in the case of the opinion attributed in the Tosefta to Tarfon, who flourished at the end of the first century, why insist that our evidence reflects opinions of the period of the closure of the document only, rather than of the time of the named authority to whom the opinion is assigned?

Rabbinic documents contain numerous sayings attributed to authorities who flourished long before the redaction of those documents. For example, many stories about the destruction of Jerusalem in 70 surface in documents of the late fourth and fifth centuries, and they claim to tell us about events of the first century, rather than presenting themselves as responses to events of the fourth century. If I could demonstrate that those sayings really *were* said by the authorities to whom they were attributed, then I should treat them as evidence of opinions from that time period (i.e., prior to the point at which the documents themselves were closed). But since this cannot be proved, I instead assume that writings closed at the end of the fourth century tell us views deemed authoritative by the framers and redactors of those writings.

Documents closed at a given point included opinions that the framers regarded as worth preserving hence and hence authoritative. Other possibilities exist, which, if confirmed, would yield other historical accounts of matters. People could have held these same views three hundred years earlier; they could have told these same stories; they could have thought these same thoughts. What is important to my argument is

---

[2] This matter is spelled out systematically in my *Rabbinic Judaism: The Documentary History of the Formative Age* (Bethesda, Md.: CDL, 1994).

not what *might* have been, but what *was*. But there is a much more urgent consideration, to which we now turn: the presentation of complete systems of thought, rather than merely random and episodic opinions on this and that. I hold that the principal (though not all) rabbinic documents set forth their data in a coherent construction, forming more than mere compilations of occasional opinions or singleton-conceptions; they portray coherent systems that accommodate a considerable corpus of well-constructed category-formations. To that claim and what is at stake in it we now turn.

The Systemic Construction of Ideas

As with the Pentateuch and the Mishnah, therefore, so too with the Talmud of the Land of Israel, *Genesis Rabbah, Leviticus Rabbah,*[3] and related compilations: the systems of thought respond to historical turning points and record the thought of a handful of reflective minds. I report, then, on the construction into a systematic statement of views held by a small circle of editors, compilers, arrangers, and redactors of a collage of sayings and stories, toward the end of the fourth century. The system of thought produced included not only earlier opinions but generated and accommodated further facts, and was subject to extension, amplification, and articulation.

To take the case in hand: Tarfon's statement in *t. Šabbat* 13:5 (see above, page 93) conveys a theology of Christianity—"had access to the truth but rejected it in favor of deception"—that both conceded the claim of Christianity ("grafted onto the olive tree") but invalidated it (in our terms, a hybrid yielding poisoned fruit). In general terms, that is precisely what we find in *Genesis Rabbah* with its portrait of Rome as Esau (a matter on which we shall concentrate): Christianity is Israel, but illegitimate Israel. The toseftan statement assigned to Tarfon adumbrates an opinion that, in *Genesis Rabbah,* would coalesce in a vast, detailed, dense and rich system. It would yield secondary developments, a hermeneutics for scriptural interpretation, doctrines and policies for concrete transactions, and even a large and compelling explanation for Christian power and prestige in a world in which the authentic Israel would find itself at the margins. The social policy embodied in Genesis Rabbah, the worldview and way of

---

[3] For the Yerushalmi, my systemic construction is in *Judaism in Society: The Evidence of the Yerushalmi. Toward the Natural History of a Religion* (Chicago: The University of Chicago Press, 1983; second printing, with a new preface: Atlanta: Scholars Press for South Florida Studies in the History of Judaism, 1991). For *Leviticus Rabbah: Judaism and Scripture: The Evidence of Leviticus Rabbah* (Chicago: The University of Chicago Press, 1986). For *Genesis Rabbah: Confronting Creation: How Judaism Reads Genesis. An Anthology of Genesis Rabbah* (Columbia, S.C.: University of South Carolina Press, 1991).

life adumbrated in its picture of Rome as Esau (and Ishmael and Moab and Edom), accords with the logic of Tarfon's statement but vastly outweighs that statement in systematic articulation.

At issue then is not episodic opinion but systematic articulation of social and public policy, and I find fully-formulated systems in the Pentateuch, in the Mishnah, and in the Talmud of the Land of Israel and its cognate midrash-compilations (and successor-documents too, as we shall see in due course). I see the turning point of the fourth century as I do because that is how the documents, read critically, portray matters. True, the Pentateuch does not commence in 450 B.C.E. but concludes then; the Mishnah was not written up all in one day in 200 C.E. but was completed then; and so with the ideas of the Talmuds and midrash-compilations. But it is only in this time, and not earlier, that those opinions came forth with everything in place and whole, in documents deemed authoritative as the official rabbinic position of Judaism. And, when I speak of a confrontation between Judaism and Christianity in the fourth century, it is the sages of that time who stand behind the documents of the day that represent Judaism. Their system animated the documents and guided the selection and arrangement of opinion in them; and their system was constituted by the governing category-formations, which dictated the selection and composition of opinion.

Variant Readings of Passages in a Document

What about the diverse versions of sayings and stories belonging to a given rabbinic document? That question shows a further point that demands consideration. The documents as we have them derive from a long period of copying, during which they received materials borrowed or made up by later copyists. Accordingly, diverse manuscripts of the Yerushalmi, *Genesis Rabbah,* and *Leviticus Rabbah* contain different versions of those documents. The materials cited here occur in most, or all, manuscripts. That is why I cite them. Still more important, my argument rests on no single item but on the repertoire of numerous and diverse materials, all well attested in manuscript evidence, and all assigned by scholarly opinion at this time to documents redacted in the late fourth or the fifth century.

On that basis I believe we have a fair sample of the sages' views in the fourth and fifth century, deriving from the writings that reached closure—it is unanimously held—at this time. But I emphasize that the varying representations of what is (or is not) in *Genesis Rabbah* or *Leviticus Rabbah* or the Talmud of the Land of Israel—not to mention the wording of various passages—do require attention, and these have received attention in two ways. The first is my careful effort to place on display materials only well attested by manuscript evidence (even though wordings may vary among the manuscripts). The second is my insistence on seeing documents as wholes and in the aggregate: what, in toto, does a document tell us? The appearance or wording of a given passage in diverse manuscript representations never plays a role in my argument, because it does not have to, and because it should not. Now to the substance of matters: the delineation of the rabbinic response to the events of the fourth century, which occupies the remainder of the present chapter and all of the next one.

The Age of Constantine and Its Meaning for Judaism

For convenience, the age of Constantine dates from 312, when Constantine extended toleration to Christianity, to 429, when the Jewish government of the land of Israel ceased to enjoy the recognition of the state. In that century Christianity joined the political world of the Roman Empire by gaining power, briefly losing it, and, finally, regaining the throne and assuring its permanent domination of the state.[4]

Enormous shifts from 312 in the political facts of the world, represented by the growing control of Christianity over the institutions of state and government, raised issues for both Judaic sages and Christian theologians that had first been defined by the Scriptures of ancient Israel. These issues focused on the meaning of history, viewed by epochs, each with its message; the identity of the Messiah; and the definition of Israel, God's people. Before Constantine no form of Christianity had ever made an impact upon the systematic thought of any of the Judaic authorships known to us. (By "authorship" I mean the group of compilers, editors, and redactors responsible for the document as we know it, as distinct from an individual author, who can have contributed a saying of his own. "Authorship" speaks of those who set forth the consensus of the collegium of sages.) For example, the Tosefta's ruling, as we saw above (page 93), captured the state of Judaic opinion concerning the inconsequence of Christianity. For their part, Christian writers did compose debates with Judaism. But the Judaic systems they fabricated represented little more than expressions of how Christians imagined Jews framed their religion—how they would have read the Hebrew Scriptures in line with Paul's and the Gospels' formulations of matters, were they not so insincere in their unbelief and merely stubborn about acknowledging the truth.

We have already seen how the one Judaic system we have fully articulated—namely, the Mishnah—is formed independent of any interests

---

[4]I summarize the main points in my *Judaism and Christianity in the Age of Constantine: Issues of the Initial Confrontation* (Chicago: University of Chicago Press, 1987).

of Christianity, e.g., the Messiah, the meaning of history, and similar eschatological questions. The mishnaic system shows us a Judaism utterly out of phase with Christianity. Only when matters of public policy—the political change represented by Constantine—demanded a clear statement on the questions at hand were issues addressed in a manner that shows a Judaic system in its own integrity, documented out of the extant Judaic sources, not only out of the writings of Church authorities. Only when both the Roman empire and Israelite nation had to assess the meaning of epochal change, with each having to reconsider the teleology of society and system, did chronic disagreement between the two become acute difference. "Messiah" stood simply for the status of a given priest or general in Judaism, whereas "The Messiah" for Christians had been Jesus Christ—the differences before 312 were straightforward and clearly distinct. But with the advent of Christian Rome, events intervened, vastly amplifying the Christians' claim in behalf of Christ the King.

While the Christian empire outlawed paganism, its policy toward the Jews accorded limited tolerance. We err if we identify the systematic destruction of Jews' lives and property later in the Christian West during the Crusades with the Roman policy of Constantine's age. Overall, the Jews of the land of Israel and of the Roman Empire in general continued to enjoy state recognition and protection. Worship was protected and not to be interrupted; synagogues were exempt from billeting; synagogue staffs were exempt from curial charges just as were Christian clergy; Jews did not have to go to court on the Sabbath; Jewish courts settled civil disputes. On the other hand, there were also disabilities, described by A. H. M. Jones as follows:

> Intermarriage between Jews and Christians was declared by Theodosius to be tantamount to adultery and subjected to the same penalties. . . . Constantine forbade Jews to circumcise their slaves considering it a capital offense and furthermore forbade Jews to buy slaves of any religion but their own. . . .

> Christianity added theological animus to the general dislike of the Jews, and the numerous diatribes against them, in the form of sermons or pamphlets, which Christian leaders produced, must have fanned the flames. It is surprising indeed that the emperors, most of whom shared the popular view, maintained such moderation in their legal enactments . . . the attitude of the emperors seems to have been mainly inspired by respect for the established law. The Jews had since the days of Caesar been guaranteed the practice of their ancestral religion and the government shrank from annulling this ancient privilege.[5]

---

[5] A. H. M. Jones, *The Decline of the Ancient World* (London: Longmans, 1964), 946–47. See also A. H. M. Jones, *The Later Roman Empire* (Oxford: Basil Blackwell, 1964), 284–602.

Still, Jones' judgment for the period at hand is positive: "Except for their exclusion from the public service and the bar the Jews . . . incurred no serious civil disabilities until the reign of Justin." True, on occasion mobs took over and burned down synagogues. But when that happened the government exacted compensation. Mass baptisms by force occurred only after our period and far from the land of Israel.

The Christian restoration, after Julian's abortive attack on Christian hegemony in 361–363, intensified over time the prior abridgement of the civil status of the Jews. Referring to the view that the Jews should be kept in a condition of misery but should not be exterminated, Ruether says, "Between 315 and 439 (from the reign of Constantine to the promulgation of the Theodosian Code), this view of the Jew was enforced through a steadily worsening legal status."[6] Avi–Yonah divides the period after Julian into three parts. The first, 363–383, until the accession of Theodosius I, was a period of "a truce between the hostile religions." The second, from the accession of Theodosius III to the death of his son, Arcadius, was marked by an

> energetic attack on Judaism by the leaders of the church, mainly through pressure on the imperial government. The government ceded here and there but did not cause serious injury to the Jewish community as a whole or to Jews as individuals. This campaign against Judaism was part of a larger program of physical attacks on paganism and pagans and their places of worship, which sharpened after 380. The third sub-period lasted from the accession of Theodosius II till the publication of his third Novella (408–438). During this time the power of the church overcame the scruples of the government and both turned against the Jews.[7]

So through the end of the period at hand, the problems of Jewish-Christian relations were those of morale, not of politics and economics. Of interest to our study are only a few facts.

The political revolution in the standing of Christianity meant that Judaism would now have to take account of Christianity as a competing formulation of Scripture's imperatives. Politics now intervened; Christians could—and did—force their presence upon Judaism. Christians also saw Israel as God's people, who were now rejected by God for rejecting the Christ. In their turn, Israel saw Christians embodied in the Christian Roman Empire as part of Israel—the bad part. Ishmael, Esau, Edom: the brother and the enemy—these scriptural figures accorded Christianity a place in the controlling narrative of history that rabbinic Judaism put forth. So while, as I have stressed, the rabbinic sages had formerly framed

---

[6] Rosemary Ruether, *Faith and Fratricide: The Theological Roots of Anti-Semitism* (N.Y.: Seabury, 1979), 186.

[7] Michael Avi–Yonah, *The Jews under Roman and Byzantine Rule* (N.Y.: Schocken, 1976), 208.

matters without taking account of the challenge of Christianity, the political revolution marked by Constantine's conversion forced them to do
so now.

Consequently, the two parties found it necessary to discuss a single
agendum—concerning history and eschatology—and Scripture would
define the terms on which each would take up that agendum. In the rabbinic documents under consideration here—those that came to closure
after the advent of the Christian Empire—we find composites of stories
and sayings that introduce the themes of theology of history and eschatological teleology, earlier so striking for their marginality to the category-
formations of the Mishnah. These composites make coherent statements,
not merely collecting sayings on a given topic.

The sequence—Constantine, then the Messiah-composites of the
Yerushalmi—proves nothing on its own. The issue is not whether those
dominant themes (namely, history and eschatology) come to prominence
after the events of the fourth century, but it is whether we can confidently
account for their prominence *by reason of* those particular turnings embodied in the specified events. I do not commit the obvious error of maintaining *post hoc ergo propter hoc* (what happened afterward happened
because of). The substance of matters settles matters. I argue that the evidence bespeaks a *focused* debate on the particular themes introduced by
the political events of the age: a point-by-point Judaic response to the
challenge of Christianity. So the sequence sets the stage for the confluence
of theological argument, with Judaic and Christian writers addressing the
same issues in the same time-frame and framing the issues in the same
terms. Not only the sequence of events and documents, but also the
meaning of those events and the consequences to be drawn from them—
that is the foundation for my construction of the turning point in the formation of Judaism that took place in, and in consequence, of events of the
fourth century.

A variety of issues were joined, but the two of greatest systemic interest involve, first, the definition of Rome in relationship to Israel, and,
second, the matter of the destruction of the temple.[8] In both cases, we find
ourselves addressing the hitherto-unwritten chapters in a Judaic theology of history. Where the Mishnah's category-formations fell silent, there
in particular the rabbinic sages produced large composites, comparable to

[8] I treat a larger repertoire in my *Constantine* and still others in *The Founda-
tions of Judaism: Method, Teleology, Doctrine* I–III (Philadelphia: Fortress, 1983–
1985). Volume I was reprinted as *Midrash in Context: Exegesis in Formative Judaism*
(Atlanta: Scholars Press for Brown Judaic Studies, 1988); Volume II was reprinted
as *Messiah in Context: Israel's History and Destiny in Formative Judaism* (Lanham,
Md.: University Press of America, 1988); Volume III was reprinted as *Torah: From
Scroll to Symbol in Formative Judaism* (Atlanta: Scholars Press for Brown Judaic
Studies, 1988).

category-formations represented in Mishnah-chapters, as we shall now see. And, as chapter five will explain, these composites—the rabbinic system that animated the Talmuds and Midrash—would realize the logic of the pentateuchal-mishnaic system and impose that logic on the antithetical themes of time and change and eschatology that that system itself had neglected.

From Enemy to (Illegitimate) Brother: The Transformation of Rome

Rabbinic Judaism responded to the events of the fourth century by framing a doctrine of Rome in relationship to Israel that matched the shift in the status and claims of Rome within the framework already present in the Torah.[9] In the Mishnah and associated documents, Rome had formed part of an undifferentiated world of idolaters, gentiles who defy God. Rome bore no more, and no less, a relationship to Israel than did Babylonia, Media, or Greece—or any of the barbarian peoples. Rome was not special, not different, not Israel's counterpoise and opposite. But that conception was to change, and Rome was to be portrayed in relationship to Israel as brother, as enemy, as illegitimate—but as part of the patrimony of Israel. That brings us to a brief exercise in the documentary history of ideas: how is Rome represented in the successive documents of rabbinic Judaism, from the Mishnah through the first of the two Talmuds and its companions?

If we ask the Mishnah its principal view of the world beyond, its answer is simple: the world beyond was essentially undifferentiated. Rome was no more, and no less, important than any other place in that undifferentiated world, and, so far as the epochs of human history were concerned, these epochs emerged solely from within Israel, and, in particular, the history of Israel's cult (*m. Zebaḥ.* 14:4–9, which lays matters out in terms of the cult's location, and *m. Roš Haš.* 4:1–4 which contrasts the *before* and the *after* of the destruction). That establishes a paradigm, not a linear history: in this pattern, the one rule prevails, in that, another.

In that context, Rome had represented what all other gentiles, without differentiation, represented: the realm of death. It was not singled out

---

[9]See, for the first systematic work on Rome in rabbinic literature, Shmuel Krauss, *Persia and Rome in Talmud and Midrash* (Jerusalem, 1947, in Hebrew), and, most recently, Mireille Hadas-Lebel, "La fiscalité romaine dans la littérature rabbinique," *Revue des études juives* (1984): 143:5–29. See also my "Stable Symbols in a Shifting Society: The Delusion of the Monolithic Gentile in Documents of Late Fourth-Century Judaism," *History of Religions* (1985): 25:163–75. Cf. also Jacob Neusner, ed., *"To See Ourselves as Others See Us:" Christians, Jews, "Others" in Late Antiquity* (Atlanta: Scholars Press Studies in the Humanities, 1985), 373–96.

and did not form a distinct species of "the gentiles." The rejection of criteria for differentiation of "gentiles" (meaning "non-Israel") or the outside world may be conveyed simply. Since the entire earth outside of the land of Israel, was, in the Mishnah's law considered to suffer from contamination by corpses, it was unclean with a severe mode of uncleanness and thus inaccessible to the holy and life-sustaining processes of the cult. If an Israelite artist were asked to paint a wall-portrait of the world beyond the land, he would paint the entire wall white, the color of death. The outside world, for the Mishnah, was entirely the realm of death. Among corpses, how are we to make distinctions? The answer is: we do not. We turn then to how the Mishnah and tractate ʾAbot treat Rome, both directly and in the symbolic form of Ishmael, Esau, and Edom. Since the system at hand treats all gentiles as essentially the same, Rome, for its part, will not present a theme of special interest. So if my description of the Mishnah's basic mode of differentiation among outsiders proves sound, then Rome should not vastly differ from other outsiders.

If we consult the Mishnah-concordance by Chayim Yehoshua Kasovsky,[10] and look for Edom, Esau, Ishmael, and Rome, we come away disappointed. "Edom" in the sense of Rome does not occur; the word "Edom" stands only for the Edomites of biblical times (*m. Yebam.* 8:3) and the territory of Edom (*m. Ketub.* 5:8). Ishmael, who like Edom later stands for Rome, supplies a name of a sage in the Mishnah, nothing more. As to the name Rome itself, the picture is not terribly different. There is a "Roman hyssop" (*m. Parah* 11:7, *m. Neg.* 14:6), and Rome occurs as a place-name (*m. ʿAbod. Zar.* 4:7). Otherwise I see not a single passage indicated by Kosovsky in which Rome serves as a topic of special interest, and, it goes without saying, in no place does "Rome" stand for an age in human history—let alone the counterpart to and opposite of Israel. Rome is part of the undifferentiated other, the outside world of death beyond. That fact takes on considerable meaning when we turn to the later fourth- and fifth-century midrash compilations.

What about the Tosefta, the Mishnah's closest companion and first systematic commentary? Relying again on C. Y. Kosovsky,[11] we find pretty much the same sort of usages, in the same proportions, as the Mishnah has already shown us. Specifically, Edom is a biblical people (*t. Yebam.* 8:1, *t. Nid.* 6:1, *t. Qidd.* 5:4). Ishmael is a proper name for several sages. More important, Ishmael never stands for Rome. And Rome itself? We have Todor of Rome (*t. Beṣah* 2:15) and Rome as a place where people live—e.g., "I saw it in Rome" (*t. Yoma* 3:8), "I taught this law in Rome" (*t. Nid.* 7:1, *t. Miqw.* 4:7). And that is all. What we do not find takes on significance in

[10] Chayim Yehoshua Kasovsky, *Otsar leshon ha-Mishnah (Thesaurus Mishnae)* (Jerusalem: Masadah, 1956).

[11] Chayim Yehoshua Kasovsky, *Otsar leshon ha-Toseftah (Thesaurus Thosephthae)* (Jerusalem, 1932–1961).

the context of what, in documents that came to closure much later, we do discover. But first let us look backward.

If we were to propose a thesis on "Rome and Christianity in the Mishnah and the Tosefta" based on the evidence at hand, it would not produce many propositions. Rome is a place, and no biblical figures or places prefigure the place of Rome in the history of Israel. Rome occupies no important place in Israel's history or in relationship to Israel. It is just another composite of idolaters, not a corporate entity comparable (but antithetical) to Israel as a moral actor. That is so even though the authors of the Mishnah and the Tosefta knew full well who had destroyed the temple and closed off Jerusalem and, by ca. 200–300, they had also fully grasped what these events had meant. And, in that same context, we realize, Christianity plays no role of consequence; no one takes the matter very seriously. Christians are people who know the truth but deny it.

The thesis consists of negatives: "Rome" did not stand for Israel's nemesis and counterpart, Rome did not mark an epoch in the history of the world, Israel did not encompass Rome in Israel's history of humanity, and Rome did not represent one of Daniel's four monarchies—the last, the worst, prior to Israel's rule. To invoke a modern category, secularity, Rome stood for a perfectly secular matter: a place where things happened. Not a mythic actor, Rome in no way symbolized anything beyond itself.

So much for documents brought to closure before Constantine. We come now to those produced in the century after two momentous events in world history. First was the conversion of Constantine to Christianity. Second was Julian's failure in allowing the temple to be rebuilt, the repression of paganism (and its affect on Judaism), the Christianization of the Holy land, and, it appears, the conversion of sizable numbers of Jews in the land of Israel to Christianity and the consequent Christianization of Palestine (no longer, in context, the land of Israel at all). We turn first to *Genesis Rabbah*, a contemporary with the Yerushalmi and generally assigned to the year 400.

The contrast between the Mishnah's Rome and the Rome of *Genesis Rabbah* (which stands for its cognate corpus, *Leviticus Rabbah*, as well), could not be more radical. Now Rome is portrayed as the anti-Israel, the counterpart and opposite to Israel. The sages saw Scripture as affording Rome a considerable place in its mythic construction. Rome is related to Israel the way Esau is related to Jacob—namely, as the illegitimate part of Israel. Indeed, in *Genesis Rabbah* the sages read the book of Genesis as if it portrayed the history of Israel in relationship to Rome—and to Rome in particular. Rome does not stand for "the gentiles," or "the idolaters," and it is not generic for all non-Israel.

Rather, Rome now functions as sui generis, like Israel. It plays a leading role in the biblical narrative, with special reference to the counterpart and opposite of the patriarchs: first Ishmael, then Esau, and, always,

Edom. Why Rome in the form it takes in *Genesis Rabbah?* And how come the obsessive character of the sages' disposition of the theme of Rome? Were their picture merely of Rome as tyrant and destroyer of the temple, we should have no reason to link their exegetical text to the problems of the age of redaction and closure. But the representation of Rome in a particular—and peculiar—relationship with Israel requires explanation. Rome is not comparable to Babylonia, Media, and Greece (prior conquerors of Israel), though Rome is commonly situated in a list made up of the four: Babylonia, Media, Greece, Rome. But if Rome belongs to a common genus, it is different from the others nonetheless. For Rome is special even among the world-empires to which it is comparable: it is a species of the genus, conqueror of Israel/world-empire, because Rome is Israel's brother, counterpart, and nemesis. Rome is the one thing standing in the way of Israel's, and the world's, ultimate salvation. So the stakes are different, and much higher.

Let us begin with a simple example of how ubiquitous the shadow of Ishmael/Esau/Edom/Rome is in *Genesis Rabbah* and the other post-Constantinian midrash-compilations, and also in the later Rabbah-compilations. Wherever the sages reflect on the future, their minds turn to their own day. They found the hour difficult because Rome, now Christian, claimed that very birthright and blessing that they understood to be theirs alone. Christian Rome posed a threat without precedent. Now another dominion, besides Israel's, claimed the rights and blessings that sustained Israel. Wherever in Scripture they turned, the sages found comfort in the iteration that the birthright, the blessing, the Torah, and the hope all belonged to them and to none other. Here is a striking statement of that constant proposition.

Genesis Rabbah LIII:xii.1–3

1. A. "[So she said to Abraham, 'Cast out this slave woman with her son, for the son of this slave woman shall not be heir with my son Isaac.'] And the thing was very displeasing to Abraham on account of his son" (Gen. 21:11):

   B. That is in line with this verse: "And shuts his eyes from looking upon evil" (Is. 33:15).[12]

2. A. "But God said to Abraham, 'Be not displeased because of the lad and because of your slave woman; whatever Sarah says to you, do

---

[12] H. Freedman, *Genesis Rabbah* (London: Soncino, 1948), 471n1: He shut his eyes from Ishmael's evil ways and was reluctant to send him away.

as she tells you, for through Isaac shall your descendants be named'" (Gen. 21:12):

B. Said R. Yudan bar Shillum, "What is written is not 'Isaac' but 'through Isaac.'" [The matter is limited, not through all of Isaac's descendants but only through some of them, thus excluding Esau.]

3. A. R. Azariah in the name of Bar Hutah, "The use of the B, which stands for two, indicates that he who affirms that there are two worlds will inherit both worlds [this age and the age to come]."

B. Said R. Yudan bar Shillum, "It is written, 'Remember his marvelous works that he has done, his signs and the judgments of his mouth' (Ps. 105:5). I have given a sign, namely, it is one who gives the appropriate evidence through what he says. Specifically, he who affirms that there are two worlds will be called 'your seed.'

C. "And he who does not affirm that there are two worlds will not be called 'your seed.'"

Section 1 makes "the matter" refer to Ishmael's misbehavior, not Sarah's proposal, so removing the possibility of disagreement between Abraham and Sarah. Sections 2–3 interpret the limiting particle *bet* ("through")— that is, among the descendants of Isaac will be found Abraham's heirs, but not all the descendants of Isaac will be heirs of Abraham. Section 2 explicitly excludes Esau, that is Rome, and Section 3 makes the matter doctrinal in the context of Israel's inner life. As the several antagonists of Israel stand for Rome in particular, so the traits of Rome, as the sages perceived them, characterized the biblical heroes. And as we shall now see, Esau provided a favorite target. From the womb Israel and Rome contended.

Genesis Rabbah LXIII:vi.1–6

1. A. "And the children struggled together [within her, and she said, 'If it is thus, why do I live?' So she went to inquire of the Lord. And the Lord said to her, 'Two nations are in your womb, and two peoples, born of you, shall be divided; the one shall be stronger than the other, and the elder shall serve the younger']" (Gen. 25:22–23):

B. R. Yohanan and R. Simeon b. Laqish:

C. R. Yohanan said, "[Because the word, 'struggle,' contains the letters for the word, 'run,'] this one was running to kill that one and that one was running to kill this one."

D. R. Simeon b. Laqish: "This one releases the laws given by that one, and that one releases the laws given by this one."

2. A. R. Berekhiah in the name of R. Levi said, "It is so that you should not say that it was only after he left his mother's womb that [Esau] contended against [Jacob].

   B. "But even while he was yet in his mother's womb, his fist was stretched forth against him: 'The wicked stretch out their fists [so Freedman] from the womb' (Ps. 58:4)."

3. A. "And the children struggled together within her:"

   B. [Once more referring to the letters of the word "struggled," with special attention to the ones that mean, "run,"] they wanted to run within her.

   C. When she went by houses of idolatry, Esau would kick, trying to get out: "The wicked are estranged from the womb" (Ps. 58:4).

   D. When she went by synagogues and study-houses, Jacob would kick, trying to get out: "Before I formed you in the womb, I knew you" (Jer. 1:5).

4. A. " . . . and she said, 'If it is thus, why do I live?'"

   B. R. Haggai in the name of R. Isaac: "This teaches that our mother, Rebecca, went around to the doors of women and said to them, 'Did you ever have this kind of pain in your life?'"

   C. "[She said to them,] '"If thus:" If this is the pain of having children, would that I had not gotten pregnant.'"

   D. Said R. Huna, "If I am going to produce twelve tribes only through this kind of suffering, would that I had not gotten pregnant."

5. A. It was taught on Tannaite authority in the name of R. Nehemiah, "Rebecca was worthy of having the twelve tribes come forth from her. That is in line with this verse:

   B. "'Two nations are in your womb, and two peoples, born of you, shall be divided; the one shall be stronger than the other, and the elder shall serve the younger.' When her days to be delivered were fulfilled, behold, there were twins in her womb. The first came forth red, all his body like a hairy mantle, so they called his name Esau. Afterward his brother came forth . . .' (Gen. 25:23–24).

   C. "'Two nations are in your womb:' thus two.

   D. "'and two peoples:' thus two more, hence four.

   E. "' . . . the one shall be stronger than the other:' two more, so six.

   F. "' . . . and the elder shall serve the younger:' two more, so eight.

G. "'When her days to be delivered were fulfilled, behold, there were twins in her womb:' two more, so ten.

H. "'The first came forth red:' now eleven.

J. "'Afterward his brother came forth:' now twelve."

K. There are those who say, "Proof derives from this verse: 'If it is thus, why do I live?' Focusing on the word for 'thus,' we note that the two letters of that word bear the numerical value of seven and five respectively, hence, twelve in all."

6. A. "So she went to inquire of the Lord:"

B. Now were there synagogues and houses of study in those days [that she could go to inquire of the Lord]?

C. But is it not the fact that she went only to the study of Eber?

D. This serves to teach you that whoever receives an elder is as if he receives the Presence of God.

Sections VI.1–3 take for granted that Esau represents Rome, and Jacob, Israel. Consequently the verse underlines the point that there is natural inborn enmity between Israel and Rome. Esau hated Israel even while he was still in the womb. Jacob, for his part, revealed from the womb those virtues that would characterize him later on, eager to serve God as Esau was eager to worship idols. The text invites just this sort of reading. Section VI.4–5 relate Rebecca's suffering to the birth of the twelve tribes. Section VI.6 makes its own point, independent of the rest and tacked on. In the next passage Rome appears as a pig—like a kosher beast because it has a cloven hoof, but different from a kosher beast because it does not chew the cud—thus a deceiver, like but unlike Israel:

Genesis Rabbah LXV:i.1

A. "When Esau was forty years old, he took to wife Judith, the daughter of Beeri, the Hittite, and Basemath the daughter of Elon the Hittite; and they made life bitter for Isaac and Rebecca" (Gen. 26:34–35):

B. "The swine out of the wood ravages it, that which moves in the field feeds on it" (Ps. 80:14).

C. R. Phineas and R. Hilqiah in the name of R. Simon: "Among all of the prophets, only two of them spelled out in public [the true character of Rome, represented by the swine], Asaf and Moses.

D. "Asaf: 'The swine out of the wood ravages it.'

E. "Moses: 'And the swine, because he parts the hoof' (Deut. 14:8).

F. "Why does Moses compare Rome to the swine? Just as the swine, when it crouches, puts forth its hoofs as if to say, 'I am clean,' so the wicked kingdom steals and grabs, while pretending to be setting up courts of justice.

G. "So Esau, for all forty years, hunted married women, ravished them, and when he reached the age of forty, he presented himself to his father, saying, 'Just as father got married at the age of forty, so I shall marry a wife at the age of forty.'

H. "'When Esau was forty years old, he took to wife Judith, the daughter of Beeri, the Hittite, and Basemath the daughter of Elon the Hittite.'"

How long would Rome rule, and when would Israel succeed? The important point is that Rome was next to last, Israel last. Rome's triumph brought assurance that Israel would be next—and last:

Genesis Rabbah LXXV:iv.2–3

2. A. "And Jacob sent messengers before him:"

B. To this one [Esau] whose time to take hold of sovereignty would come before him [namely, before Jacob, since Esau would rule, then Jacob would govern].

C. R. Joshua b. Levi said, "Jacob took off the purple robe and threw it before Esau, as if to say to him, 'Two flocks of starlings are not going to sleep on a single branch' [so we cannot rule at the same time]."

3. A. " . . . to Esau his brother:"

B. Even though he was Esau, he was still his brother.

Esau remains Jacob's brother, and Esau rules before Jacob will. The application to contemporary affairs cannot be missed, both in the recognition of the true character of Esau—a brother!—and in the interpretation of the future of history.

So the main point is clear. In the minds of the compilers of *Genesis Rabbah* and authors of its composites and even discrete compositions, Genesis portrays the events of the day: the struggle of two equal powers, Rome and Israel, Esau and Jacob, Ishmael and Isaac. The world-historical changes of the fourth century, with the confirmation in politics and power of the Christians' claim that Christ was king over all humanity, demanded from the rabbinic sages an appropriate—and, to Israel, per-suasive—response.

When we turn to *Leviticus Rabbah*, conventionally dated to some fifty years after *Genesis Rabbah* (ca. 450 C.E.), we find the same view of Rome not simply another one of the gentile non-peoples but as correlated with Israel. Here we see how the sages absorb events into their system of classification. In such a context, we find no interest (except in relationship to Israel) either in the outsiders and their powers, or in the history of the empires of the world, or in redemption and the messianic fulfillment of time. What is important for our purpose in the following is the representation of Rome, and I trim the passage, which is massive, to focus on that:

Leviticus Rabbah XIII:v.1–6, 8–9, 13

1. A. Said R. Ishmael b. R. Nehemiah, "All the prophets foresaw what the pagan kingdoms would do [to Israel].

   B. "The first man foresaw what the pagan kingdoms would do [to Israel].

   C. "That is in line with the following verse of Scripture: 'A river flowed out of Eden [to water the garden, and there it divided and became four rivers]' (Gen. 2:10). [The four rivers stand for the four kingdoms, Babylonia, Media, Greece, and Rome.]"

2. A. R. Tanhuma said it, [and] R. Menahema [in the name of] R. Joshua b. Levi: "The Holy One, blessed be he, will give the cup of reeling to the nations of the world to drink in the world to come.

   B. "That is in line with the following verse of Scripture: 'A river flowed out of Eden' (Gen 2:10), the place from which justice [DYN] goes forth."

3. A. "[There it divided] and became four rivers" (Gen 2:10)—this refers to the four kingdoms.

   B. "The name of the first is Pishon (PSWN); [it is the one which flows around the whole land of Havilah, where there is gold; and the gold of that land is good; Bdellium and onyx stone are there]" (Gen. 2:11–12).

   C. This refers to Babylonia, on account [of the reference to Babylonia in the following verse:] "And their [the Babylonians'] horsemen spread themselves (PSW)" (Hab. 1:8).

4. A. "The name of the second river is Gihon; [it is the one which flows around the whole land of Cush]" (Gen. 2:13).

B. This refers to Media, which produced Haman, that wicked man, who spit out venom like a serpent.

5. A. "And the name of the third river is Tigris (HDQL), [which flows east of Assyria]" (Gen. 2:14).

B. This refers to Greece [Syria], which was sharp (HD) and speedy (QL) in making its decrees, saying to Israel, "Write on the horn of an ox that you have no portion in the God of Israel."

6. A. "And the fourth river is the Euphrates (PRT)" (Gen. 2:14).

B. This refers to Edom [Rome], since it was fruitful (PRT), and multiplied through the prayer of the elder [Isaac at Gen. 27:39].

C. Another interpretation: It was because it was fruitful and multiplied, and so cramped his world.

D. Another explanation: Because it was fruitful and multiplied and cramped his son.

E. Another explanation: Because it was fruitful and multiplied and cramped his house.

F. Another explanation: "Parat"—because in the end, "I am going to exact a penalty from it."

G. That is in line with the following verse of Scripture: "I have trodden (PWRH) the winepress alone" (Is. 63:3).

8. A. Daniel foresaw what the evil kingdoms would do [to Israel].

B. "Daniel said, I saw in my vision by night, and behold, the four winds of heaven were stirring up the great sea. And four great beasts came up out of the sea, [different from one another. The first was like a lion and had eagles' wings. Then as I looked, its wings were plucked off . . . And behold, another beast, a second one, like a bear . . . After this I looked, and lo, another, like a leopard . . . After this I saw in the night visions, and behold, a fourth beast, terrible and dreadful and exceedingly strong; and it had great iron teeth]" (Dan. 7:3–7).

K. "The first was like a lion [and had eagles' wings]" (Dan. 7:4).

L. This refers to Babylonia.

V. "And behold, another beast, a second one, like a bear. [It was raised up one side; it had three ribs in its mouth between its teeth, and it was told, Arise, devour much flesh]" (Dan. 7:5).

W. This refers to Media.

BB. "'A leopard watches over their cities' (Jer. 5:6) refers to Greece.

CC. " 'Whoever goes out from them will be savaged' (Jer. 5:6) refers to Edom.

DD. "Why so? 'Because their transgressions are many, and their backslidings still more' (Jer. 5:6)."

9. A. Moses foresaw what the evil kingdoms would do [to Israel].

B. "The camel, rock badger, and hare" (Deut. 14:7). [Compare: "Nevertheless, among those that chew the cud or part the hoof, you shall not eat these: the camel, because it chews the cud but does not part the hoof, is unclean to you. The rock badger, because it chews the cud but does not part the hoof, is unclean to you. And the hare, because it chews the cud but does not part the hoof, is unclean to you, and the pig, because it parts the hoof and is cloven-footed, but does not chew the cud, is unclean to you" (Lev. 11:4–8).]

C. The camel (GML) refers to Babylonia, [in line with the following verse of Scripture: "O daughter of Babylonia, you who are to be devastated!] Happy will be he who requites (GML) you, with what you have done to us" (Ps. 137:8).

D. "The rock badger" (Deut. 14:7)—this refers to Media.

E. Rabbis and R. Judah b. R. Simon.

F. Rabbis say, "Just as the rock badger exhibits traits of uncleanness and traits of cleanness, so the kingdom of Media produced both a righteous man and a wicked one."

G. Said R. Judah b. R. Simon, "The last Darius was Esther's son. He was clean on his mother's side and unclean on his father's side."

H. "The hare" (Deut 14:7)—this refers to Greece. The mother of King Ptolemy was named "Hare" [in Greek: *lagos*].

I. "The pig" (Deut. 14:7)—this refers to Edom [Rome].

J. Moses made mention of the first three in a single verse and the final one in a verse by itself [(Deut. 14:7, 8)]. Why so?

K. R. Yohanan and R. Simeon b. Laqish.

L. R. Yohanan said, "It is because [the pig] is equivalent to the other three."

M. And R. Simeon b. Laqish said, "It is because it outweighs them."

N. R. Yohanan objected to R. Simeon b. Laqish, " 'Prophesy, therefore, son of man, clap your hands [and let the sword come down twice, yea thrice]' (Ez. 21:14)."

O. And how does R. Simeon b. Laqish interpret the same passage? He notes that [the threefold sword] is doubled (Ez. 21:14).

13. A. Another interpretation [now treating "bring up the cud" (GR) as "bring along in its train" (GRR)]:

B. "The camel" (Lev. 11:4)—this refers to Babylonia.

C. "Which brings along in its train"—for it brought along another kingdom after it.

D. "The rock badger" (Lev. 11:5)—this refers to Media.

E. "Which brings along in its train"—for it brought along another kingdom after it.

F. "The hare" (Lev. 11:6)—this refers to Greece.

G. "Which brings along in its train"—for it brought along another kingdom after it.

H. "The pig" (Lev. 11:7)—this refers to Rome.

I. "Which does not bring along in its train"—for it did not bring along another kingdom after it.

J. And why is it then called "pig" (HZYR)? For it restores (MHZRT) the crown to the one who truly should have it [namely, Israel, whose dominion will begin when the rule of Rome ends].

K. That is in line with the following verse of Scripture: "And saviors will come up on Mount Zion to judge the Mountain of Esau [Rome], and the kingdom will then belong to the Lord" (Obad 1:21).

We should not miss the proposition that is demonstrated out of the facts of Scripture: Rome is different from the other world-rulers, special and final, because beyond Rome comes Israel, Rome's opposite and nemesis. The future is in hand even now, because God had told the prophets what would happen to Israel at the hands of the pagan kingdoms, Babylonia, Media, Greece, and Rome. (These are also represented by Nebuchadnezzar, Haman, Alexander, and Edom or Esau, interchangeably, for Rome.) The same vision came from Adam, Moses, and Daniel. The same policy toward Israel—oppression, destruction, enslavement, alienation from the true God—emerged from all four kingdoms. How does Rome stand out? First, it was made fruitful through the prayer of Isaac on behalf of Esau (Gen 27:39–40). Second, Rome is related through Esau, as Babylonia, Media, and Greece are not. Edom is represented by the fourth and final beast. The fourth beast was seen in a vision separate from the first three. It was worst of all and outweighed the rest. In apocalypticizing the animals of Lev. 11:4–8/Deut. 14:7, the pig, standing for Rome, again emerges as different from the others (camel, rock badger, hare) and more threatening than the rest. Just as the pig pretends to be a clean beast by showing the cloven hoof but in fact is an unclean one, so Rome pretends to be just but in fact governs by thuggery. Edom does not pretend to praise God but only blasphemes. It does not exalt the righteous but kills them.

Rome is like but unlike the other empires. It is like them as world-ruler by reason of Israel, but unlike them because it comes at the end, ultimately to be succeeded by Israel. While all the other beasts "bring along" further ones in their wake, the pig does not: "It does not bring another kingdom after it" (Section 13.5.I above). It will restore the crown to the one who will truly deserve it, namely, Israel. Esau will be judged by Zion, so Obad 1:21. The symbolization has delivered an implicit message in the treatment of Rome as distinct from but essentially equivalent to, the former kingdoms. This seems to me a stunning way of saying that the now-Christian empire in no way requires differentiation from its pagan predecessors. Nothing has changed, except that matters have gotten worse. Beyond Rome, standing in a straight line with the others, lies the true shift in history: the rule of Israel and the cessation of the dominion of the (pagan) nations.

The upshot of the contrast between the Mishnah and Tosefta, on the one hand, and *Genesis Rabbah* and *Leviticus Rabbah,* on the other, may be simply stated. When the sages of the Mishnah and the Tosefta spoke of "Edom" and "Edomites," they meant biblical Edom, a people in the geographic vicinity of the land of Israel. By "Rome" they meant the city—that alone. That fact bears meaning when we turn to documents produced two centuries later, and one hundred years beyond the triumph of Christianity. When the sages of *Genesis Rabbah* spoke of "Rome," it was not a political Rome but a messianic Rome that was at issue: Rome as surrogate for Israel, Rome as obstacle to Israel. Why? The substance of the doctrine of Rome defines the answer. From the sages' foci and emphases we reconstruct the challenge to which they responded. The sages accorded to Christian Rome a position and standing vis-à-vis Israel that no other nation or people or empire received: "Indeed, it is as you say, a kind of Israel, an heir of Abraham as your texts explicitly claim. But we remain the sole legitimate Israel, the bearer of the birthright—we and not you. So you are our brother: Esau, Ishmael, Edom." And the rest follows.

By rereading the story of the beginnings, the sages discovered the answer and the secret of the end. Rome claimed to be Israel and, indeed, the sages conceded that Rome shared the patrimony of Israel. That claim took the form of the Christians' appropriation of the Hebrew Bible as "the Old Testament," so the sages acknowledged a simple fact in acceding to the notion that, in some way, Rome too formed part of Israel. But it was the rejected part: the Ishmael, not the Isaac; the Esau, not the Jacob. The advent of Christian Rome precipitated the sustained, polemical, and, I think, rigorous and well-argued rereading of beginnings in light of the end. Rome then marked the conclusion of human history as Israel had known it. What lies beyond? The coming of the true Messiah, the redemption of Israel, the salvation of the world, the end of time. So the issues were not inconsiderable, and when the sages spoke of Esau/Rome, as they often did, they confronted the life-or-death decision of the day.

When we come to *Leviticus Rabbah,* the passage we examined places us several steps down the path explored by the compilers of *Genesis Rabbah.* The polemic represented in *Leviticus Rabbah* by the symbolization of Christian Rome makes the simple point that Christians are no different from, and no better than, pagans; they are essentially the same. Moreover, just as Israel had survived Babylonia, Media, and Greece, so would they endure to see the end of Rome (whether pagan or Christian). But of course the symbolic polemic rested on false assumptions, and hence conveyed a message that misled Jews by misrepresenting their new enemy. The new Rome really *did* differ from the old. Christianity was not merely part of a succession of undifferentiated modes of paganism but something quite different. True, the symbols assigned to Rome attributed to it worse, more dangerous traits than those assigned to the earlier empires. The pig pretends to be clean, just as the Christians give the signs of adherence to the God of Abraham, Isaac, and Jacob. That much the passage concedes. But it is not enough. For out of symbols should emerge a useful public policy, and the mode of thought represented by symbols in the end should yield an accurate confrontation with that for which the symbol stands.

Writing History: The Temple and the Failure of Julian's Project in Jerusalem—A Null-Hypothesis

I referred earlier to the Emperor Julian's project of rebuilding the temple of Jerusalem. The failure of that project made its impression, as we shall see, on Christian dialogue with Judaism. But does it define the context for the retelling of the stories of the destruction of 70 that began in the post-Constantinian rabbinic documents? The answer is both yes and no. On the one side, the destruction of the temple in 70 first makes its appearance as a focus of narrative in these documents. That leads us to anticipate a response to the Christian challenge. But, on the other side, I find here no counterpart to the innovative representation of Rome. Still, the sages speak by indirection. Perhaps in their representation of the destruction of the second temple we may find some detail that invokes the fiasco of Julian's project.

The stories the sages tell concerning the destruction define in terms particular to the interior issues of the rabbinic sages themselves, what matters in the destruction of the temple. The eschatological-messianic motif does not register in the context of the pertinent narratives. Accordingly, Julian's edict, counterpart to that of Cyrus 900 years earlier elicits no comment, even by indirection, in the rabbinic literature, which never refers to or acknowledges the fourth-century fiasco. We have to turn only to Christian theologians of the last quarter of the fourth century to find out what the other side thought the event meant. Let us begin from the beginning: the events of 362–363 and the articulated reaction to them in Christianity. We will then proceed to Judaic accounts of comparable events and the emphasis and focus thereof.

Why did the rebuilding of the temple matter to Christianity? From the Gospels' attribution to Jesus of the prediction that the temple would be destroyed ("No stone on stone" [Mark 13:2]), Christians had long cited the destruction of the temple of Jerusalem as proof of the prophetic powers of Jesus. The ruin of Jerusalem had served for three centuries to testify to the truth of Christianity. The Judaic response, dictated by the scriptural paradigm, pointed to the coming restoration—if not this morning, then wake up tomorrow and see. The Christian critics of Judaism attest to Israel's serene affirmation of the restoration: temple, Jerusalem, land—Eden. Julian, then, corresponded to Cyrus, and the paradigm of Scripture would impose itself once again.

Then came the rebuilding—in the very context of the Empire's anti-Christian politics. Julian, as part of his policy of opposing Christianity, gave orders in 362–363 to permit the Jews to rebuild their temple and resume animal sacrifices, just as the pagan temples were to be restored and their animal sacrifices renewed. Like Cyrus, Julian accommodated Israel's hopes within a broader state policy. But Julian in general favored Jews, remitted taxes that had applied to them in particular, and allowed them to rebuild their temple as part of a broader policy. Forbidden to worship in Jerusalem for the preceding three centuries, the Jews took the emperor's decree as a mark of friendship and began work. Some may have even assumed that the emperor's action forecast the coming of the Messiah. Julian had moreover issued edicts of toleration but, singling out Christianity, he pressured Christians to give up the faith and revert to paganism. He further declared war on Christianity by forbidding Christians to teach in the philosophical schools, since Christians could not teach the classical authors, for Christians "despise the gods the [classics] honored." He took away the clergy's former legal power, withdrew recognition of bishops as judges in civil matters, and subjected the clergy to taxation.

So, as Bowersock says, "Julian and the Jews had a common enemy in the Christians; their allegiance could be valuable in the Near East, particularly in Mesopotamia, where the emperor was going to conduct his campaign against the Persians."[13] Julian undertook a more general policy of

---

[13] G. W. Bowersock, *Julian the Apostate* (Cambridge, Mass.: Harvard University Press, 1978), 87–88.

restoring pagan temples Christians had closed. For their part, the Christians had turned Jerusalem into a Christian city, and Constantine and his mother had built churches and shrines there. Since Julian intended to restore sacrifices as part of normal pagan prayer, he wanted the Jews to restore their cult as well. By securing the restoration of the temple, he moreover would invalidate the prophecy of Jesus that not one stone of the temple would be left upon another.[14] But when Julian died in battle in 363, nothing had been accomplished. Frend explains the matter very simply:

> His aim may have been . . . to strike at the heart of Constantinian Jerusalem, to upstage the Holy Places by a new, rebuilt "sacred city of Jerusalem." Unfortunately workers struck hidden gaseous deposits when they began to lay the new foundations. Explosions and fire greeted their efforts, and the attempt was abandoned in confusion.[15]

So ended the last attempt to rebuild the temple of Jerusalem from then to now. Julian's successors dismantled all of his programs and restored the privileges the Church had lost. How did Christianity and Judaism respond? For the former, we need not speculate; for the latter, we have no basis for speculation at all.

The Christian response is articulated; The Judaic one is not. Let us turn first to the one we have in so many words. It comes to us in accessible form scarcely a quarter-century after the fiasco from John Chrysostom ("of the golden mouth"). A preacher in Antioch, Chrysostom (347–407) addressed the issue of Judaism in 386–387, in a series of sermons accusing Christians of backsliding. He dwelt on the matter of the destruction of the temple—and the Jews' failure to rebuild it—as proof of the divinity of Jesus. He drew upon the failure of that project to demonstrate that Judaic rites no longer held any power. He further cited that incident to prove that Israel's salvation lay wholly in the past, in the time of the return to Zion, and never in the future. In this context, the destruction of the temple and the fiasco of Julian's day discredit Judaism. In Chrysostom's case the relationship of the destruction of Jerusalem and the divinity of Jesus took pride of place. His longest homily and the most theological-historical, the fifth, is summarized by Wilken as follows:

> . . . the chief topic of the sermon: The greatest proof that Christ is truly God is that he "predicted the temple would be destroyed, that Jerusalem would be captured, and that the city would no longer be the city of the Jews as it had been in the past." If only ten, twenty, or fifty years had passed since the destruction of the temple, one might understand doubts about Jesus' prophecy, but over three centuries have passed and there is not "a shadow of the change for which you are waiting." . . . If the Jews had never at-

---

[14] Ibid., 89.
[15] W. H. C. Frend, *The Rise of Christianity* (Philadelphia: Fortress, 1984), 606.

tempted to rebuild the temple during this time, one might say that they could do so only if they made the effort. But the course of events shows the reverse, for the Jews have attempted to rebuild the temple, not once, but three times, and were unsuccessful in every effort. . . . The failure of Julian's effort to rebuild the temple in Jerusalem, then, is proof that Christ was not an ordinary man among men, but the divine son of God. His word was more powerful than the feeble efforts of men, for by his word alone he defeated the emperor Julian and the "whole Jewish people." . . . The prophecy of Christ is proven true by the historical "facts." . . . the fulfillment of the ancient prophecies and the continued existence of the Church is evidence of the power and divinity of Christ.[16]

So everything depended on the temple, whether restored or in permanent ruin. Jesus had said no stone would rest on stone, and none did. Julian had tried to rebuild the temple and had failed. Chrysostom pointed to the Jews' exile as proof of their defeat: "It is illegitimate to keep their way of life outside of Jerusalem . . . for the city of Jerusalem is the keystone that supports the Jewish rite."

What about the Judaic response within the rabbinic sages' view of matters? The rabbinic sages' idiom taught them a more circumspect and subtle mode of discourse than that characteristic of Chrysostom. They spoke in the Talmuds and midrash-compilations not through proposition and explicit philosophical syllogism as in the Mishnah and the Tosefta. Rather, they framed their syllogisms in a more subtle way in narrative and exegetical context, proving their point by drawing upon facts of Scripture, on the one side, and the lives and deeds of the sages, on the other. Through their choice of topics and the points they made in telling stories about those topics, the sages found it possible to deliver with great power and enormous effect the syllogistic message of contemporary polemics that others presented in a more abstract and general mode of discourse. And that brings us to the issue at hand: the rabbinic formulation of the issues of 362–363.

We do not know what that response to those events was. We have no explicit reference in the sages' writings to the failure of the project. To be sure, from what the sages said on intersecting topics, we can readily reconstruct an appropriate response (if not one particular to the event). It is the one fully exposed in chapter five: the temple will be rebuilt when the Messiah comes, and not before. That is because the Messiah will only come when Israel attains that sanctification that the Torah requires, and the model of the sage provides the ideal for which Israel should strive. The attitude of mind required of Israel was humility and acceptance—humility before God and acceptance of the sages' authority. These attitudes,

[16] Robert L. Wilken, *John Chrysostom and the Jews: Rhetoric and Reality in the Late Fourth Century* (Berkeley: University of California Press, 1983), 155–58, cf. also 62–63.

joined with actions aimed at living the holy life, will in due course prove Israel worthy of the arrival of (receiving) the Messiah. That message, written across the pages of the Talmud of the Land of Israel (but not in any earlier rabbinic documents) assuredly addressed the crisis of disappointment.

But that generic response does not exhaust our options in recovering the rabbinic sages' comment on the fiasco of 362–363. A further question awaits its answer, the question natural to the documentary reading of matters set forth in section B of this chapter (see above, pages 94–99). It is as follows: When did the unfolding Judaic system of the sages, fully documented in the canon of rabbinic compilations from the Mishnah through the Babylonian Talmud (Bavli), recognize the destruction of the temple and the cessation of the cult as finalities of history? And what lessons do narratives of the destruction mean to teach? What we want to know, therefore, is: When, in the unfolding of the canonical documents, do narratives about the temple's destruction first make their appearance—and what are the lessons drawn from the narratives? When we know in which documents the destruction of the temple in 70 becomes a principal focus of interest—and in which documents the matter is ignored or treated in a routine manner—we can produce a measure of insight into the state of mind of the documents' compilers and the authors of the documents' compositions and composites.

The fourth-century calamity of starting the restoration and failing to complete it simply does not define the context and focus of the stories about the events of the first century. What we should expect is some sort of reflection, in the usual veiled terms to be sure, about the mistake of rebuilding the temple without God's explicit intervention. The closest we come to a comment that can pertain to the fiasco of 362–363 is the elliptical counsel contained in the following:

Song of Songs Rabbah XXIV:ii.1, 4–5

1. A. R. Yosé b. R. Hanina said, "The two oaths [Song 2:7: 'I adjure you, O daughters of Jerusalem,' and Song 3:5, 'I adjure you, O daughters of Jerusalem, by the gazelles or the hinds of the field'] apply, one to Israel, the other to the nations of the world.

   B. "The oath is imposed upon Israel that they not rebel against the yoke of the kingdoms.

   C. "And the oath is imposed upon the kingdoms that they not make the yoke too hard for Israel.

   D. "For if they make the yoke too hard on Israel, they will force the end to come before its appointed time."

4. A. R. Helbo says, "There are four oaths that are mentioned here [Song 2:7, 'I adjure you, O daughters of Jerusalem,' Song 3:5, 'I adjure you, O daughters of Jerusalem, by the gazelles or the hinds of the field,' Song 5:8, 'I adjure you, O daughters of Jerusalem, if you find my beloved, that you tell him I am sick with love,' Song 8:4, 'I adjure you, O daughters of Jerusalem, that you not stir up nor awaken love until it please'], specifically,

B. "he imposed an oath on Israel not to rebel against the kingdoms and not to force the end [before its time], not to reveal its mysteries to the nations of the world, and not to go up from the exile by force.

C. "For if so [that they go up from the exile by force], then why should the royal messiah come to gather together the exiles of Israel?"

5. A. R. Onia said, "The four oaths he imposed upon them corresponded to the four generations that forced the end before its time and stumbled in the effort.

B. "And what are they?

C. "Once in the days of Amram, once in the days of Dinai, once in the days of Koziba, and once in the days of Shutelah son of Abraham: 'The children of Ephraim were as archers handling the bow' (Ps. 78:9)."

D. Some say, "One in the days of Amram, once in the generation of the repression, once in the days of the son of Koziba, and once in the days of Shutelah son of Abraham: 'The children of Ephraim were as archers handling the bow' (Ps. 78:9)."

E. "For they were reckoning the hour from the time that the Holy One, blessed be He, made the decree when he speak with our father, Abraham, between the pieces [Gen. 15:13–17], but the time actually commenced from the moment at which Isaac was born.

F. "[Basing their actions upon this erroneous reckoning,] they assembled and went forth to battle and many of them fell slain.

G. "How come? 'Because they did not believe in the Lord and did not trust in his salvation' (Ps. 78:9),

H. "but they forced the end and violated the oath."

Of indeterminate date but generally assumed to belong in the period in which the Bavli took shape, *Song of Songs Rabbah* offers an inviting composite indeed. The promising passage concerns the four oaths: in the days of Amram, Koziba, Shutelah son of Abraham, and in the generation of the repression (after Bar Kokhba). But I see no basis for introducing the reconstruction of the temple in response to the ukase of a pagan emperor into the pattern. All cases represent Israel's own initiatives.

The project of 362–363 really does not match the admonition at hand, since Israel did not rebel against now-pagan Rome any more than Israel had rebelled against Cyrus. The rebuilding in both cases came about through the initiative of the pagan emperor, not of Israel's own undertaking. In the passage before us, Israel is admonished not to rebel against the nations and attempt on its own to recover Jerusalem and rebuild the temple. God will see to it at a time of his choosing and under the auspices not of a pagan king but of the Messiah. For our part, we may find here rueful reflection on what was learned from the failure of 362–363.

But the account before us hardly requires such a particular reading of matters, because the authors are perfectly able to specify examples, such as "Koziba"—and yet we do not find the case at hand. When Ben Koziba is represented in a messianic context, as we shall see in chapter five, he is in conflict with the rabbinic sages, not with pagan emperors. We do not confuse verisimilitude with identity; too many other reference-points present themselves to allow us to conclude that the sages at hand refer to Julian's project in particular. So here we might hear echoes of the events of 362–363 only if we knew that the Jews' share in the enterprise was undertaken by a Messiah-figure who opposed rabbinic opinion. We have no evidence of that allegation.

It would be tempting but ill-founded to present the stories of the destruction of the temple as evidence of the response to the failed project of 362–363; the documents came to closure well after that time. Only in the latest documents of rabbinic Judaism's formative age, the Talmud of Babylonia and its cognates, do we find narratives of the events of 70. Perhaps there is something to be learned from them about the fourth-century calamity?

Here too, formidable obstacles, both formal and substantive, stand in our way. The first formal obstacle is that the stories concern the destruction, not the rebuilding! The second is that they derive in one case from Babylonian documents, not those of the land of Israel. In the other case, the document is of indeterminate date and venue. So even on the surface they cannot be asked to attest to opinion held in the land of Israel in the late fourth and fifth centuries. We do not know that that is the case. But, more to the point, they represent the matter in other terms than those defined by the failed project, e.g., as adumbrated in the oaths of *Song of Songs Rabbah*. What they deemed the critical issue of 70 does not suggest anyone had in mind a false Messiah (as with Ben Koziba) or poor timing by reason of forcing God's hand (as with *Song of Songs Rabbah*'s four oaths). Then what is at stake and why introduce destruction-narratives at all? Let me frame matters to specify what counts in the present exercise.

Of interest is how documents address the events of the fourth century and deal with the theme raised by those events: It is in terms dictated by the interior concerns of the rabbinic sages. The narratives then prove asymmetrical to the events of the fourth century. They match other situations, events we can readily imagine (but can in no way document). What we do learn is how the rabbinic system, in its telling of the tales of the destruction, responds on its own terms and framework to events as portrayed in its own imagination, not in the terms and framework set forth by the fourth-century confrontation with Christian Rome (let alone the first-century confrontation with pagan Rome!).

What difference does it make? I have made much of the documentary reading of the figure of Rome. I now have the opportunity to show how such a reading might have yielded no determinate result, which underscores the compelling quality of the concrete results already reviewed. So what I present is a species of a null-hypothesis. If I am right in reading in the context of the advent of the Christian empire the fabrication of Rome by the cited midrash-compilations, then how would I know I was wrong? That is, what would the rabbinic compilations look like, if they dealt with issues comparable to those in play in the fourth century—but not in the framework of the meanings imputed to those events that to begin with made those events urgent? That answer is now clear. Here I show what is asymmetrical, so underscoring the symmetry of rabbinic sayings that I hold truly are symmetrical to events—the advent of Rome the brother, the illegitimate one for example.

We start from the beginning and establish our base-line for contrast. Chapters two and three have already established that for the Mishnah, Tosefta, and ʾAbot, the destruction of the temple is subsumed within the renewal of the scriptural paradigm. The dramatic accounts of the destruction as a singular event, complete with narratives of precisely what happened and why, make their appearance long after the failure of Julian's plan. One account makes its appearance in the second of the two Talmuds, Bavli, and the other account in its companion, *The Fathers According to Rabbi Nathan.* And the lesson to be learned from those stories concerns the priority of the rabbinic sage and the study of the Torah in which he engages, over the priesthood and the sacrifices they present. Israel endures in the schoolhouse, which (for the interim determined by God) succeeds the temple and sustains Israel until the arrival of the Messiah and the restoration of the temple. The destruction of the temple teaches the lesson that, from the loss of the second temple to the building of the third, Israel serves God in the schoolhouse, under the guidance of the rabbinic sage. The Messiah, himself a rabbinic sage, will eventually come in response to Israel's realization of the entire Torah on a single Sabbath—a matter of restoration of Eden in the end of days that will be taken up in context in chapter five.

Let me now present the two stories that take a paramount position in the documentary presentation of the destruction of the temple, the one in the Bavli (ca. 600 C.E.) and the other in *The Fathers According to Rabbi Nathan* (of no determinate date or venue but most likely belonging to the period of the Bavli). I give the Bavli's version in an abridged version, except where Yohanan ben Zakkai figures, and then I present in greater detail the destruction as portrayed in *The Fathers According to Rabbi Nathan,* where Yohanan ben Zakkai forms the focus. Italics represent the translation from the Aramaic in the original text, while plain type represents the translation from the Hebrew.

Here is the story as portrayed in the Talmud of Babylonia, which came to closure in ca. 600 C.E.:

Bavli *Giṭṭin* 55B–56A

I.2.A. Said R. Yohanan, "What is the meaning of the verse, 'Happy is the man who fears always, but he who hardens his heart shall fall into mischief' (Prov. 28:14)? On account of Qamsa and Bar Qamsa Jerusalem was destroyed, on account of a cock and a hen Tur Malka was destroyed, on account of a shaft of leather Betar was destroyed."

I.3.A. On account of Qamsa and Bar Qamsa Jerusalem was destroyed:

B. There was a man whose friend was Qamsa and whose enemy was Bar Qamsa. He made a party and said to his slave, "Go, invite Qamsa." He went and brought Bar Qamsa. The host came and found him seated. He said to him, "Since you're the one who tells stories about me, what in the world are you doing here. Get up, get out."

C. He said to him, "Since I've come, let me stay, and I'll pay you for whatever I eat and drink."

D. **[56A]** He said to him, "No."

E. He said to him, "Then I'll pay you half the cost of your whole banquet."

F. He said to him, "No."

G. He said to him, "I'll give you the whole cost of your banquet."

H. He said to him, "No." He grabbed him by the hand and took him and threw him out.

I. The man thought, "Since the rabbis were sitting right there and they didn't object, it follows that they're perfectly happy with such a thing. I'll go and report them to the government."

J. He went and told Caesar, "The Jews are rebelling against you."

K. He said to him, "How shall I know?"

L. He said to him, "Send them an offering. See if they offer it up!"

M. He went and sent with him a third-grown calf. On the way, he made a blemish on its upper lip—some say, in the white of the eye—in a place that we regard as a blemish but they don't.

N. Rabbis considered offering it up, to keep peace of the government. Said to them R. Zechariah b. Abequlos, "People will say, 'They're offering blemished animals on the altar.'"

O. They considered killing him, so that he wouldn't go and report what had happened.

P. Said to them R. Zechariah, "They will say, 'One who makes a blemish on Holy Things is to be put to death.'"

Q. Said R. Yohanan, "The excess of scruples of R. Zechariah b. Abequlos is what destroyed our house, burned our Temple, exiled us from our land."

I.4.A. The emperor sent against them Caesar Nero. As he was coming, he shot an arrow to the east and it went and fell on Jerusalem; he shot it to the west, and it came and fell on Jerusalem, and so in the four directions of the heavens, the arrow came and fell on Jerusalem.

B. He said to a child, "Tell me, what verse you are learning just now?"

C. He said to him, "'And I will lay my vengeance upon Edom by the hand of my people Israel' (Ezek. 25:14)."

D. He said, "It is the Holy One, blessed be He, who wants to destroy his house and then go and lay the blame on me." He ran away and fled and converted to Judaism, and from him came forth R. Meir.

I.5.A. He sent against them Caesar Vespasian. He came and besieged Jerusalem for three years. There were in the city three nobles, Naqdimon ben Gurion, Ben Kalba Sabua, and Ben Sisit Hakkeset.

B. Naqidmon ben Gurion: For the sun shown for him.

C. Ben Kalba Sabua: For whoever entered his house as hungry as a dog would go out stuffed.

D. Ben Sisit Hakkeset: For his show fringes would trail on cushions.

E. There are those who say: Because his seat was set among the nobles of Rome.

F. One of them said to them, "I shall provide food for them in wheat and barley," the next, "I will provide wine, oil, and salt" and the third, "I'll provide wood."

G. Rabbis praised most of all the offer of wood, for R. Hisda would hand over all his keys to his slave except for the key to the wood-shed, for R. Hisda would say, "A storehouse of wheat needs sixty storehouses of wood."

H. So these men had enough food for the city for twenty-one years.

I.6.A. There were zealots [biryoni] there. Said to them rabbis, "Let's go out and make peace with them."

B. They wouldn't let them.

C. They said to them, "Let's go out and make war with them."

D. Rabbis said, "Nothing good will come of it."

E. They went and burned the stores of wheat and barley, so there was a famine.

I.7.A. Marta bar Beitos was one of the richest women in Jerusalem. She sent for her messenger and said to him, "Go, bring me some fine flour." But by the time he went, it sold out.

B. He came and said to her, "There's no fine flour, but there's white flour."

C. She said to him, "Go bring that to me." But by the time he went, it sold out.

D. He came and said to her, "There's no white flour, but there's dark flour."

E. She said to him, "Go bring that to me." But by the time he went, it sold out.

F. He came and said to her, "There's no dark flour, but there's barley flour."

G. She said to him, "Go bring that to me." But by the time he went, it sold out.

H. In the meantime she had taken off her shoes. She said, "I'll go out and see whether I can find something to eat." Some dung stuck to her foot and she died.

I. Rabban Yohanan ben Zakkai recited in her regard the verse, "The tender and delicate woman among you, who would not venture to set the sole of her foot upon the open ground . . . ' (Deut. 28:57).

J. There are those who say, "She ate a date left by R. Sadoq and got sick and died."

I.8.A. For R. Sadoq sat in fasts for forty years that Jerusalem not be destroyed. When he ate something, the food could be seen as it passed through his throat. When he wanted to get well, they would bring him a fig, and he would suck the juice and toss out the rest.

I.9.A. When she was dying, she brought out all the gold and silver and threw it into the marketplace, saying, "What in the world do I need this for?"

B. That is in line with the verse, "They will throw their silver into the streets" (Ezek. 7:19).

I.10.A. Abba Siqara was the chief of the zealots in Jerusalem. He was the son of Rabban Yohanan b. Zakkai's sister. He sent word to him, "Come to me in secret."

B. He came.

C. He said to him, "How long are you going to act in this way and kill everybody through famine?"

D. He said to him, "What should I do? If I say anything to them, they'll kill me, too."

E. He said to him, "Find some sort of remedy for me to get out of here, maybe there will be the possibility of saving something."

F. He said to him, "Pretend to be sick, and have everybody come and ask about you; have something bad smelling and put it by you, so people will think you're dead. Then let your disciples carry you— but nobody else—so that no one will feel that you're still light, since people know that a living being is lighter than a corpse."

G. They did so. R. Eliezer came in at one side, and R. Joshua at the other. When they got to the gate, they wanted to stab him. He said to them, "People will say they stabbed their master." They wanted to shove him over the wall. He said to them, "People will say they shoved their master [over the wall]." They opened the gate for him, and he got out.

H. When he got there, he said, "Peace be unto you, O king, peace be unto you, O king."

I. He said to him, "You are subject to the death penalty on two counts; first of all, I'm not a king, and you called me king; second, if I really am king, then how come you didn't come to me up till now?"

J. He said to him, "As to your statement, 'I'm not king,' **[56B]** the truth is you really are king, because if you weren't king, then Jerusalem wouldn't have been handed over to you, for it has been written, 'Lebanon shall fall by a mighty one' (Isa. 10:34), and 'mighty one' refers only to a king, in line with the verse, 'And their mighty one shall be of themselves' (Jer. 30:21). Not only so, but Lebanon speaks of the Temple, 'This goodly mountain and Lebanon' (Deut. 3:25). And as to what you have said, 'If I really am king, then how come you didn't come to me up till now?' up to now, the zealots among us wouldn't let me come."

K. He said to him, "So if there's a jar of honey, with a lizard wrapped around it, wouldn't you break the honey to get rid of the lizard?"

L. He shut up.

M. R. Joseph, and some say, R. Aqiba, recited in his regard: "'God turns wise men backward and makes their knowledge foolish' (Isa. 44:25). He ought to have said to him, 'We would take a pair of tongs and grab the lizard and kill it but leave the jar whole.'"

N. In the meantime an agent [parastak/frestak] came to him from Rome. He said to him, "Arise, for the Caesar is dead, and the citizens of Rome propose to enthrone you at the head."

O. At that moment he had finished putting on one boot. He wanted to put on the other, but it wouldn't go on. He wanted to take off that one, but it wouldn't go off. He said, "What's going on?"

P. He said to him, "Don't be distressed. Good news has come to you, for it is written, 'Good news makes the bone fat' (Prov. 15:30). So what's the solution? Bring someone you despise and let him walk before you: 'A broken spirit dries up the bones' (Prov. 17:22)." He did so and the boot went on.

Q. He said to him, "Well, if you're so smart, how come you didn't come to me before now?"

R. He said to him, "Well, didn't I already tell you?"

S. He said to him, "So I told you, too!"

T. He said to him, "Now I'm going away, and I'm sending someone else. So ask something from me, which I'll give you."

U. He said to him, "Give me Yavneh and its sages, and the chain of Rabban Gamaliel, and a physician to heal R. Sadoq."

V. R. Joseph, and some say, R. Aqiba, recited in his regard the verse, "'God turns wise men backward and makes their knowledge foolish' (Isa. 44:25). He ought to have said to him to leave the place alone this time." But he thought that maybe that much he won't do, and there would not be the possibility of saving anything at all.

I.11.A. What was the healing that the physicians brought to R. Sadoq? On the first day they gave him to drink water in which bran had been soaked, on the next, water in which coarse meal had been soaked, on the next day, water in which flour had been mixed, so that his stomach grew little by little.

I.12. A. He went and sent Titus, who said, "'Where is their God, the rock in whom they trusted?' (Deut. 32:37)."

B. This is that wicked Titus, who blasphemed and raged against Heaven. What did he do? He took a whore by her hand, and went into the house of the Holy of Holies; he spread out a scroll of the Torah, and on it he ravished her.

C. He took a sword and slashed the curtain.

D. A miracle was done, and blood spurted out. He thought he had killed himself: "Your adversaries have roared in the midst of your assembly, they have set up their ensigns for signs" (Ps. 74:4).

E. Abba Hanan said, "'Who is a mighty one like you, O Lord' (Ps. 89:9)—who is like you in having so thick a skin that you could hear the blaspheming and raging of that wicked man and keep dumb?"

F. The household of R. Ishmael set forth this Tannaite statement: "'Who is like you among the gods' (Ex. 15:11)—who is like you among the dumb [the word for dumb and gods sharing the same consonants]."

G. What did he do? He took the veil and made it into a kind of basket, and he brought all the utensils that were in the sanctuary and put them in it, and he set them onto a boat to go to serve in his triumph his city: "And withal I saw the wicked buried, and they that come to the grave and they that had done right went away from the holy place and were forgotten in the city' (Qoh. 8:10)—don't read the letters that spell buried in that way, but rather, as 'collected'; don't read the letters that spell 'and were forgotten' in that way, but rather, 'and served as a triumph.'"

H. There are those who say, "They were literally buried. For even things that were buried were revealed to them."

I. A gale arose at sea, to swamp him. He said, "It appears to me that the god of these people is mighty only through water. Pharaoh came along, and he drowned him in water. Sisera came along, and he drowned him in water. So he's now standing against me to drown me in water. So if he's so mighty, let him come up onto dry land and make war with me there."

J. An echo came forth and said to him, "Wicked man, son of a wicked man, son of the wicked Esau, I have a small creature in my world, called a gnat."

K. Why is it called a gnat? Because it has a little aperture for taking in but not for excreting.

L. "Disembark on dry land and go, make war with it."

M. He disembarked on dry land. A gnat came and entered his nostril and picked away at his brain for seven years.

N. One day he was going by the gate of a smithy, the gnat heard the sound of the hammer and stopped gnawing. He said, "So I see, there's a solution." So every day they brought a smithy, and he hammered before him. To a gentile smithy they gave four zuz, to an Israelite he said, "Just enjoy the satisfaction of seeing your enemy's suffering."

O. This went on for thirty days. From that point, the creature got used to it [following Simon].

Now let us consider the version of the same event as portrayed in *The Fathers According to Rabbi Nathan,* a commentary on tractate ʾAbot lacking a determinate date but possibly of the period of the Bavli:

The Fathers According to Rabbi Nathan IV:vi.1

A. Now when Vespasian came to destroy Jerusalem, he said to [the inhabitants of the city,] "Idiots! why do you want to destroy this city and burn the house of the sanctuary? For what do I want of you, except that you send me a bow or an arrow [as marks of submission to my rule], and I shall go on my way."

B. They said to him, "Just as we sallied out against the first two who came before you and killed them, so shall we sally out and kill you."

C. When Rabban Yohanan ben Zakkai heard, he proclaimed to the men of Jerusalem, saying to them, "My sons, why do you want to destroy this city and burn the house of the sanctuary? For what does he want of you, except that you send him a bow or an arrow, and he will go on his way."

D. They said to him, "Just as we sallied out against the first two who came before him and killed them, so shall we sally out and kill him."

E. Vespasian had stationed men near the walls of the city, and whatever they heard, they would write on an arrow and shoot out over the wall. [They reported] that Rabban Yohanan ben Zakkai was a loyalist of Caesar's.

F. After Rabban Yohanan ben Zakkai had spoken to them one day, a second, and a third, and the people did not accept his counsel, he sent and called his disciples, R. Eliezer and R. Joshua, saying to them, "My sons, go and get me out of here. Make me an ark and I shall go to sleep in it."

G. R. Eliezer took the head and R. Joshua the feet, and toward sunset they carried him until they came to the gates of Jerusalem.

H. The gatekeepers said to them, "Who is this?"

I. They said to him, "It is a corpse. Do you not know that a corpse is not kept overnight in Jerusalem."

J. They said to them, "If it is a corpse, take him out," so they took him out and brought him out at sunset, until they came to Vespasian.

K. They opened the ark and he stood before him.

L. He said to him, "Are you Rabban Yohanan ben Zakkai? Indicate what I should give you."

M. He said to him, "I ask from you only Yavneh, to which I shall go, and where I shall teach my disciples, establish prayer [Goldin: a prayer house], and carry out all of the religious duties."

N. He said to him, "Go and do whatever you want."

O. He said to him, "Would you mind if I said something to you."

P. He said to him, "Go ahead."

Q. He said to him, "Lo, you are going to be made sovereign."

R. He said to him, "How do you know?"

S. He said to him, "It is a tradition of ours that the house of the sanctuary will be given over not into the power of a commoner but of a king, for it is said, And he shall cut down the thickets of the forest with iron, and Lebanon [which refers to the Temple] shall fall by a mighty one (Is. 10:34)."

T. People say that not a day, two or three passed before a delegation came to him from his city indicating that the [former] Caesar had died and they had voted for him to ascend the throne.

U. They brought him a catapult and drew it up against the wall of Jerusalem.

V. They brought him cedar beams and put them into the catapult, and he struck them against the wall until a breach had been made in it. They brought the head of a pig and put it into the catapult and tossed it toward the limbs that were on the Temple altar.

W. At that moment Jerusalem was captured.

X. Rabban Yohanan ben Zakkai was in session and with trembling was looking outward, in the way that Eli had sat and waited: Lo, Eli sat upon his seat by the wayside watching, for his heart trembled for the ark of God (1 Sam. 4:13).

Y. When Rabban Yohanan ben Zakkai heard that Jerusalem had been destroyed and the house of the sanctuary burned in flames, he tore his garments, and his disciples tore their garments, and they wept and cried and mourned.

As is clear, the two versions of the same event differ. Let us consider the differences.

The focus of the Bavli's story is not on Yohanan b. Zakkai, who takes a subordinate part. It provides a cause for the catastrophe, explaining who brought the Romans down on the Jews. *The Fathers According to Rabbi Nathan* does not address that issue. The story in the Bavli further stresses the zealots' destruction of the stores of food and drink and fuel, then proceeds to the story of Martha, yielding the homily on Deut 28:5 and then turns to Sadoq. Yohanan is introduced only by making him an uncle of the head of the zealots, who is the principal actor in this version. The initiatives all belong to Abba Sikra, who tells Yohanan what to do. The disciples of Abba Sikra ("he") have the wit to get Yohanan out safely. Yohanan does nothing to impress Vespasian, and gets little enough from him.

The Bavli's version of events does not accomplish what the version of *The Fathers According to Rabbi Nathan* does, which is to place the sage into the balance as the opposite and equal of the emperor and Israel's principal actor and active intellect. What is fresh and indicative in *The Fathers According to Rabbi Nathan*? The sage takes the central part: he undertakes all initiatives and he does more than merely react to the decisions and errors of others. He moreover forms the bridge from temple to Torah by rising from his bier and pointing toward a center of Torah-study as the next step, out of Jerusalem. He further identifies a surrogate for the offerings, so long as the temple lies in ruins, in acts of lovingkindness—a doctrine that, in concrete deed, forms the counterpart to the sages' stress on the tamed emotions, conciliatory attitude, and ethic of self-abnegation (characteristic of both *m. ʾAbot* and *The Fathers According to Rabbi Nathan*), as well as of the other accounts of the same theme elsewhere.

Of the stories about the destruction of the temple, none of them occurs in the Mishnah, Tosefta, *m. ʾAbot*, or the other documents that reached closure prior to 400. Among the eighty-eight distinct components of which the tradition and legend of Yohanan ben Zakkai is composed, his role in the encounter with Vespasian figures in these: (1) Zechariah 11:1 predicted the destruction, first in Bavli; (2) Isaiah 14:14 and the destruction of the first temple, first in Bavli; (3) escape in a coffin, first in *The Fathers According to Rabbi Nathan;* and (4) the temple rites are really hocus pocus, first in the *Pesiqta deRab Kahana.* This last item carries us to the fifth century and to the land of Israel, so it is worth notice:

Pesiqta deRab Kahana IV:vii.5

A. A gentile asked Rabban Yohanan ben Zakkai, saying to him, "These rites that you carry out look like witchcraft. You bring a cow and slaughter it, burn it, crush the remains, take the dust, and if one of you contracts corpse uncleanness, you sprinkle on him two or three times and say to him, 'You are clean.' "

B. He said to him, "Has a wandering spirit never entered you?"

C. He said to him, "No."

D. He said to him, "And have you ever seen someone into whom a wandering spirit entered?"

E. He said to him, "Yes."

F. He said to him, "And what do you do?"

G. He said to him, "People bring roots and smoke them under him and sprinkle water on the spirit and it flees."

H. He said to him, "And should your ears not hear what your mouth speaks? So this spirit is the spirit of uncleanness, as it is written, 'I will cause prophets as well as the spirit of uncleanness to flee from the land'" (Zech. 13:2)."

I. After the man had gone his way, his disciples said to him, "My lord, this one you have pushed off with a mere reed. To us what will you reply?"

J. He said to them, "By your lives! It is not the corpse that imparts uncleanness nor the water that effects cleanness. But it is a decree of
the Holy One, blessed be He.

K. "Said the Holy One, blessed be He, 'A statute have I enacted, a
decree have I made, and you are not at liberty to transgress
my decree: "This is the statute of the Torah" (Num. 19:1).' "

Whatever is at stake in this colloquy, one issue seems remarkably remote: the restoration of the temple and its animal sacrifices! Yohanan ben
Zakkai, the principal figure of rabbinic lore in the events of 70, is here represented as dismissing as beyond all rationality the rite of temple purification that Scripture prescribes. I see no point of intersection between that
issue and the aborted project of 362–363.

What lesson do the stories of the destruction in Bavli and *The Fathers
According to Rabbi Nathan* register? They portray Yohanan ben Zakkai, the
sage of sages, as the critical figure in both predicting the destruction of the
temple and then forming the bridge between the destruction and the continuing life of Israel through the way of the Torah. The issue is the pri-
macy of the sage in Israel's movement from temple to the age beyond,
and the message is that all things depend on the sage and his Torah. The
story of *Pesiqta deRab Kahana* is congruent with that message.

Where then do we find the issue that animates the rabbinic narratives, and is that issue particular to the fiasco of 362–363? We may say that
the account of Israel's history as embodied in the figure of the sage—who
balances and outweighs the emperor, who embodies Rome's history—
makes its original appearance in the narratives of the destruction. I find
the key in the particular role of the sage in opposition to the emperor:
Yohanan ben Zakkai and Vespasian embodying Israel and Rome, respectively. The sage-versus-emperor representation of matters comes late in
the unfolding of the rabbinic canon. It forms part of the sages' conventional policy vis-à-vis secular authority, whether Jewish, in the form of the
exilarch (for Babylonia) or patriarch (for the land of Israel), or pagan. That
issue not only is not particular to the fiasco of 362–363, it in no way
intersects with that event.

What about the Messiah? When we wish to find a context in which
the sage confronts a secular, military authority treated as a (or the) Messiah, it is in the Yerushalmi's account of Bar Kokhba's conduct in 132–135
(which we will meet in chapter five). There the point is that Israel should
place its hopes in the sage and the Torah, not in Israel's own military
power; the temple restoration does not figure. At issue then is the coming
of the Messiah through the ministry of the Rabbi-sage: "Today, if you will
it" (as we shall see). The upshot is that the sage now forms the model of Israel's salvation, and, therefore, also the definition of the Messiah and
other eschatological components of Judaism.

The destruction-narratives, as I argue, show us how matters appear when we ask documents to respond to determinate events. Sometimes the documents yield significant data; sometimes they do not. The null-hypothesis accompanying the affirmative results for Rome in Talmud and Midrash is now fully exposed: we know what failure looks like, so we can recognize success when we find it. Simply stated: the tension and its resolution in the two destruction-narratives do not require our introducing the events of 362–363. They do not even sustain doing so. What is at stake is an issue of salvific theology. Who saves Israel? It is not the emperor but his counterpart, the sage. That conclusion (to us banal and commonplace) then points toward the further theological principle that the sage stands for Israel's salvation, with the consequence that the Messiah will be the quintessential sage, just as the later rabbinic-compilations represent David as a rabbi. The many stories about the sagacity of David (therefore of the Messiah)—his mastery of the Torah, his formation in the model of the ideal sage—point toward profound reflection on Israel's true history and destiny. These stories do not respond to the particularities of the events of Julian's reign. And in the rabbinic compilations of the late fourth and fifth centuries, we have no others that pertain.

Rabbinic Judaism and the Meaning of History

Where do we now stand? It is at the juncture between the penta-teuchal-mishnaic system and the events of the fourth century, a turning point in the formation of rabbinic Judaism. The approach of the pentateuchal-mishnaic system to cataclysmic events cannot have proved commensurate to the issues. No stoic indifference, no policy of patient endurance could shelter Israel, the Jewish people, from the events that swept over them. For if Constantine had become a Christian, if Julian's promise of rebuilding the temple had produced nothing, if Christian emperors had secured control of the Empire for Christ and even abridged long-standing rights and immunities of Israel, as they did, then what hope could possibly remain for Israel? Of greater consequence: was not history vindicating the Christian claim that God had saved humanity through the suffering people of God, the Church? Christians believed that the conversion of Constantine and the Roman government proved beyond a doubt that Christ was King-Messiah. For Israel, the interpretation of the political happenings of the day required deep thought about the long-term history of humanity. Conceptions of history carried with them the most profound judgments on the character of the competing nations: Israel, and the Christians, a third race, a no-people—as some called themselves—now become the regnant nation, the Church.

The scriptural record of Israel, shared by both parties to the dispute, took as its premise a single fact. When God wished to lay down a judgment, he did so through the medium of events. History, composed of singular events, therefore spoke God's message. Prophets found vindication through their power to enunciate and even (in the case of Moses) to make, and change, history. Revealing God's will, history moreover consisted of a line of one-time events, all of them heading in a single direction—a line that began at creation and will end with redemption or salvation.

Both parties—Judaic sages and Christian theologians —proposed to answer one and the same question: what does it all mean? Specifically, how shall we interpret the momentous events of the day? Which events matter? What patterns do we discern in them? And what, finally, do they prove? The rabbinic sages effectively framed a doctrine of history and an eschatological teleology that responded to these questions. We now turn to these matters.

5

Symmetries: History and Messiah in the Talmudic-Midrashic System

History Returns and Rabbinic Judaism Takes Shape

A set of documents that accomplished the complete union of the pentateuchal system, with its historical mode of thought and expression, and the mishnaic system built upon, but asymmetrical with, the pentateuchal system defined the outcome of the crisis of the fourth century. In these documents—the Talmud of the Land of Israel (the Yerushalmi or Jerusalem Talmud) and its associated midrash-compilations *(Genesis Rabbah* and *Leviticus Rabbah)*—the pentateuchal and the pentateuchal-mishnaic systems once more were made symmetrical. The pentateuchal engagement with history found its counterpart in the talmudic interest in selected events and their lessons. The systemic teleology came to expression, now, in eschatological terms, embodied by the figure of the Messiah. Matching these two systems helped create the fully articulated system of rabbinic Judaism, encompassing both history and eschatology. This Judaic system for Israel's social order taught that Israel should attain sanctification in the here and now, in line with the Mishnah's focus, so as to merit salvation at the end of days, in line with the pentateuchal belief in messianic eschatology that its use of the medium of historical narrative invited.

But rendering the systems symmetrical took place on the Mishnah's own terms: the realization of norms of conduct as a means of attaining sanctification. Consequently, Judaism was to emerge from late antiquity richly eschatological, obsessed with the Messiah and his coming, engaged by the history of Israel and the nations. Judaism at the end of late antiquity did indeed provide an ample account and explanation of Israel's history and destiny—but in terms of sanctification. In rabbinic Judaism, then, the end of days would come when all Israel kept a single Sabbath. "Today, if you will it," and similar sayings underscored that the sanctification of Israel would bring on the salvific fulfillment, as we shall see.

When constructing a systematic account of Judaism—that is, the worldview and way of life for Israel presented in the Mishnah—the philosophers of the Mishnah did not use the Messiah myth in constructing a teleology for their system. They found it possible to present a statement of goals for their projected life of Israel that was separate from appeals to history and eschatology. They certainly knew, and even alluded to, long-standing and widely held eschatological beliefs beginning with those in Scripture, but the framers nevertheless made choices different from others, both before and after them. Their document reflects these choices, both affirmative and negative.

The appearance of a messianic eschatology fully consonant with other characteristics of the rabbinic system—its stress on the viewpoints and prooftexts of Scripture, its interest in what was happening to Israel, its focus upon the national-historical dimension of the life of the group—indicates that, in its mythic repertoire, the later encompassing rabbinic system stands essentially autonomous of the prior, mishnaic system. True, what had gone before was absorbed and fully assimilated. But the rabbinic system first appearing in the Talmud of the Land of Israel is different in the aggregate from the mishnaic system. It represents more, however, than a negative response to its predecessor. The rabbinic system of the two Talmuds, emerging in the first of the two at the end of the fourth century, took over the Mishnah's fundamental worldview about the importance of Israel's constructing for itself a life beyond time. The rabbinic system then transformed the Messiah myth in its totality into an essentially ahistorical force. If people wanted to reach the end of time, they had to rise above time (that is, history) and stand off at the side of great political and military, that is, historical events.

That is the message of the Messiah myth as it reaches full exposure in the rabbinic system of the two Talmuds. At its foundation, it is precisely the message of teleology without eschatology expressed by the Mishnah and its associated documents. Accordingly, we cannot claim that the rabbinic or talmudic system in this regard constitutes a reaction against the mishnaic one. We must conclude, quite to the contrary, that in the Talmuds and their associated documents we see the restatement in classical-mythic form of the ontological convictions that had informed the minds of the second-century philosophers. The new medium contained the old and enduring message: Israel must turn away from time and change, submitting to whatever happens, so as to win for itself the only government worth having—that is, God's rule, accomplished through God's anointed agent, the Messiah.

The Conception of History in the Talmud of the Land of Israel

The Talmud of the Land of Israel—a commentary to thirty-nine of the Mishnah's sixty-two tractates—takes events seriously and treats as unique and remarkable those happenings it deems eventful. There we find, first, a willingness to include events of far greater diversity than those in the Mishnah, and second, an interest in the periodization of history.

First, the broadening of the definition of consequential events: So far as things happen that demand attention and so constitute "events," within the Mishnah these fall into two classifications: (1) biblical history, and (2) events involving the temple. In the Yerushalmi, by contrast, we also find two other sorts of stories: (1) Torah-events, that is, important stories about the legal and supernatural doings of rabbis, and also (2) political events, e.g., including Rome, Israel's wars with Rome, and the Messiah. These events, moreover, involved people not considered in the Mishnah: gentiles as much as Jews, Rome as much as Israel.

The Mishnah's history, such as it is, knows only Israel. The Yerushalmi greatly expands the range of historical interest when it develops a theory of Rome's relationship to Israel and, of necessity also, Israel's relationship to Rome. Only by taking account of the world at large can the Talmud's theory of history yield a philosophy of history worthy of the name—that is, an account of who Israel is, the meaning of what happens to Israel, and the destiny of Israel both in this world and at the end of time. Israel by itself—as the Torah had claimed—lived in eternity, beyond time. But Israel and Rome together struggled in historical time: an age with a beginning, a middle, and an end. That is the importance of the expanded range of historical topics found in the present Talmud. In the Bavli we find a still broader interest, in Persia as much as Rome, in the sequence of world empires past and present; there we see how rich and encompassing a theory of historical events begins with a simple step toward a universal perspective. It was a step that the authors of the Mishnah were incapable of taking.

And second, the concept of periodization—the raw material of historical thought—hardly presents surprises, since apocalyptic writers began their work by differentiating one age from another. When the Mishnah includes a statement (*m. Zebaḥ.* 10:4–8) of the "periods" into which time is divided, however, it speaks only of stages of the cult: Shiloh, Nob, Jerusalem. One age is differentiated from the next not by reference to world-historical changes but only by the location of the sacrificial sanctuary. The rules governing each locale impose taxa upon otherwise undifferentiated time. So periodization constitutes a function of the larger system of sanctification through sacrifice. The contrast between "this world" and "the world to come," which is not a narrowly historical conception in the Mishnah, now finds a counterpart in the Talmud's contrast between "this age" and "the age in which the Temple stood." And that distinction is very much an act of this-worldly historical differentiation. It not only yields apocalyptic speculation, but also generates sober and worldly reflection on the movement of events and the meaning of history in the prophetic-apocalyptic tradition. Accordingly, the Yerushalmi presents both the expected amplification of the established concepts familiar from the Mishnah, and also a separate set of ideas—perhaps rooted in prior times, but still autonomous of what the Mishnah in particular had encompassed.

From the viewpoint of the Mishnah, the single most unlikely development is interest in the history of any nation other than Israel. For the Mishnah, the world beyond the sacred land was unclean, tainted in particular with corpse-uncleanness: Outside the holy lies the realm of death. Only within the range of the sacred do things happen. There, events may be classified and arranged, all in relationship to the temple and its cult. But, standing majestically unchanged by the vicissitudes of time, the cult rises above history. But it is just such an interest in the history of the great empires of the world—perceived, to be sure, in relationship to the history of Israel—that reemerges within the framework of the documents that succeeded the Mishnah. Naturally, in the land of Israel in the fourth century only one empire mattered: Rome, which the Yerushalmi viewed solely as the counterpart to Israel. The world then consists of two nations: Israel, the weaker, and Rome, the stronger. Jews enjoy a sense of vastly enhanced importance when they contemplate such a world, containing as it does only two peoples that matter, of whom one is Israel. But from our perspective, the utility for the morale of the defeated people holds no interest. What strikes us is the evidence of the formation of a second and separate system of historical interpretation, beyond that of the Mishnah.

History and doctrine merge, with history made to yield doctrine. What is stunning is the perception of Rome as an autonomous entity, with a point of origin and a tradition of wisdom, just as Israel has. These are the two points at which the large-scale conception of historical Israel finds a counterpart in the present literary composition. This sense of poised opposites, Israel and Rome, comes to expression in two ways. The first is that it is Israel's own history that calls into being its counterpoint, the anti-history of Rome. Without Israel, there would be no Rome—a wonderful consolation to the defeated nation. For if Israel's sin created Rome's power, then Israel's repentance will bring Rome's downfall. Here is the way in which the Talmud presents the match:

Yerushalmi ʿAbodah Zarah 1:2.i.4

E. Saturnalia means "hidden hatred" [sina'ah temunah]: [The Lord] hates, takes vengeance, and punishes.

F. This is in accord with the following verse: "Now Esau hated Jacob" (Gen. 27:41).

G. Said R. Isaac b. R. Eleazar, "In Rome they call it Esau's Saturnalia."

H. Kratesis: It is the day on which the Romans seized power.

K. Said R. Levi, "It is the day on which Solomon intermarried with the family of Pharaoh Necho, King of Egypt. On that day Michael came down and thrust a reed into the sea, and pulled up muddy alluvium, and this was turned into a huge pot, and this was the great city of Rome. On the day on which Jeroboam set up the two golden calves, Remus and Romulus came and built two huts in the city of Rome. On the day on which Elijah disappeared, a king was appointed in Rome: "There was no king in Edom, a deputy was king" (1 Kings 22:47).

The important point here is that Solomon's sin is seen as provoking Heaven's founding of Rome. Thus we have history, lived by Israel, and anti-history, provoked by Israel and lived out by Rome. Quite naturally, the conception of history and anti-history will assign to the actors in the anti-history (i.e., the Romans) motives explicable in terms of history (i.e., the history of Israel). The entire world and what happens in it enter into the framework of meaning established by Israel's Torah. So what the Romans do—their historical actions—can be explained in terms of Israel's conception of the world.

The most important change is the shift in historical thinking adumbrated in the pages of the Yerushalmi, a shift from focus upon the temple and its supernatural history to close attention to the people, Israel, and its natural, this-worldly history. Once Israel, holy Israel, had come to form the counterpart to the temple and its supernatural life, that other history—Israel's—would stand at the center of things. Accordingly, a new sort of memorable event came to the fore in the Talmud of the Land of Israel. It was the story of the suffering of Israel, and remembering of that suffering, on the one side, and the effort to explain events of that tragic kind, on the other. So a composite "history" constructed out of the Yerushalmi's units of discourse pertinent to consequential events would contain long chapters on what happened to Israel, the Jewish people—and not only (or even mainly) what had earlier occurred in the temple.

This expansion in the range of historical interest and theme forms the counterpart to the emphasis throughout the law of Judaism (Mishnah, Tosefta, Yerushalmi, and Bavli) upon the enduring sanctity of the people Israel, which paralleled the sanctity of the temple. What is striking in the Yerushalmi's materials on Israel's suffering is the sages' interest in finding a motive for what the Romans had done. That motive derived specifically from the repertoire of explanations already available in Israelite thought. In adducing scriptural reasons for the Roman policy, sages extended to the world at large that same principle of intelligibility, in terms of Israel's own Scripture and logic that, in the law itself, made everything sensible and reliable. So the labor of history-writing (or at least, telling stories about historical events) went together with the work of lawmaking. The whole formed a single exercise in explanation of things that had happened—that is, historical explanation. True, one enterprise involved historical events, the other legal constructions. But the outcome was one and the same.

Clearly, for the authors of Yerushalmi, as much as for the ancient prophets, history taught lessons, and in their view, Israel had best learn the lesson of its history. When it did so, it also would take command of its own destiny. So the stakes were very high. What lesson, precisely, did Israel need to learn? Stated first negatively, then positively, the framers of Yerushalmi were not telling the Jews to please God by fulfillng commandments in order to gain control of their own destiny. On the contrary, the paradox of the Yerushalmi's system lies in the fact that Israel frees itself from control by other nations only by humbly agreeing to accept God's rule instead.

The heavy weight of prophecy, apocalyptic, and biblical historiography, with their emphasis upon history as the indicator of Israel's salvation, stood against the Mishnah's quite separate thesis of what truly mattered. What, from the rabbinic viewpoint, demanded description and analysis and required interpretation? It was the category of *sanctification,* for eternity. The true issue framed by history and apocalypse was how to move toward salvation, how to act in this-worldly time so as to attain salvation at the end of time. The Mishnah's teleology beyond time, its capacity to posit an eschatology completely lacking a historical Messiah—these take a position beyond the imagination of the entire antecedent sacred literature of Israel. Only one strand or stream, the priestly one, had ever taken so extreme a position on the centrality of sanctification and the peripherality of salvation. Wisdom had stood in between: by drawing attention both to what happened and to what endured it pointed toward the significance of eschatological salvation. But to wisdom, what ultimately mattered was not nature or supernature, but rather abiding relationships in historical time.

Genesis Rabbah and Israel's History

Israel's sages in *Genesis Rabbah* and the great Church historian Eusebius have much in common: Both went back to beginnings. Both parties wanted to draw lessons for present and future history seeking meaning for their own times from the history of former times, from the story of the beginnings of the world and of Israel. To that end, they proposed to identify the patterns in events that would convey the will of God for Israel. The issue was the same, the premise the same, the facts the same; only the conclusions differed. In the initial encounter, in the age of Constantine, therefore, the Judaic philosophers of history and the Christians represented by Eusebius conducted a genuine argument, with different people talking to each other about essentially the same thing.

The common ground was the book of Genesis. In looking to the past to explain the present, the Judaic sages turned to the story of the beginnings of creation, humanity, and Israel found in Genesis. In doing so, they addressed precisely the same range of historical questions that occupied Eusebius: Where did it all start? Both parties shared the supposition that if we can discern beginnings, we can understand the end. The Israelite sages took up the beginnings that, to Eusebius too, marked the original pattern for ongoing history. Sages, of course, would not have added what to Eusebius was critical: "Where did it all start—now that we know where it was all heading all the time?" Sages could not imagine, after all, the events of their own day marked the goal and climax of historical time. Rome formed a single episode, not the end. But then, sages had to state what they thought constituted the real history of the world and of Israel.

The book of Genesis became the principal mode of historical reflection and response for the sages of the age. They chose that book to deal in precisely the same manner and setting with exactly the same questions that occupied Eusebius: to understand the end (for Eusebius) or critical turning (for the sages), one must look back to the beginning. In fact, in the present context of debate, *only* the book of Genesis could have served both parties so well. For Eusebius, the end would impart its judgment of the meaning of the beginning: this is where things all along had been heading. For the sages of *Genesis Rabbah*, the beginning would tell us where, in time to come, things will end up. That is the point on which the parties differed, making it possible to reconstruct their argument.

The Israelite sages took up the beginnings that marked the original pattern for ongoing history. Sages could not imagine, after all, that what had happened in their own day marked the goal and climax of historical time. Rome formed an episode, not the end. But then, sages had to state what they thought constituted the real history of the world and of Israel.

Accordingly, sages read Genesis as the history of the world with an emphasis on Israel. The lives portrayed, the domestic quarrels and petty conflicts with the neighbors, all yield insight into what was to be. Why? Because the deeds of the patriarchs taught lessons about how the children were to act, and, it further followed, the lives of the patriarchs signaled the history of Israel. The nation of Israel constituted one extended family, and the metaphor of the family imparted the character of a family record to the stories of Genesis. History–become–genealogy conveyed the message of salvation. These propositions really laid down the same judgment—one for the individual and the family, the other for the community and the nation—since there was no differentiating. Every detail of the narrative therefore served to prefigure what was to be, and Israel found itself, time and again, in the revealed facts of the history of the creation of the world, the decline of humanity down to the time of Noah, and, finally, its ascent to Abraham, Isaac, and ultimately Israel.

What are the laws of history, and, more important, how do they apply to the crisis at hand? The principal message of the story of the beginnings, as sages read Genesis, is that the world depends upon the *zekhut* or legacy of acts of uncoerced self-sacrifice or merit, produced by Abraham, Isaac, and Jacob; Israel, for its part, enjoys access to that unearned grace, being today the descendants of the patriarchs and matriarchs. That conception of matters constitutes the sages' doctrine of history: the family forms the basic and irreducible historical unit. Israel is not so much a nation as a family, and the heritage of the patriarchs and matriarchs sustains that family from the beginning even to the end. The sages read history as genealogy, effecting the symbolization of the conflict between (Christian) Rome and eternal Israel through family relationships. The rivalry of the twin brothers Esau and Jacob then contains the history of the fourth century—from sages' viewpoint a perfectly logical mode of historical reflection. That, then, expresses the main viewpoint of history in *Genesis Rabbah*.

Genesis now is read as both a literal statement and also as an effort to prefigure the history of Israel's suffering and redemption. Ishmael, now standing for Christian Rome, claims God's blessing, but Isaac gets it, as Jacob will take it from Esau. Details, as much as the main point, yielded laws of history. In the following passage, the sages take up the detail of Rebecca's provision of "a little water," showing what that act had to do with Israel's later history. The passage at hand is somewhat protracted, but it contains in a whole and cogent way the mode of thought and the results: salvation is going to derive from the *zekhut* of the matriarchs and patriarchs.

Genesis Rabbah XLVIII:x.2

A. "Let a little water be brought" (Gen. 18:4):

B. Said to him the Holy One, blessed be he, "You have said, 'Let a little water be brought' (Gen. 18:4). By your life, I shall pay your descendants back for this: 'Then sang Israel this song, "spring up O well, sing you to it"' (Num. 21:7)."

C. That recompense took place in the wilderness. Where do we find that it took place in the land of Israel as well?

D. "A land of brooks of water" (Deut. 8:7).

E. And where do we find that it will take place in the age to come?

F. "And it shall come to pass in that day that living waters shall go out of Jerusalem" (Zech. 14:8).

G. ["And wash your feet" (Gen. 18:4)]: [Said to him the Holy One, blessed be he,] "You have said* 'And wash your feet.' By your life, I shall pay your descendants back for this: 'Then I washed you in water' (Ez. 16:9)."

H. That recompense took place in the wilderness. Where do we find that it took place in the land of Israel as well?

I. "Wash you, make you clean" (Is. 1:16).

J. And where do we find that it will take place in the age to come?

K. "When the Lord will have washed away the filth of the daughters of Zion" (Is. 4:4).

L. [Said to him the Holy One, blessed be he,] "You have said, 'And rest yourselves under the tree' (Gen. 18:4). By your life, I shall pay your descendants back for this: 'He spread a cloud for a screen' (Ps. 105:39)."

M. That recompense took place in the wilderness. Where do we find that it took place in the land of Israel as well?

N. "You shall dwell in booths for seven days" (Lev. 23:42).

O. And where do we find that it will take place in the age to come?

P. "And there shall be a pavilion for a shadow in the daytime from the heat" (Is. 4:6).

Q. [Said to him the Holy One, blessed be he,] "You have said, 'While I fetch a morsel of bread that you may refresh yourself' (Gen. 18:5). By your life, I shall pay your descendants back for this: 'Behold I will cause to rain bread from heaven for you' (Ex. 16:45)."

R. That recompense took place in the wilderness. Where do we find that it took place in the land of Israel as well?

S. "A land of wheat and barley" (Deut. 8:8).

T. And where do we find that it will take place in the age to come?

U. "He will be as a rich grain field in the land" (Ps. 82:6).

V. [Said to him the Holy One, blessed be he,] "You ran after the herd ['And Abraham ran to the herd' (Gen. 18:7)]. By your life, I shall pay your descendants back for this: 'And there went forth

a wind from the Lord and brought across quails from the sea'
(Num. 11:27)."

W. That recompense took place in the wilderness. Where do we find
that it took place in the land of Israel as well?

X. "Now the children of Reuben and the children of Gad had a very
great multitude of cattle" (Num. 32:1).

Y. And where do we find that it will take place in the age to come?

Z. "And it will come to pass in that day that a man shall rear a young
cow and two sheep" (Is. 7:21).

AA. [Said to him the Holy One, blessed be he,] "You stood by them:
'And he stood by them under the tree while they ate' (Gen. 18:8).
By your life, I shall pay your descendants back for this: 'And the
Lord went before them' (Ex. 13:21)."

BB. That recompense took place in the wilderness. Where do we find
that it took place in the land of Israel as well?

CC. "God stands in the congregation of God" (Ps. 82:1).

DD. And where do we find that it will take place in the age to come?

EE. "The breaker is gone up before them . . . and the Lord at the head
of them" (Mic. 2:13).

The passage presents a sizable and beautifully disciplined construction, making one point again and again: Everything that the matriarchs
and patriarchs did brought a reward to their descendants. The enormous
emphasis on the way in which Abraham's deeds prefigured the history of
Israel—in the wilderness, in the land, and, finally, in the age to come—
provokes us to wonder who held that there were children of Abraham besides Israel. The answer then is clear. We note that there are five statements of the same proposition, each drawing upon a clause in the base
verse. The extended statement moreover serves as a sustained introduction to the treatment of the individual clauses that now follow, item by
item. The rabbinic sages now understood the meaning of what had happened back then, and, from what had happened then, they also grasped
the sense and direction of events of their own day.

So history yielded patterns, patterns proved points, and the points
at hand indicated the direction of Israel. The substance of historical doctrine remains social in its focus. Sages present their theory of the meaning
of history within a larger theory of the identification of Israel. Specifically,
they see Israel as an extended family, children of one original ancestral
couple, Abraham and Sarah. Whatever happens, then, constitutes family
history, which is why the inheritance of zekhut from the ancestors protects
their children even now, in the fourth century C.E. In this typological read-

ing, Israel's history takes place under the aspect of eternity. Events do not take place one time only; in order to make a difference and so to matter, events must constitute paradigms and generate patterns. Salvation is all the same; its particularization is all that history records. The lessons of history therefore do not derive from sequences of unique moments but from patterns that generate recurring and reliable rules. Accordingly, sages read the present in light of the past, rather than reading the past in light of the present. Given their despondent present circumstances, they had little choice.

Sages found a place for Rome in Israel's history only by assigning to Rome a place in the family. Their larger theory of the social identity of Israel left them no choice. But it also permitted them to assign to Rome an appropriately significant place in world history, while preserving for Israel the climactic role. Jacob struggles with Esau and Isaac plays his part in the matter. Rome does have a legitimate claim, and that claim demands recognition—an amazing, if grudging concession—on the part of sages that Christian Rome at least is Esau.

Genesis Rabbah LXVII:iv.1–2

1. A. "When Esau heard the words of his father, he cried out with an exceedingly great and bitter cry [and said to his father, 'Bless me, even me also, O my father!']" (Gen. 27:34):

   B. Said R. Hanina, "Whoever says that the Holy One, blessed be he, is lax, may his intestines become lax. While he is patient, he does collect what is coming to him."

   C. "Jacob made Esau cry out one cry, and where was he penalized? It was in the castle of Shushan: 'And he cried with a loud and bitter cry' (Est. 4:1)."

2. A. "But he said, 'Your brother came with guile and he has taken away your blessing'" (Gen. 27:35):

   B. R. Yohanan said, "[He came] with the wisdom of his knowledge of the Torah."

So Rome really *is* Israel's brother. No other pagan empire ever enjoyed an equivalent place; no other pagan era ever found identification with an event in Israel's family history. The passage presents a stunning concession and an astounding claim. The history of the two brothers forms a set of counterpoints, the rise of one standing for the decline of the other. There can be no more powerful claim for Israel: the ultimate end, Israel's final glory, will mark the permanent subjugation of Esau. Israel then will follow, as the fifth and final monarchy (of Dan 7:9–14). The point of section 1 in the passage above is to link the events of Genesis to the history of Israel's later redemption. In this case, however, the matter concerns Israel's paying recompense for causing anguish to Esau. The second section above introduces Jacob's knowledge of Torah in place of Esau's view of Jacob as full of guile.

From Scripture's Historical Thinking to Rabbinic Judaism's Paradigmatic Structure

The Hebrew Scriptures set forth Israel's life as history: it had a beginning, middle, and end, a purpose and a coherence, a teleological system. The Bible distinguished past from present and present from future—and it composed a sustained narrative, made up of one-time, irreversible events. In Scripture's historical portrait, Israel's present condition appealed for explanation to Israel's past, perceived as a coherent sequence of weighty events, each unique, all formed into a great chain of meaning. The rabbinic sages, by contrast, found in Scripture's words paradigms of an enduring present, by which all things must take their measure; they possessed no conception whatsoever of the absolute pastness of the past. In other words, the modes of thought that governed the Mishnah guided sages' reading of Scripture as well. Rabbinic Judaism in the Yerushalmi and cognate midrash-compilations kept all time—past, present, and future—within a single framework. For that purpose, a model was constructed, with selected events forming a pattern that imposes order and meaning on the chaos of what happens, whether past, present, or future. The paradigm obliterates distinctions between past, present, and future, between here and now and then and there. The past participates in the present, the present recapitulates the past, and the future finds itself determined—predetermined really—within the same free-standing structure comprised by God's way of telling time.

One paradigm is marked by the history of humanity set forth in Scripture: Eden, then after Eden; or Adam vs. Israel, Eden vs. the land; Adam's fall vs. Israel's loss of the land. The sages will impose a further, critical variable on the pattern of Eden vs. land of Israel, Adam vs. Israel, and that is: Sinai. A pattern then will recognize the divisions of time between pre-Sinai and post-Sinai. These general definitions should be made still more concrete in the setting of rabbinic Judaism. Let me give a single example of paradigmatic time, in contrast to the conceptions of time that govern in the Hebrew Scriptures. The character of paradigmatic thinking in the mishnaic manner about history and time is captured in the following passage, which encompasses the entirety of Israel's being (its "history," in conventional language) within the conversation that is portrayed between Boaz and Ruth. I abbreviate the passage to highlight only the critical components:

Ruth Rabbah Parashah V:XL.i.1–5

1. A. "And at mealtime Boaz said to her, 'Come here and eat some bread, and dip your morsel in the wine.' So she sat beside the reapers, and he passed to her parched grain; and she ate until she was satisfied, and she had some left over":

   B. R. Yohanan interested the phrase "come here" in six ways:

   C. "The first speaks of David.

   D. "'Come here:' means, to the throne: 'That you have brought me here' (2 Sam. 7:18).

   E. "'. . . and eat some bread:' the bread of the throne.

   F. "'. . . and dip your morsel in vinegar:' this speaks of his sufferings: 'O Lord, do not rebuke me in your anger' (Ps. 6:2).

   G. "'So she sat beside the reapers:' for the throne was taken from him for a time."

   I. "'and he passed to her parched grain:' he was restored to the throne: 'Now I know that the Lord saves his anointed' (Ps. 20:7).

   J. "'. . . and she ate and was satisfied and left some over:' this indicates that he would eat in this world, in the days of the messiah, and in the age to come.

2. A. "The second interpretation refers to Solomon: 'Come here:' means, to the throne.

   B. "'. . . and eat some bread:' this is the bread of the throne: And Solomon's provision for one day was thirty measures of fine flour and three score measures of meal' (1 Kgs. 5:2).

   C. "'. . . and dip your morsel in vinegar:' this refers to the dirty of the deeds [that he did].

   D. "'So she sat beside the reapers:' for the throne was taken from him for a time."

   G. "'and he passed to her parched grain:' for he was restored to the throne.

   H. "'. . . and she ate and was satisfied and left some over:' this indicates that he would eat in this world, in the days of the messiah, and in the age to come.

3. A. "The third interpretation speaks of Hezekiah: 'Come here:' means, to the throne.

   B. "'... and eat some bread:' this is the bread of the throne.

   C. "'... and dip your morsel in vinegar:' this refers to sufferings [Is. 5:1]: 'And Isaiah said, Let them take a cake of figs' (Is. 38:21).

   D. "'So she sat beside the reapers:' for the throne was taken from him for a time: 'Thus says Hezekiah, This day is a day of trouble and rebuke' (Is. 37:3).

   E. "'... and he passed to her parched grain:' for he was restored to the throne: 'So that he was exalted in the sight of all nations from then on' (2 Chr. 32:23).

   F. "'... and she ate and was satisfied and left some over:' this indicates that he would eat in this world, in the days of the messiah, and in the age to come.

4. A. "The fourth interpretation refers to Manasseh: 'Come here:' means, to the throne.

   B. "'... and eat some bread:' this is the bread of the throne.

   C. "'... and dip your morsel in vinegar:' for his dirty deeds were like vinegar, on account of wicked actions.

   D. "'So she sat beside the reapers:' for the throne was taken from him for a time: 'And the Lord spoke to Manasseh and to his people, but they did not listen. So the Lord brought them the captains of the host of the king of Assyria, who took Manasseh with hooks' (2 Chr. 33:10–11)."

   K. "'and he passed to her parched grain:' for he was restored to the throne: 'And brought him back to Jerusalem to his kingdom' (2 Chr. 33:13).

   N. "'... and she ate and was satisfied and left some over:' this indicates that he would eat in this world, in the days of the messiah, and in the age to come.

5. A. "The fifth interpretation refers to the Messiah: 'Come here:' means, to the throne.

   B. "'... and eat some bread:' this is the bread of the throne.

   C. "'... and dip your morsel in vinegar:' this refers to suffering: 'But he was wounded because of our transgressions' (Is. 53:5).

D. "'So she sat beside the reapers:' for the throne is destined to be taken from him for a time: 'For I will gather all nations against Jerusalem to battle and the city shall be taken' (Zech. 14:2).

E. "' . . . and he passed to her parched grain:' for he will be restored to the throne: 'And he shall smite the land with the rod of his mouth' (Is. 11:4)."

G. "Just as the first redeemer was revealed and then hidden from them"

I. "so the last redeemer will be revealed to them and then hidden from them."

The paradigm here may be formed of these units: (1) David's reign; (2) Solomon's reign; (3) Hezekiah's reign; (4) Manasseh's reign; (5) the Messiah's reign. So paradigmatic time compresses events to the dimensions of its model. All things happen on a single plane of time. Past, present, and future are undifferentiated, and that is why a single action contains within itself an entire account of Israel's social order under the aspect of eternity.

The foundations of the paradigm, of course, rest on the fact that David, Solomon, Hezekiah, Manasseh (and, therefore, also the Messiah) all descend from the union of Ruth and Boaz. Then, within the framework of the paradigm, the event that is described here—"And at mealtime Boaz said to her, 'Come here and eat some bread, and dip your morsel in the vinegar.' So she sat beside the reapers, and he passed to her parched grain; and she ate until she was satisfied, and she had some left over" (Ruth 2:14)—forms not an *event* but a *pattern,* counterpart to a mishnaic case. The pattern transcends time; or more accurately, aggregates of time, the passage of time, the course of events—these are all simply irrelevant to what is in play in Scripture. Rather we have a tableau, joining persons who lived at widely separated moments, linking them all as presences at this simple exchange between Boaz and Ruth; imputing to them all, whenever they came into existence, the shape and structure of that simple moment: the presence of the past, for David, Solomon, Hezekiah, and so on, but also the pastness of the present in which David or Solomon—or the Messiah for that matter—lived or would live (it hardly matters, verb tenses prove hopelessly irrelevant to paradigmatic thinking). As in the Mishnah's approach to history, here too, time is simply ignored. A variety of interpretations of the passage may yield a range of paradigms but the model of paradigmatic time will remain one and the same. The paradigm serves to select events endowing them with order and meaning, structure and familiarity. Paradigmatic time, like mishnaic hierarchical classification, organizes events in patterns, and invokes a model that everywhere pertains.

The rabbinic sages found in Scripture a set of paradigms that served without regard to circumstance or context. A very small number of models, all of which emerged from Scripture, governed. These are (1) Eden and Adam, (2) Sinai and the Torah, (3) the land and the people Israel, and (4) the temple and its building, destruction, rebuilding. These paradigms served severally and jointly: for example, Eden and Adam on its own but also superimposed upon the land and Israel; Sinai and the Torah on its own but also superimposed upon the land and Israel; the temple, on its own or superimposed upon any and all of the other paradigms. In many ways, then, we have the equivalent of a set of two- and three- or even four-dimensional grids. A given pattern forms a grid on its own, one set of lines being set forth in terms of, for example, Eden (that is, timeless perfection) in contrast to the other set of lines, such as Adam (that is, temporal disobedience). But upon that grid, a comparable grid can be superimposed, the land and Israel being an obvious one; and upon the two, yet a third and fourth, Sinai and Torah, temple and the confluence of nature and history.

Any paradigmatic case—personality, event, idea—imposes structure and order on all data; and the structure will be the same for the small and the large, the now and the then. By that criterion of paradigmatic structuring of "history," we should be able to tell the story of Israel's past, present, and future, by appeal to any identified model, and we need not predict which model will yield what pattern, for the patterns are always the same, whatever the choice of the model. In the following example, we are able to define the paradigm of Israel's history out of the lives of the founders of the Israelite tribes. The tribal progenitors moreover correspond to the kingdoms that will rule over Israel, so there is a correspondence of opposites. In the following, as the single best formulation of paradigmatic thinking in the rabbinic canon, Israel's history is taken over into the structure of Israel's life of sanctification, and all that happens to Israel forms part of the structure of holiness built around cult, Torah, synagogue, sages, Zion, and the like; I give only a small part:

Genesis Rabbah LXX:viii.2–3, 5, 7

2. A. "As he looked, he saw a well in the field:"

C. "'As he looked, he saw a well in the field:' this refers to the well [of water in the wilderness, Num. 21:17].

D. "'. . . and lo, three flocks of sheep lying beside it:' specifically, Moses, Aaron, and Miriam.

E. "'. . . for out of that well the flocks were watered:' from there each one drew water for his standard, tribe, and family."

F. "And the stone upon the well's mouth was great:"

G. Said R. Hanina, "It was only the size of a little sieve."

H. [Reverting to Hama's statement:] "'. . . and put the stone back in its place upon the mouth of the well:' for the coming journeys. [Thus the first interpretation applies the passage at hand to the life of Israel in the wilderness.]

3. A. "'As he looked, he saw a well in the field:' refers to Zion.

B. "'. . . and lo, three flocks of sheep lying beside it:' refers to the three festivals.

C. "'. . . for out of that well the flocks were watered:' from there they drank of the holy spirit.

D. "'. . . The stone on the well's mouth was large:' this refers to the rejoicing of the house of the water-drawing."

E. Said R. Hoshaiah, "Why is it called 'the house of the water drawing'? Because from there they drink of the Holy Spirit."

F. [Resuming Hama b. Hanina's discourse:] "'. . . and when all the flocks were gathered there:' coming from 'the entrance of Hamath to the brook of Egypt' (1 Kgs. 8:66).

G. "'. . . the shepherds would roll the stone from the mouth of the well and water the sheep:' for from there they would drink of the Holy Spirit.

H. "'. . . and put the stone back in its place upon the mouth of the well:' leaving it in place until the coming festival. [Thus the second interpretation reads the verse in light of the temple celebration of the Festival of Tabernacles.]

5. A. "'As he looked, he saw a well in the field:' this refers to Zion.

B. "'. . . and lo, three flocks of sheep lying beside it:' this refers to the first three kingdoms [Babylonia, Media, Greece].

C. "'. . . for out of that well the flocks were watered:' for they enriched the treasures that were laid upon up in the chambers of the Temple.

D. "'. . . The stone on the well's mouth was large:' this refers to the merit attained by the patriarchs.

E. "'. . . and when all the flocks were gathered there:' this refers to the wicked kingdom, which collects troops through levies over all the nations of the world.

F. "'. . . the shepherds would roll the stone from the mouth of the well and water the sheep:' for they enriched the treasures that were laid upon up in the chambers of the Temple.

G. "'. . . and put the stone back in its place upon the mouth of the well:' in the age to come the merit attained by the patriarchs will stand [in defense of Israel]." [So the fourth interpretation interweaves the themes of the Temple cult and the domination of the four monarchies.]

7. A. "'As he looked, he saw a well in the field:' this refers to the synagogue.

B. "'. . . and lo, three flocks of sheep lying beside it:' this refers to the three who are called to the reading of the Torah on weekdays.

C. "'. . . for out of that well the flocks were watered:' for from there they hear the reading of the Torah.

D. "'. . . The stone on the well's mouth was large:' this refers to the impulse to do evil.

E. "'. . . and when all the flocks were gathered there:' this refers to the congregation.

F. "'. . . the shepherds would roll the stone from the mouth of the well and water the sheep:' for from there they hear the reading of the Torah.

G. "'. . . and put the stone back in its place upon the mouth of the well:' for once they go forth [from the hearing of the reading of the Torah] the impulse to do evil reverts to its place." [The sixth and last interpretation turns to the twin themes of the reading of the Torah in the synagogue and the evil impulse, temporarily driven off through the hearing of the Torah.]

So much for the correlation of the structures of the social and cosmic order with the condition of Israel. In the passage just reviewed, paradigms take over the organization of events. Time is no longer sequential and linear. What endures are the structures of cosmos and society: prophets, Zion, Sanhedrin, holy seasons, and on and on. Clearly, the one thing that plays no role whatsoever in this tableau and frieze is Israel's linear history; past and future take place in an eternal present.

Even in this new, paradigmatic reading of history—which subverted the biblical mode of thought—Scripture nonetheless defined how matters were to be understood. Scripture laid matters out, and the sages then drew conclusions from that layout that conformed to their own experience. The second destruction, then, precipitated thinking about paradigms of Israel's life: the midrash-compilations we have surveyed reflect the aftermath of the fiasco precipitated by the Emperor Julian in 362–363. The events of the fourth century stretched the paradigm in different ways than the ones of 586 had, because the sages brought to Scripture different premises and drew from Scripture different conclusions. But in point of fact, not a single paradigm set forth by sages can be distinguished in any important component from the counterpart in Scripture—not Eden and Adam in comparison to the land of Israel and Israel, and not the tale of Israel's experience in the spinning out of the tension between the word of God and the will of Israel.

The upshot is simple. Israel's own deeds defined the events of history. Rome's role, like Assyria's and Babylonia's before, depended upon Israel's provoking divine wrath to be executed by the great empire. Israel had to learn the lesson of its history to also take command of its own destiny. But this notion of determining one's own destiny should not be misunderstood. The framers of the Talmud of the Land of Israel were not telling the Jews that by doing commandments they would gain control of their own destiny. On the contrary, the paradox of Yerushalmi's system lies in the fact that Israel can free itself of control by other nations only by humbly agreeing to accept God's rule. The nations—Rome, in the present instance—rest on one side of the balance, while God rests on the other. Israel must then choose between them. There is no such thing for Israel as freedom from both God and the nations, total autonomy and independence. There is only a choice of masters: a ruler on earth or a ruler in heaven.

The Messiah Comes to Rabbinic Judaism

The Messiah-theme, trivial in the Mishnah, moves to the forefront in the Yerushalmi. Texts that expose a fully-realized Messiah-doctrine first surface in the unfolding of the rabbinic canon, in the Yerushalmi. That correlates with the same document's keen interest in history and its patterns. While the Mishnah provided a teleology without eschatology, the framers of the Yerushalmi and related midrash-compilations could not conceive of any but an utterly eschatological goal. Accordingly, historical events entered into the construction of a teleology for the Yerushalmi's system of Judaism as a whole.

What the law demanded reflected the consequences of wrongful action on the part of Israel. So, again, Israel's own deeds defined the events of history. Rome's role, like Assyria's and Babylonia's, depended upon Israel's provoking divine wrath as it was executed by the great empires. This mode of thought comes to simple expression in what follows.

Yerushalmi *'Erubin* 3:9.i.4

B. R. Ba, R. Hiyya in the name of R. Yohanan: "Do not gaze at me because I am swarthy, because the sun has scorched me. My mother's sons were angry with me, they made me keeper of the vineyards; but, my own vineyard, I have not kept!" [Song 1:6]. What made me guard the vineyards? It is because of not keeping my own vineyard.

C. What made me keep two festival days in Syria? It is because I did not keep the proper festival day in the Holy Land.

D. "I imagined that I would receive a reward for the two days, but I received a reward only for one of them.

E. "Who made it necessary that I should have to separate two pieces of dough-offering from grain grown in Syria? It is because I did not separate a single piece of dough-offering in the land of Israel."

Israel had to learn the lesson of its history to also take command of its own destiny. But what that lesson was would come to full realization only in the exposition of the Messiah-theme. The framers of the Mishnah will certainly have concurred with propositions such as these. And why not? For the fundamental affirmations of the Mishnah about the centrality of Israel's perfection in stasis—sanctification—readily prove congruent to the attitudes at hand. Once the Messiah's coming had become dependent upon Israel's condition (and not upon Israel's actions in historical time), then the Mishnah's system will have imposed its fundamental and definitive character upon the Messiah-myth. An eschatological teleology framed through that myth then would prove wholly appropriate to the Mishnah's overall method. That is for a simple, striking reason. The Messiah-theme is made to repeat, in its terms, the doctrine of virtuous attitudes and emotions that prevail throughout; the condition of the coming of the Messiah is Israel's humility, its submission to the tides and currents of history. What, after all, makes a Messiah a false Messiah? In this Talmud, it is not his claim to save Israel, but his claim to save Israel without the help of God. The meaning of the true Messiah is Israel's total submission, through the Messiah's gentle rule, to God's yoke and service.

Keeping the commandments as a mark of submission, loyalty, and humility before God defines the rabbinic system of salvation, as much as it sets forth the pentateuchal-mishnaic system of sanctification. So Israel does not "save itself;" Israel never completely controls its own destiny, either on earth or in heaven. The only choice is whether to cast one's fate into the hands of cruel, deceitful men, or to trust in the living God of mercy and love. The stress that Israel's arrogance alienates God, whereas Israel's humility and submission win God's favor, cannot surprise us. We shall now see how this position is spelled out in the setting of discourse about the Messiah in the Talmud of the Land of Israel.

In the Yerushalmi we first see the emblematic stories of the failed Messiah of the second century, Bar Kokhba (Ben Kozeba), as he exemplifies arrogance against God. He lost the war against Rome because of that arrogance. His emotions, attitudes, sentiments, and feelings form the model of how the virtuous Israelite is not to conceive of matters. In particular, he ignored the authority of sages:

Yerushalmi *Ta^canit* 4:5.vii.1

J. Said R. Yohanan, "Upon orders of Caesar Hadrian, they killed eight hundred thousand in Betar."

K. Said R. Yohanan, "There were eighty thousand pairs of trumpeters surrounding Betar. Each one was in charge of a number of troops. Ben Kozeba was there and he had two hundred thousand troops who, as a sign of loyalty, had cut off their little fingers.

L. "Sages sent word to him, 'How long are you going to turn Israel into a maimed people?'

M. "He said to them, 'How otherwise is it possible to test them?'

N. "They replied to him, 'Whoever cannot uproot a cedar of Lebanon while riding on his horse will not be inscribed on your military rolls.'

O. "So there were two hundred thousand who qualified in one way, and another two hundred thousand who qualified in another way."

P. When he would go forth to battle, he would say, "Lord of the world! Do not help and do not hinder us! 'Hast thou not rejected us, O God? Thou dost not go forth, O God, with our armies'" (Ps. 60:10).

Q. Three-and-a-half years did Hadrian besiege Betar.

R. R. Eleazar of Modiin would sit on sackcloth and ashes and pray every day, saying "Lord of the ages! Do not judge in accord with strict judgment this day! Do not judge in accord with strict judgment this day!"

S. Hadrian wanted to go to him. A Samaritan said to him, "Do not go to him until I see what he is doing, and so hand over the city [of Betar] to you. [Make peace . . . for you.]"

T. [The Samaritan] got into the city through a drainpipe. He went and found R. Eleazar of Modiin standing and praying. He pretended to whisper something in his ear.

U. The townspeople saw [the Samaritan] do this and brought him to Ben Kozeba. They told him, "We saw this man having dealings with your friend."

V. [Bar Kokhba] said to him, "What did you say to him, and what did he say to you?"

W. He said to [the Samaritan], "If I tell you, then the king will kill me, and if I do not tell you, then you will kill me. It is better that the king kill me, and not you.

X. "[Eleazar] said to me, 'I should hand over my city.' ['I shall make peace . . .']"

Y. He turned to R. Eleazar of Modiin. He said to him, "What did this Samaritan say to you?"

Z. He replied, "Nothing."

AA. He said to him, "What did you say to him?"

BB. He said to him, "Nothing."

CC. [Ben Kozeba] gave [Eleazar] one good kick and killed him.

DD. Forthwith an echo came forth and proclaimed the following verse:

EE. "Woe to my worthless shepherd, who deserts the flock! May the sword smite his arm and his right eye! Let his arm be wholly withered, his right eye utterly blinded! [Zech. 11:17].

FF. "You have murdered R. Eleazar of Modiin, the right arm of all Israel, and their right eye. Therefore may the right arm of that man wither, may his right eye be utterly blinded!"

GG. Forthwith Betar was taken, and Ben Kozeba was killed.

That kick—an act of temper, a demonstration of untamed emotions— tells the whole story. We notice two complementary themes. First, Bar Kokhba treats heaven with arrogance, asking God merely to keep out of the way. Second, he treats an especially revered sage with a parallel arrogance. The sage had the power to preserve Israel. Bar Kokhba destroyed Israel's one protection. The result was inevitable.

In the sages' view Israel had to choose between wars, either the war fought by Bar Kokhba or the "war for Torah." "Why had they been punished? It was because of the weight of the war, for they had not wanted to engage in the struggles over the meaning of the Torah" (y. Ta῾an. 3:9).

Those struggles, which were ritual arguments about ritual matters, promised the only victory worth winning. Then Israel's history would be written in terms of wars over the meaning of the Torah and the decision of the law. The Talmud of Babylonia would then declare that the principal result of Israel's loyal adherence to the Torah and its religious duties will be Israel's humble acceptance of God's rule. The humility, under all conditions, makes God love Israel.

Bavli *Ḥullin* VI:7.i.7

A. Said R. Abba, "How severe is the sin of a theft of something that is consumed. For even the completely righteous cannot return it. As it says, 'I will take nothing but what the young men have eaten, [and the share of the men who went with me; let Aner, Eshcol, and Mamre take their share]' (Gen. 14:24)."

B. Said R. Yohanan in the name of R. Eleazar b. R. Simeon, "Everywhere you find the words of R. Eliezer the son of R. Yosé the Galilean, make your ear like a funnel [to receive them]."

C. [He said], "It was not because you were more in number than any other people that the Lord set his love upon you and chose you, for you were the fewest of all peoples" (Deut. 7:7). Said the Holy One Blessed be He to Israel, "I adore you. For even at the time that I bestow upon you greatness, you humble yourselves before me.

D. "I bestowed greatness upon Abraham and he said before me, 'I am but dust and ashes' (Gen. 18:27). [I bestowed greatness upon] Moses and Aaron and they said, 'What are we? Your murmurings are not against us but against the Lord' (Exod. 16:8). [I bestowed greatness upon] David and he said, 'But I am a worm, and no man' (Ps. 22:6).

E. "But the idolaters are not [humble] like this.

F. "I bestowed greatness upon Nimrod and he said, 'Come let us build ourselves a city, and a tower with its top in the heavens, and let us make a name for ourselves . . .' (Gen. 11:4).

G. "[I bestowed greatness upon] Pharaoh and he said, 'Who is the Lord?' (Exod. 5:2).

H. "[I bestowed greatness upon] Sennacherib and he said, 'Who among all the gods of the countries have delivered their countries out of my hand, that the Lord should deliver Jerusalem out of my hand?' (II Kings 18:35).

I. "[I bestowed greatness upon] Nebuchadnezzar and he said, 'I will ascend above the heights of the clouds, I will make myself like the Most High' (Is. 14:14).

J. "[I bestowed greatness upon] Hiram king of Tyre and he said, 'I am a god, I sit in the seat of the gods, in the heart of the seas' (Ezek. 28:2)."

The issue of the Messiah and the meaning of Israel's history framed through the Messiah-myth, is here consistent with its presentation elsewhere in the rabbinic canon. The heart of the matter is Israel's subservience to God's will, as expressed in the Torah and embodied in the teachings and lives of the great sages. When Israel fully accepts God's rule, then the Messiah will come. Until that time, the Jews will be subjugated to pagan domination.

Israel can act to redeem itself through the opposite of self-determination, namely, by subjugating itself to God. Israel's power lies in its negation of power. Its destiny lies in giving up all pretense at deciding its own destiny. So weakness is the ultimate strength, forbearance the final act of self-assertion, passive resignation the sure step toward liberation. Israel's freedom is engraved on the tablets of the commandments of God: to be free is freely to obey.

The passage, praising Israel for its humility, completes the circle begun with the description of Bar Kokhba as arrogant and boastful. Gentile kings are boastful; Israelite kings are humble. The theory of Israel's history and destiny as it was expressed within the Messiah-myth interprets matters in terms of a single criterion. Whatever other notions existed within the Israelite world about God sending a (or the) Messiah at the end of time to "save" Israel, it was a single idea for the rabbinic sages. And that conception stands at the center of their system; it shapes and is shaped by their system. In context, the Messiah expresses the system's meaning and so makes it work.

The rabbinic system of the Talmuds and Midrash then transformed the Messiah-myth in its totality into an essentially ahistorical force. If Israel wanted to reach the end of time, they had to rise above time, that is, history, and stand off at the side of great movements of political and military character. That is the full-blown message of the Messiah-myth. At its foundation it is precisely the message of teleology without eschatology expressed by the Mishnah and its associated documents. In the Talmuds and their associated documents we see the restatement in classical-mythic form of the ontological convictions that had informed the minds of the second-century philosophers. The new medium contained the old and enduring message: Israel must turn away from time and change, submit to whatever happens, so as to win for itself the only government worth having, that is, God's rule, accomplished through God's anointed agent, the Messiah.

Once the figure of the Messiah has appeared, there arises discussion on who, among the living, the Messiah might be. The identification of the

Messiah begins with the person of David himself: "If the Messiah-King comes from among the living, his name will be David. If he comes from among the dead, it will be King David himself" (*y. Ber.* 2:2.4.2.3.A). A variety of evidence announced the advent of the Messiah as a figure in the larger system of formative Judaism. The rabbinization of David constitutes one kind of evidence. Serious discussion, within the framework of the accepted documents of mishnaic exegesis and the law, concerning the identification and claim of diverse figures asserted to be Messiahs, presents still more telling proof.

Yerushalmi *Berakot* 2:4
(Translated by Tzvee Zahavy)

A. Once a Jew was plowing and his ox snorted once before him. An Arab who was passing and heard the sound said to him, "Jew, loosen your ox and loosen the plow and stop plowing. For today your Temple was destroyed."

B. The ox snorted again. He [the Arab] said to him, "Jew, bind your ox and bind your plow, for today the Messiah-King was born."

C. He said to him, "What is his name?"

D. "Menahem."

E. He said to him, "And what is his father's name?"

F. The Arab said to him, "Hezekiah."

G. He said to him, "Where is he from?"

H. He said to him, "From the royal capital of Bethlehem in Judea."

I. The Jew went and sold his ox and sold his plow. And he became a peddler of infant's felt-cloths [diapers]. And he went from place to place until he came to that very city. All of the women bought from him. But Menahem's mother did not buy from him.

J. He heard the women saying, "Menahem's mother, Menahem's mother, come buy for your child."

K. She said, "I want to bring him up to hate Israel. For on the day he was born, the Temple was destroyed."

L. They said to her, "We are sure that on this day it was destroyed, and on this day of the year it will be rebuilt."

M. She said to the peddler, "I have no money."

N. He said to her, "It is of no matter to me. Come and buy for him and pay me when I return."

O. A while later he returned to that city. He said to her, "How is the infant doing?"

P. She said to him, "Since the time you saw him a spirit came and carried him away from me."

Q. Said R. Bun, "Why do we learn this from [a story about] an Arab? Do we not have explicit scriptural evidence for it? 'Lebanon with its majestic trees will fall' (Is. 10:34). And what follows this? 'There shall come forth a shoot from the stump of Jesse' (Is. 11:1). [Right after an allusion to the destruction of the temple the prophet speaks of the Messianic age.]"[1]

This is a set-piece story, adduced to prove that the Messiah was born on the day the temple was destroyed. Since the Messiah was born when the temple was destroyed, God had prepared for Israel a better fate than had appeared.

A more concrete matter—the identification of the Messiah with a known historical personality—was associated with the name of Akiba, in the *y. Ta'an.* text below. He is said to have claimed that Bar Kokhba, leader of the second-century revolt, was the Messiah. The important aspect of the story, however, is the rejection of Akiba's view. The discredited Messiah figure (if Bar Kokhba actually was such in his own day) finds no apologists in the later rabbinical canon. What is striking in what follows, moreover, is that we really have two stories. At section G Akiba is said to have believed that Bar Kokhba was a disappointment. In sections H–I, he is said to have identified Bar Kokhba with the King-Messiah. Both cannot be true, so what we have is simply two separate opinions of Akiba's judgment of Bar Kokhba/Bar Kozeba.

Yerushalmi *Ta'anit* 4:5.iv

G. R. Simeon b. Yohai taught, "Aqiba, my master, would interpret the following verse: 'A star (kokhab) shall come forth out of Jacob' (Num. 24:17). 'A disappointment (Kozeba) shall come forth out of Jacob.'"

H. R. Aqiba, when he saw Bar Kozeba, said, "This is the King Messiah."

I. R. Yohanan ben Toreta said to him, "Aqiba! Grass will grow on your cheeks before the Messiah will come!"[2]

---

[1] *The Talmud of the Land of Israel: A Preliminary Translation* (vol. 1, Berakhot, trans. Tzvee Zahavy; Chicago: University of Chicago Press, 1989), 88–89.

[2] Jacob Neusner, *Besah and Taanit* (vol. 18 of *Talmud of the Land of Israel*; Chicago: University of Chicago Press, 1987), 269–70.

The important point is not only that Akiba had been proved wrong. It is that the very verse of Scripture adduced in behalf of his viewpoint could be treated more generally and made to refer to righteous people in general, not to the Messiah in particular. And that leads us to the issue of the age, as sages had to face it: what makes a Messiah a false Messiah? The answer, we recall, is arrogance.

What the framers of the document have done is to assemble materials in which the eschatological, therefore Messianic, teleology is absorbed within the ahistorical, and therefore sagacious, one. The Messiah turned into a sage is no longer the Messiah embodied in the figure of the arrogant Bar Kokhba (in the Yerushalmi's representation of the figure; *Ta'anit* 4:5 above). The reversion to the prophetic notion of learning history's lessons carried in its wake a reengagement with the Messiah-myth. But the reengagement does not represent a change in the unfolding system. Why not? Because the climax comes in an explicit statement that the conduct required by the Torah will bring the coming Messiah. That explanation of the holy way of life focuses upon the end of time and the advent of the Messiah—both of which therefore depend upon the sanctification of Israel. So sanctification takes priority, but salvation depends on it. The framers of the Mishnah had found it possible to construct a complete and encompassing teleology for their system with scarcely a single word about the Messiah's coming when the system would be perfectly achieved. So with their interest in explaining events and accounting for history, third- and fourth-century sages invoked what their predecessors had at best found of peripheral consequence to their system. The following contains the most striking expression of the viewpoint at hand.

Yerushalmi *Ta'anit* 1:1.ii.5

F. "They went into exile to Rome, and the presence of God went into exile with them. What is the scriptural basis for this claim? '[The oracle concerning Dumah]. One is calling to me from Seir, "Watchman, what of the night? Watchman, what of the night?" Is. 21:11).'"

G. The Israelites said to Isaiah, "O our Rabbi, Isaiah, What will come for us out of this night?"

H. He said to them, "Wait for me, until I can present the question."

I. Once he had asked the question, he came back to them.

J. They said to him, "Watchman, what of the night? What did the Guardian of the ages say [a play on 'of the night' and 'say']?"

K. He said to them, "The watchman says: 'Morning comes; and also the night. [If you will inquire, inquire; come back again]'" (Is. 21:12).

L. They said to him, "Also the night?"

M. He said to them, "It is not what you are thinking. But there will be morning for the righteous, and night for the wicked, morning for Israel, and night for idolaters."

N. They said to him, "When?"

O. *He said to them, "Whenever you want, He too wants [it to be]—if you want it, he wants it."*

P. They said to him, "What is standing in the way?"

Q. He said to them, "Repentance: 'come back again'" (Is. 21:12).

R. R. Aha in the name of R. Tanhum b. R. Hiyya, "If Israel repents for one day, forthwith the son of David will come.

S. "What is the scriptural basis? 'O that today you would hearken to his voice!'" (Ps. 95:7).

T. Said R Levi, "If Israel would keep a single Sabbath in the proper way, forthwith the son of David will come.

U. "What is the scriptural basis for this view? 'Moses said, Eat it today, for today is a Sabbath to the Lord; [today you will not find it in the field]' (Ex. 16:25).

V. "And it says, '[For thus said the Lord God, the Holy One of Israel], "In returning and rest you shall be saved; [in quietness and in trust shall be your strength." And you would not]'" (Is. 30:15). By means of returning and [Sabbath] rest you will be redeemed.

The discussion of the power of repentance would hardly have surprised a Mishnah-sage. What is new is at R–V, the explicit linkage of keeping the law with achieving the end of time and the coming of the Messiah. That motif stands separate from the notions of righteousness and repentance, which surely do not require it. So the condition of "all Israel," a social category in historical time, comes under consideration, and not only the status of individual Israelites in life and in death. The latter had formed the arena for 'Abot's account of the Mishnah's meaning. Now history as an operative category, drawing in its wake Israel as a social entity, comes once more on the scene. But, except for the Mishnah's sages, it had never left the stage.

We must not lose sight of the importance of this passage, with its emphasis on repentance, on the one side, and the power of Israel to re-form itself, on the other. The Messiah will come any day that Israel makes it possible. If all Israel will keep a single Sabbath in the proper (rabbinic) way, the Messiah will come. If all Israel will repent for one day, the Messiah will come. "Whenever you want . . ." the Messiah will come. Now, two things are happening here. First, the system of religious observance, including study of Torah, is explicitly endowed with salvific power. Second, the persistent hope of the people for the coming of the Messiah is linked to the system of rabbinic observance and belief. In this way, the austere program of the Mishnah, with no trace of a promise that the Messiah will come if and when the system is fully realized, finds a new motive. A teleology lacking all eschatological dimension here gives way to an explicitly Messianic statement that the purpose of the law is to attain Israel's salvation: "If you want it, God wants it too." The one thing Israel commands is its own heart; the power it yet exercises is the power to repent. These suffice. The entire history of humanity will respond to Israel's will, to what happens in Israel's heart and soul. And, with temple in ruins, repentance can take place only within the heart and mind. The Messiah will come any day that Israel makes it possible. Let me underline the most important statement of this large conception: If all Israel will keep a single Sabbath in the proper (rabbinic) way, the Messiah will come. If all Israel will repent for one day, the Messiah will come. "Whenever you want . . . ," the Messiah will come. Now that the project of rebuilding the temple has come to nothing, that remains the one compelling message.

Judaism despite Christianity

The fourth century—and especially the events from 312 to 363—produced an actual debate between Jews and Christians on issues defined in the same terms, through the medium of the same modes of argument, with appeal to the same facts supplied by the same Scripture. This had not happened before. For the first time Judaic sages and Christian theologians now met in a head-on argument on a shared agenda and confronted the fundamental issues of the historical existence of politics and society in the West: doctrine (specifically, the meaning of history) teleology (specifically, the eschatological teleology formed by the Messianic doctrine identifying Jesus as Christ) and the symbolism of the godly society (specifically, the identity of God's social medium—Israel—in the making of the world).

Before that time, Judaic sages had talked about their issues to their own private audience, while Christian theologians had for three centuries pursued their arguments on their distinctive agenda. The former pretended the latter did not exist. The latter framed doctrines concerning the former solely within their internal arguments within Christianity. When they spoke of "Judaism" it was a Christian fabrication, for Christian theological purposes. There had been no confrontation of an intellectual character, since neither party had addressed the issues important to the other in such a way that the issues found a mutually agreeable definition. Nor did the premises of argument, the core of shared facts and shared reason, form a mutually acceptable protocol of discourse. Later on, for many centuries, the confrontation would shift, so that no real debate on a shared set of issues, defined in the same way by both parties could unfold. The politics would not require it, and the circumstances would prevent it.

In the fourth century, by contrast, issues urgent for Christians proved of acute, not merely chronic, concern for Jews as well. In my view, this came about not because differences on Scripture and its meaning by themselves could produce debate. Those differences became urgent only when matters of public policy, specifically, the ideology of state (empire, for the Christians; supernatural nation or family, for the Jews) demanded a clear statement on the questions at hand: how long? by whom? When the Roman Empire and Israelite nation had to assess the meaning of epochal change, when each had to reconsider the teleology of society and system as the identity of the Messiah defined that teleology, when each had to reconsider the appropriate metaphor for the political unit, namely, people, nation, extended family, only then did chronic disagreement become acute difference. It was the progressive but remarkable change in the character of the Roman government—at the beginning of the century pagan and hostile to Christianity, at the end of the century Christian and hostile to paganism—that was decisive. The terms of the confrontation between Judaism and Christianity reached conclusive formulation in the age of Constantine.

Christians and Jews in the first century had not argued with one another. Each—the family of Christianities, the family of Judaisms—had gone its own way. When Christianity originally came into being in the first century, one important strand of the Christian movement stressed issues of salvation, maintaining in the Gospels that Jesus was and is Christ, come to save the world and impose a radical change on history. At that same time, an important group within the diverse Judaic systems of the age, the Pharisees, emphasized issues of sanctification, maintaining that the task of Israel was to attain that holiness of which the temple was a singular embodiment. When, in the Gospels, we find the record of the Church placing Jesus into opposition with the Pharisees, we witness the confrontation of different people talking about different things to different people. The issues presented to Jews by the triumph of Christianity in the fourth century (which *do* inform the documents shaped in the land of Israel in the period of that triumph) did not play an important role in prior ages—in particular, the composition of the Mishnah and closely allied documents (e.g., Tosefta, *m. ʾAbot, Sifra, Sifrê*) which reached closure before the fourth century. These present, as we have seen, a Judaism not despite Christianity, but in utter indifference to Christianity. The contrast between the Mishnah and the Judaic system emerging in the fourth-century documents tells the tale.

The shift in the condition of Israel marked by Christ's rise to political power and the Torah's loss of a place in political institutions moreover defined the context and setting of Judaism from then to nearly the present day. And, it must be said, the response of the day—represented by the Judaism defined in the documents of the late fourth and fifth centuries—proved remarkably successful. Judaism did endure, and the Jews did persist, from then to now. So the Judaism that emerged from the Yerushalmi in the fourth century (and that reached fruition and full statement in the Bavli two hundred years later) enjoyed stunning success. The fourth century also marks the first century of Christianity as the West would know it. When Rome became Christian, Judaism as it would flourish in Western civilization reached that familiar form and definition that we know today. Rabbinic Judaism was born in the matrix of Christianity's political triumph.

Christianity's explicit claims, now validated in world-shaking events of the age, demanded a reply. The sages of the Talmud of the Land of Israel, *Genesis Rabbah,* and *Leviticus Rabbah* provided it. When the Christian challenge met Israel's worldview head-on, the sages' doctrines responded. What did Israel's sages have to present as the Torah's answer to the cross? It was the Torah, with its doctrine of history, Messiah, and Israel. History in the beginning, in Genesis, accounted for the events of the day. The Messiah will be a sage of the Torah. Israel today comprises the family, after the flesh, of the founders of Israel. The Torah therefore served as the encompassing symbol of Israel's salvation. The Torah would be embodied in the person of the Messiah who, of course, would be a sage, a rabbi. The Torah confronted the cross, with its doctrine of the triumphant Christ, Messiah and king, ruler now of earth as of heaven. In the formulation of the sages who wrote the fourth- and early-fifth-century documents, the Talmud of the Land of Israel and *Genesis Rabbah* and *Leviticus Rabbah,* the Torah thus confronted the challenge of the cross of Christianity as, later on, the Torah would again meet and overcome the sword and crescent of Islam. Within Israel the Torah everywhere triumphed. That is why, when Christianity came to power and commenced to define the civilization of the West, Judaism met and overcame its greatest crisis before modern times. And it held. As a result, Jews remained within the Judaic system of the dual Torah. That is why they continued for the entire history of the West to see the world through the worldview of the dual Torah and to conduct life in accord with the way of life of the Torah as the rabbis explained it. And their explanation accorded with the paradigm of the Pentateuch, with its self-sustaining pattern of resentment and remission, exile and return. Rabbinic Judaism would show the way to return to the people defined as holy and elect and separate—and in exile from its true home, the land, its Eden.

6

Stability and the Next Turning Point

The Beginning of Western Civilization and the Birth of Christianity and Judaism

Defining the terms of Judaic existence, rabbinic Judaism prospered, with remarkably slight competition from other Judaic religious systems for Israel's social order. This was the case so long as the Christianity to which it responded continued to set the norms for the world beyond Israel's framework.[1] Christianity raised the questions that pressed, and rabbinic Judaism answered those questions for its Israel. When other questions proved urgent, other Judaic systems would have to answer them—or the Israel that deemed those questions critical would perish of despair. Let me explain.

From the fourth century to the eighteenth century, rabbinic Judaism remained stable, adapting to change and adopting its own evolving powerful forces of intellect and piety. It endured for more than fourteen centuries, through time and through change, with a stable symbolic structure, a coherent mythic formulation, a continuous canon, and a particular definition of who and what is Israel. During that time, it encountered very little competition from other Judaic systems in the framework of Israel. But with the political revolutions at the end of the eighteenth century, Christianity entered a new political context, and right alongside, rabbinic Judaism came to the next turning point in its history.[2]

---

[1] Rabbinic Judaism in the setting of Islamic civilization requires study in its own terms. The theory offered in this chapter concerns only Christendom, East and West.

[2] That is not for one minute to suggest that the rabbinic system remained intact. But it was, as I have said in the text, essentially unimpaired. It absorbed

From the end of the eighteenth century, with challenges to the hegemony of Christianity in Western civilization came competition for rabbinic Judaism, within the Judaic framework, from other Judaic religious systems. These represented different systems from the rabbinic one (though initially generally claiming continuity with the rabbinic system). They differed because they found their core and focus by answering different questions from the ones that rabbinic Judaism had addressed in the Mishnah, Talmuds, and Midrash. They consequently would set forth their own structures of symbols and distinctive mythic accounts, they would produce a different mode of learning and revise and redefine the canon, and they would each set forth their own definition of who and what is Israel among the nations.

Through the nineteenth and into the twentieth centuries, the Judaic religious system of the Pentateuch, Mishnah, Talmuds, and Midrash continued in the received form and in secondary, recognizable forms. But it also found itself competing with other Judaic religious systems for the authoritative definition of Israel's social order. So we may say that Constantine inaugurated the politics in which Christianity defined the civilization of the West, but the American Constitution (1787) and the French Revolution (with its Declaration of the Rights of Man, 1791, and its sustained assault against Christianity) brought to a conclusion the age in which a politically-paramount Christianity alone set the norm for Europe and North America, Christian and Judaic, respectively. When Christianity in its orthodox, catholic formulation, East and West, ceased alone to define the questions addressed by civilization in Christendom, then Judaism in its rabbinic formulation, normative for so long, found itself answering questions that no longer enjoyed a monopoly within Israel. The upshot was (and remains): when other generations of Jews found other questions urgent, other Judaisms took shape to answer them.

In the preceding two chapters, I have tried to explain why the advent of Christian rule in the Roman Empire made so profound an impact as to produce a Judaism. A move of the empire from reverence for Zeus to

---

entirely unprecedented modes of thought and expression, such as philosophy and Kabbalah. Massive movements such as Hasidism would take shape. But these developments augmented the initial canon—Pentateuch and Prophets, Mishnah, Talmud and Midrash. Their foci and emphases reshaped what was a continuous religious tradition, perfectly able to make its own developments beyond its original limits. The Torah found a place for the kabbalistic writings, and the halakah as social system strengthened itself through the piety generated thereby. So I make reference to the fundamental stability of rabbinic Judaism until the nineteenth century in the West, and until the twentieth century in much of Eastern Europe. Only in the nineteenth century did important Judaic religious systems of the social order, as well as Jewish secular systems, present large-scale and weighty competition to the rabbinic structure—and from outside of its limits altogether.

adoration of Mithra meant nothing. To Jews paganism was what it was, lacking all differentiation. Christianity was something else, because it was like Judaism. In terms of our explanation, Christians claimed that theirs *was* a Judaism—in fact, the only Judaism, Judaism without qualifications—now fulfilled in the Christian Christ. Christians read the Torah and claimed to declare its meaning. They furthermore alleged, like Israel, that they alone worshiped the one true God. And they challenged Israel's claim to know that God—and even to be Israel, continuator of the Israel of the promises and grace of ancient Scripture. Accordingly, Israel's sages cannot have avoided the issue of the place, within the messianic pattern, of the remarkable turn in world history represented by the triumph of Christianity. Since the Christians celebrated confirmation of their faith in Christ's Messiahship and Jews were hardly prepared to concur, it falls surely within known patterns for us to suppose that Constantine's conversion would have been identified with some dark moment to prefigure the dawning of the messianic age.

At that time through the late fourth and into the fifth century, important Judaic documents, particularly the Talmud of the Land of Israel, *Genesis Rabbah,* and *Leviticus Rabbah,* were completed. These writings undertook to deal with an agenda defined by the political triumph of Christianity. The questions facing Jews concerned both the meaning of history and the coming of the Messiah. Christian thinkers, for their part, reflected on issues presented by the political revolution in the status of Christianity. Issues of the interpretation of history from creation to the present, the restatement of the challenge and claim of Christ the King as Messiah against the continuing expectation of Israel that the Messiah is yet to come—these made their appearance in both Judaic and Christian writings of the day. Issues of Judaism as laid forth in documents redacted in the late fourth and early fifth century—but not before that time—exhibit remarkable congruence with the contours of the intellectual program presented by Christian thinkers. So in the period at hand, in political conditions that would persist in the West, Judaic sages and Christian theologians addressed precisely the same questions, questions critical to the self-understanding of Israel, the Jewish people. That fact in my view accounts for the stability and success of the Judaism at hand—its self-evident truth for Israel, the Jewish people—in the long centuries in which that Judaic system defined the way of life and the worldview of the Jewish people: Judaism.

The Christian *Défi* and the Success of Judaism

The Judaic and Christian systems of the first and second centuries had prepared their respective groups for worlds that would never exist. Israel was conceived by the Jewish community as autonomous, the Christian community as subordinate and commanding little more than its own rites and doctrines. The Judaism of the pentateuchal-mishnaic system addressed a self-governing people, secure within its own political institutions. By contrast the Christianity that emerged in Paul's letters, the Gospels, and the early church fathers never envisioned a Christian state. But in the fourth century the two systems traded places: Judaism prepared for politics, lost its political system, while Christianity, unprepared for power, inherited the world. In many ways, therefore, the fourth century marks the intersection of trajectories of the history of the two groups of religious systems, Judaic and Christian.

Judaism and Christianity in late antiquity present histories that mirror one another. When Christianity began, Judaism was the dominant tradition in the Holy Land and it continued to frame its ideas within a political framework until the early fourth century. Christianity there was subordinate and from the beginning had to work out its self-understanding against the background of a politically definitive Judaism at that time. So Judaism in its principal expressions produced deep thought on political issues. But Christianity, never anticipating that it would inherit an empire and rule the world, scarcely made itself ready for its coming political power. The roles reversed themselves when the politically well-framed Judaism lost all access to an effective polity, while a politically mute Christianity entered onto responsibilities scarcely imagined a decade before they came into being.

From the time of Constantine onward, therefore, matters reversed themselves. Now Christianity predominated, expressing its ideas in political and institutional terms. Judaism, by contrast, had lost its political foundations and faced the task of working out its self-understanding in a world defined by Christianity, now everywhere triumphant and in charge of politics. So we must call the fourth Christian century the West's first century. That is because the fourth century was when the West began, in the union of Christian religion and Roman rule. It also was when the Judaism that thrived in the West reached the normative definition it was to exhibit for the next fourteen centuries.

Under Constantine the religious systems of Christianity became licit, then favored, and finally dominant in the government of the Roman empire, and Christians then confronted a world for which nothing had prepared them. But they did not choose to complain. For the political triumph of Christ, now ruler of the world in dimensions wholly unimagined, brought its own lessons. All of human history required fresh consideration, from the first Adam to the last. The writings of churches now asked to be sorted out so that the biblical canon, Old and New, might correspond to the standing and clarity of the new Christian situation. So too one powerful symbol, the cross (selected by Constantine for his army, under which he won), took a position of dominance and declared its distinctive message of a Christianity in charge of things. Symbol, canon, systemic teleology—all three responded to the unprecedented and hitherto not-to-be-predicted circumstance of Christ on the throne of the nations.

Just beyond the end of that century of surprises, in 429, Israel in the land of Israel lost its institution of autonomous government. That year marked the end of the Patriarchate, the government that had ruled the Jews of the land of Israel for the preceding three centuries. It was the end of their political entity, their instrument of self-administration and government in their own land. Tracing its roots back for centuries and claiming to originate in the family of David, the Patriarchate had succeeded the regime of the priests in the temple and the kings, first as allies and then as agents of Rome. Israel's tradition of government, of course, went back to Sinai. No one had ever imagined that the Jews would define their lives other than as a people, a political society with collective authority and shared destiny and a public interest. The revelation of Sinai addressed a nation, the Torah gave laws to be kept and enforced, and, as is clear, Israel found definition in comparison to other nations. It would have rulers, subject to God's authority to be sure; it would have a king now, and a king-Messiah at the end of time.

So the fourth century brought a hitherto unimagined circumstance: an Israel lacking the authority to rule itself under its own government now lost even the ethnic and patriarchal government that had held things together beyond 70 (that is, beyond the long centuries of priestly rule in the temple and royal rule in Jerusalem). The two systems had, from the end of the first century to the eve of the fourth, prepared for worlds that neither would inhabit—the one for the status of the governed, not the governor, the other for the opposite. Christianity, in politics, would define not the fringes but the very fabric of society and culture. Judaism, out of politics altogether, would find its power in the donated obedience of people in no way to be coerced, except from within or from on high. Lacking access to the legitimate violence of its own politics, Judaism became a voluntary community. However Christianity and Judaism would choose to define themselves beyond the time of turning, therefore, would constitute mediating systems, with the task to emerge, responding to a new world out of an inappropriate old one. The Judaism that would take shape beyond the fourth century would use writings produced in one religious system to address a quite different one, and so too would the Christianity that would rule, both in its Western and in its Eastern expressions.

The outcome of the sages' doctrine of the dual Torah was a stunning success. Judaism in the rabbis' statement did endure in the Christian West, imparting to Israel the secure conviction of constituting that Israel after the flesh to which the Torah continued to speak. On what basis do I claim that the rabbinic sages' Judaism won? Because despite great pressure and intense competition from Christianity (and then Islam) the Jews chose to practice Judaism. That fact emerged with great force in the con-

trast between the fate of Christianity and the fate of Judaism in the face of
Islam. When, in its turn, Islam gained its victory, Christianity throughout
the Middle East and North Africa gave way. Lands Christian for many
centuries became Muslim. But the sages' Judaism in those same vast terri-
tories retained the loyalty and conviction of the people of the Torah. The
cross would rule only where the crescent and its sword did not, but
the Torah of Sinai everywhere and always sanctified Israel in time and
promised secure salvation for eternity.

Christianity and the Indicative Traits of Normative Judaism

I claim that the christianization of Rome affected the formation of
rabbinic Judaism. I have now to specify those aspects of Judaism in which
Christianity made its impact: How, precisely, do I allege that that is so, and
how not? The answer derives from the political facts that changed and
those that did not change when Constantine officially recognized Christianity. When Rome at its political apex became Christian, and when
Christianity became first tolerated, then established, and finally triumphant, the condition of Israel changed in some ways but not in others.

What remained the same? The politics and social context of a defeated nation. Israel in the land of Israel had long ago lost its major war as
an autonomous political unit of the Roman Empire. In the year 70 the
Romans had conquered the capitol and destroyed the temple there. In
132, a war broke out and Israel again suffered defeat, this time worse than
before. Jerusalem was now transformed into a forbidden city to Jews.
With the temple in permanent ruins, Israel, the Jewish people, took up
the task of finding an accommodation with enduring defeat, with its exit
from political history. So whether Rome accepted pagan or Christian rule
had no bearing on the fundamental fact of Israel's life: a vanquished
nation, a broken heart.

Then what did change with Constantine? It was the circumstance
and context of the religious system of Judaism. While the political situation
of Israel did not change, the political situation of Christianity did—*and
therefore, with impact upon Judaism.* How so? Jews in the land of Israel persisted as a subject-people. That is what they had been, and that is what they
remained. But Judaism now confronted a world in which its principal components—hermeneutic, teleology, symbol—were challenged by the corresponding components of the now-triumphant faith in Christ. The Judaism
that emerged dealt with that challenge in a way particular to Christianity.
The doctrines that assumed central significance—those concerning the
Messiah, on the one side, and the character of God's revelation in the Torah
to Moses at Sinai, on the other—took up questions addressed to Judaism by
Christianity and only by Christianity. So the changes in the Talmuds and

midrash-compilations that took over the pentateuchal-mishnaic system were due to the distinctive claims of Christianity, and what remained intact in the antecedent heritage endured because politics continued as before. Israel continued as a subjugated people, and the prior heritage had already proved its compatibility with that condition.

Now, as we know, the Hebrew Scriptures, in Christian view, demanded a reading as the Old Testament, predicting the New. Why? Because history now proved that Scripture's prophetic promises of a king-Messiah had pointed toward Jesus, now Christ enthroned. Concomitantly, the teleology of the Israelite system of old, focused as it was on the coming of the Messiah, now found confirmation and realization in the rule of Jesus, again, as Christ enthroned. And the symbol of the whole—hermeneutics and teleology alike—rose in heaven's heights: the cross that had triumphed at the Milvian Bridge. No wonder, then, that the critical components of the prior system of Judaism now came under sharp revision. To be concrete, let me specify the changes I think indicative.

(1) The written Torah found completion in the oral one, granting legitimacy to Judaism's extra-scriptural traditions. The Mishnah and its exegetical continuators, the Talmuds, alongside the Pentateuch and its exegetical continuators, the midrash-compilations, entered the status of tradition of Sinai.

(2) As we saw in chapter five, the system as a whole was now made to point toward an eschatological teleology, to be realized in the coming of the Messiah when Israel's condition, defined by the one whole Torah of Sinai, itself warranted.

(3) And, it would necessarily follow, the symbol of the Torah would expand to encompass the teleology and hermeneutic at hand. Salvation comes from the Torah, not the cross—a matter that does not require amplification.

So point by point, the principles of Judaism responded point by point to the particular challenge of the principal event of that century, and produced the fresh reading of the Talmud of the Land of Israel, coming to closure at the end of the fourth century. So the fourth century marked the first century of Judaism as it would flourish in the West. It further indicated the first century of Christianity, as Christianity enthroned would define and govern the civilization of the West.

If, now, we inquire into exactly what in fact sages did at that time—meaning, what documents did they produce and what did they say in them that they had not said earlier—the answer is clear. They composed the Talmud of the Land of Israel as we know it. They collected exegeses of Scripture and made them into systematic and sustained accounts of the meaning of the Pentateuch. (I assume late third- through early-fifth-century dates, for *Sifra* and the two *Sifrés*; ca. 300 C.E., *Genesis Rabbah,* and *Leviticus Rabbah,* ca. 400–450 C.E.). Let us dwell on this matter of composing collections of exegeses of the Hebrew Scriptures, with special reference to the Pentateuch—something that, in the Christian world, contemporaries worked out as well.

First, the exegetical work continued to privilege the Pentateuch, which, as we have seen, constitutes a definitive marker of a Judaic religious system. The earliest rabbinic exegetical compilations all focused on pentateuchal books. When we recall what Christians had to say to Israel, we may find entirely reasonable the view that compiling scriptural exegeses constituted part of a Jewish apologetic response. One Christian message had been that Israel "after the flesh" had distorted and continually misunderstood the meaning of its own Scripture. Failing to read the Old Testament in the light of the New, especially the prophetic promises in the perspective of Christ's fulfillment of those promises, Israel "after the flesh" had lost access to God's revelation to Moses at Sinai. A suitably powerful, yet appropriately proud, response by the sages would have two qualities. First, it would supply a complete account of what Scripture had meant, and must always mean, as Israel read it. Second, it would do so without dignifying the position of the other side with the grace of an explicit reply at all. And the enterprise would lay its heavy emphasis on the centrality of the Pentateuch.

The midrash-compilations of exegeses and the Talmud of the Land of Israel compiled at this time assuredly take up the challenge of restating the meaning of the Torah revealed by God to Moses at Mount Sinai. This the sages did in a systematic and thorough way. At the same time, if the charges of the other side precipitated the work of exegetical compilation and composition, the consequent collections in no way suggest this. The issues of the documents are made always to emerge from the inner life not even of Israel in general, but of the sages' estate in particular. Scripture was thoroughly rabbinized, as earlier it had been Christianized. None of this suggests the other side had won a response for itself. Only the net effect—a complete picture of the whole, as Israel must perceive the whole of revelation—suggests the extraordinary utility for apologetics, outside as much as inside the faith, served by these same compilations.

It follows that the changes at the surface, in articulated doctrines of teleology, hermeneutics, and symbolism, respond to changes in the political condition of Israel as well as in the religious foundations of the politics of the day. Not engaged with Judaism except in a philosophical framework, paganism had presented a different and simpler problem to sages. Christianity's explicit claims, validated in world-shaking events of the age, demanded a reply. The sages of the fourth century provided it. So it is at those very specific points at which the Christian challenge met head-on Israel's old worldview that sages' doctrines change from what they had been.

What did Israel have to present in the face of the cross? The *Torah*—in the doctrine of the status, as oral and memorized revelation, of the Mishnah, and, by implication, of other rabbinical writings. The *Torah*, moreover, in the encompassing symbol of Israel's salvation. The *Torah*, finally, in the person of the Messiah who, of course, would be a rabbi. The Torah in all three modes confronted the cross, with its doctrine of the triumphant Christ, Messiah and king, ruler now of earth as of heaven. So what changed? Those components of sages' worldview that now stood in direct confrontation with counterparts on the Christian side. What remained the same? Doctrines governing fundamental categories of Israel's social life, to which the triumph of Christianity made no material difference.

The Stability of Rabbinic Judaism and the Next Turning Point

The rabbinic system answered the urgent questions of the hour—and of the Christian centuries. The rabbinic sages therefore presented remarkably pertinent doctrines in documents closed at the end of the first Christian century of the West (4th century C.E.). These encompassed an explanation of the authority of the dual Torah taught by the rabbinic sages, an account of the meaning of Scripture as sages read it, and a clear statement on the now-urgent Messiah-question. Not only so, but in their writings sages composed a position on issues defined by Christian theologians in the same way, worked out through the same arguments, and on the foundation of the same body of facts. These shared issues concerned the meaning of history, the character and identity of the Messiah, and the definition of Israel. In all, therefore, we find a systematic confrontation on a program confronting both parties for a single reason. And what was that reason? It was the political revolution accomplished by Constantine's Christian continuators.

Here we find ourselves confronting the thesis of this book: the claim that religion is public, social, and by its nature therefore, political: a response to worldly power-relationships. The fact that Judaic sages conceived and articulated doctrines on issues shared with Christianity would shape the future history of the Judaism formed by those same sages. For as Christianity continued to harp on the same points, as it did, the Judaic party to the dispute for centuries to come could refer to the generative symbols and determinative myths of the sages' Judaism, which dealt with these very issues. And the Judaic party did so as well. The Christian challenge, delivered through instruments of state and society, demanded a Judaic response, one involving not merely manipulation of power but exercise of intellect. Jews, continuing as a distinct society, took to heart the negative message of Christianity—"the Messiah has already come, you have no hope in the future, you are not Israel anyhow, and history proves we are right." Sages produced responses to these questions, with doctrines of the meaning of history, of the conditions in which the Messiah will come to Israel, and of the definition of Israel. The symbolic system of rabbinic Judaism, with its stress on Torah; the eschatological teleology of that system, with its stress on the Messiah-sage coming to obedient Israel; the insistence on the equivalence of Israel and Rome, Jacob and Esau, with Esau penultimate and Jacob at the end of time—these constituted in Israel powerful responses to the Christian question.

In a profound sense, therefore, the Judaism that reached canonical expression in the late fourth century succeeded because it dealt in a strikingly relevant way with both the issues and the politics of the Christian world within which Jews lived. The issues carried intellectual weight, and the politics imparted to those issues urgency and power. Because of politics the issues demanded attention. Had the doctrines focused on matters not at issue at all, and had the points of direct confrontation not elicited a response within Judaism, then the Judaism at hand would have proved itself simply irrelevant—it would have died of the attrition of sheer disinterest. We know that that is the fact, for when we deal with a world that confronted the Jewish people with other challenges enjoying self-evident urgency, the Judaism of the sages lost its standing as self-evidently true and right in large sectors of Israel.

Specifically, when we come to a world no longer defined by Christian politics and culture in any form, such as the beginning of the nineteenth century in the West (Germany, France, Britain, and the USA), we deal with precisely a situation in which the inherited Judaism ceased to address Jews' urgent questions—in specified places, under specified circumstances, and in particular classes of Jewish society. Then, for those places and classes of society, new compositions of symbols and systems of ideas—invented in some measure out of the received writings of ancient times, to be sure—would emerge to do so. The sages' Judaism of the late fourth century and beyond flourished when the world to which it spoke found persuasive not the answers alone, but the very questions that that Judaism had deemed pressing. And that Judaism ceased to speak to those Jews for whom its message proved incongruent to the questions those Jews found they had to answer. The critical issue, therefore, was congruence to circumstance, rather than truth or self-evidence of answers. And circumstance, to begin with, found salient traits in the conditions of politics: people acting together in an organized way, legitimately exercising power, even violence. But when we speak of politics, the definition of Israel as a political entity in this world's terms—a people, one people, in quest of its state, the Jewish state, the state of Israel—we move beyond the limits set for this account. But we remain well within the thesis announced at the outset concerning despair as the provocation, and the renewal of received tradition as the response.

Index of Ancient Sources

HEBREW BIBLE

Genesis
2:10   111
2:11–12   111
2:13   111
2:14   112
2:15   16
2:16   16
3:9   17
3:11   17
3:23   17
3:24   17
11:4   159
14:24   159
15:1–3   22
15:13–14   22
15:13–17   121
18:4   144, 145
18:5   145
18:7   145
18:8   146
18:27   159
21:11   106
21:12   107
25:22–23   107
25:23–24   108
26:34–35   109
27:34   147
27:35   147
27:39   112
27:39–40   114
27:41   141

Exodus
5:2   159
13:21   146

15:11   129
16:8   159
16:25   164
16:45   145
27:20   17

Leviticus
11:4   114
11:4–8   113, 114
11:5   114
11:6   114
11:7   114
13   52
14   52
15   52
17:5   77
17:5–7   79
17:8–9   78
19:1–18   20
23:42   145
24:2   17
26   15
26:3   22
26:6   22
26:34   22

Numbers
3:12–15   76
8:16–18   76
11:27   146
19:1   134
21:7   144
21:17   152
24:17   162
32:1   146

Deuteronomy
3:25   128
7:7   159
8:7   144
8:8   145
12:9   77
12:13   78, 79
12:14   78, 79
14:7   113, 114
14:8   110, 113
28   15
28:5   132
28:57   127
32:37   129

Joshua
4:19ff.   77
18:1   77

1 Samuel
4:13   132
21:2   77
21:7   77

2 Samuel
7:18   149

1 Kings
3:4   77
5:2   149
8:66   153
22:47   141

2 Kings
18:35   159

2 Chronicles
32:23   150
33:10–11   150
33:13   150

Esther
4:1   147

Psalms
6:2   149
20:7   149
22:6   159
58:4   108
60:10   157
74:4   129
78:9   121
80:14   109
82:1   146
82:6   145
89:9   129
95:7   164
105:5   107
105:39   145
137:8   113

Proverbs
15:30   128
17:22   128
28:14   124

Qoheleth
8:10   129

Song of Songs
1:6   156
2:7   120, 121
3:5   120, 121

5:8   121
8:4   121

Isaiah
1:16 145
4:4   145
4:6   145
7:21 146
10:34 128, 131, 162
11:1 162
11:4 151
14:14 133, 160
21:11 163
21:12 164
30:15 164
33:15 106
37:3 150
38:21 150
44:25 128, 129
53–54 3
53:5 150
57:8 93
63:3 112

Jeremiah
1:5   108
2:7   17
5:6   112, 113
15:1 17
30:21 128

Lamentations
1:1   17

Ezekiel
7:19 127
16:9 145
21:14 113, 114
25:14 125
28:2 160

Daniel
7:3–7 112
7:4   112
7:5   112
7:9–14 147
9:11 17

Hosea
6:7   16
9:15 17

Obadiah
1:21 114, 115

Micah
2:13 146
7:6   84

Habbakuk
1:8   111

Zechariah
11:1 133
11:17 158
13:2 133
14:2 151
14:8 145

NEW TESTAMENT

Mark
13:2 117

RABBINIC WORKS

Mishnah

ᶜAbodah Zarah
4:7   104

ᵓAbot
1:1   55
1:1–11 86

Ketubbot
5:8   104

Maᶜaśerot
1:1   45
1:2   45

Negaᶜim
14:6 104

Parah
11:7 104

Qiddušin
4:1   72

Roš Haššanah
4:1–3 72
4:1–4 103
4:4   74

Šabbat
2:6   71

Soṭah
7:1   82
9:15 65, 83

Sukkah
3:12 73

Taᶜanit
4:6–7 75
4:7   80

Yebamot
8:3   104

Zebaḥim
5:3   77
5:5   77
5:6–8 77
10:4–8 139
13:1 78
14:4 79
14:4–8 76, 78, 79
14:4–9 103
14:5 79, 80
14:6 79
14:7 79, 80
14:8 80
14:9 78, 80
14:10 79, 80

Tosefta

Beṣah
2:15 104

Miqwaᵓot
4:7   104

Niddah
6:1   104
7:1   104

Qiddušin
5:4   104

Šabbat
13:5 93, 97

Yebamot
8:1   104

Yoma
3:8   104

Bavli

Giṭṭin
55B–56A 124
56B   128

Ḥullin
VI:7.i.7 159

Yerushalmi

ᶜAbodah Zarah
1:2.i.4 140

Berakot
2:2.4.2.3.A 161
2:4   161

ᶜErubin
3:9.i.4 156

Taᶜanit
1:1.ii.5 163
3:9   158
4:5.iv 162
4:5.vii.1 157

OTHER RABBINIC WORKS

The Fathers According to Rabbi Nathan
IV:vi.1 130

Genesis Rabbah
XIX:ix.2 16
XLVIII:x.2 144
LIII:xii.1–3 106
LXIII:vi.1–6 107
LXV:i.1 109
LXVII:iv.1–2 147
LXX:viii.2–3 152
LXX:viii.5 153
LXX:viii.7 154
LXXV:iv.2–3 110

Leviticus Rabbah
XIII:v.1–6 111
XIII:v.8–9 112
XIII:v.13 114

Pesiqta deRab Kahana
IV:vii.5 133

Ruth Rabbah
V:LX.i.1–5 149

Song of Songs Rabbah
XXIV:ii.1 120
XXIV:ii.4–5 121

Tanhuma Qedoshim
10 51